The Reminiscences of

Vice Admiral Charles Wellborn, Jr.

U. S. Navy (Retired)

U. S. Naval Institute
Annapolis, Maryland
1972

Preface

This manuscript is the result of a series of tape recorded interviews with Vice Admiral Charles Wellborn, Jr., U. S. Navy (Retired), in the Westchester Apartments, Washington, D. C. They were conducted by John T. Mason, Jr., during the period ranging from November, 1971 to May, 1972 and were done in behalf of the Oral History program of the U. S. Naval Institute.

Some minor emendations and corrections were made by Admiral Wellborn to the original typescript but otherwise the MS remains essentially as it was given on tape. The reader is reminded that this is a record of the spoken word rather than the written word.

A fairly comprehensive subject index has been compiled and is appended for the convenience of the researcher.

DECLARATION OF TRUST

The undersigned does hereby appoint and designate as his (her) Trustee herein, the Secretary-Treasurer and Publisher of the United States Naval Institute to perform and discharge the following duties, powers, and privileges in connection with the possession and use of a certain taped interview between the undersigned and the Oral History Department of the United States Naval Institute.

1. Classification of Transcript.

    ( )a. If classified OPEN, the transcript(s) may be read or the recording(s) audited by the qualified personnel upon presentation of proper credentials, as determined by the Secretary-Treasurer of the U. S. Naval Institute.

    (✓)b. If classified PERMISSION REQUIRED TO CITE OR QUOTE, the user will be required to obtain permission in writing from the interviewee prior to quoting or citing from either the transcript(s) or the recording(s).

    ( )c. If classified PERMISSION REQUIRED, permission must be obtained in writing from the interviewee before the transcribed interview(s) can be examined or the tape recording(s) audited.

    ( )d. If classified CLOSED, the transcribed interview(s) and the tape recording(s) will be sealed until a time specified by the interviewee. This may be until the death of the interviewee or for any specified number of years.

2. It is expressly understood that in giving this authorization, I am in no way precluded from placing such restrictions as I may desire upon use of the interview at any time during my lifetime, nor does this authorization in any way affect my rights to the copyright of my literary expressions that may be contained in the interview.

Witness my hand and seal this 22nd day of May 1972.

I hereby accept and consent to the foregoing Declaration of Trust and the powers therein conferred upon me as Trustee:

5/26/72

Interview No. 1 with Vice Admiral Charles Wellborn, Jr. U.S. Navy
(Retired)

Place: His residence in Washington, D.C.

Date: Tuesday morning, 9 November 1971

Subject: Biography

By: John T. Mason, Jr.

Q: It certainly is delightful to meet you, Admiral. I have been looking forward to this series with you. I've reviewed your career and I find it immensely interesting as it covers many points of historical interest. Inasmuch as it is to be an oral biography, I wonder if you'd begin in the proper way and tell me where you were born, when you were born, and a little about your family background.

Adm. W.: I'd be delighted. I can't remember when I was born, but I'm told that it was on January 30, 1901 in Los Angeles, California. I came from quite a long line of lawyers. My grandfather was a lawyer and a judge, as was my father and all the male members of my family except me. I grew up in Los Angeles, went to public schools there, but I'm a high-school dropout.

Q: That's an interesting fact.

Adm. W.: Yes. As World War I developed I became interested, of course, in getting into uniform and began to take competitive examinations for the Naval Academy. Ultimately, I achieved an appointment and went into the Naval Academy about six months before

I was due to graduate from high school, so I have no high-school diploma.

Q: How did your family with its total legal background look upon this departure?

Adm. W.: Well, my father had always had a sort of secret yearning to be a seafaring person, so he approved of this very highly. In fact, he helped me a very great deal in managing it.

Q: And how did your mother react?

Adm. W.: As far as she was concerned, she seemed to be quite neutral. Whatever he and I wanted was quite all right with her.

Q: Tell me, Sir, did you have brothers and sisters?

Adm. W.: Yes. I have an older brother - or had an older brother. He died some years ago, but I still have two sisters, one two years older and one two years younger. So I grew up in a family where a sense of humor was pretty necessary.

Q: You must have been a pretty good student in school if you could dispense with a high-school diploma and still pass the examinations for the Naval Academy?

Adm. W.: At the time I was in school in California, I think their public schools were very good, and while I didn't have a diploma my own assessment of my educational background was pretty good. I didn't have any real difficulty at the Naval Academy.

Q: What were your strong points in school? Mathematics and that

Wellborn #1 - 3

sort of thing?

Adm. W.: Yes, I think so. Mathematics was a subject I seemed to have little difficulty with and did reasonably well with. English and languages didn't seem to be my strong points. They were the ones with which I had such difficulties as I did have.

Q: In preparation for the appointment which came from your local congressman?

Adm. W.: Yes.

Q: Did you have to do any special prepping?

Adm. W.: I didn't attend any special prep school. I did, prior to taking the entrance examination, play hooky from normal high-school courses - classes - and devoted myself pretty exclusively for several weeks to studying up the subjects that were included in the entrance exam. At that time, the entrance requirements didn't involve any sort of accreditation from the schools you had attended. It was strictly on the basis of the entrance examination, which you either passed or failed.

Q: Were you getting a principal appointment?

Adm. W.: Originally I had an alternate appointment. Finally Congress, as World War I developed, increased the size of the Naval Academy and I fell heir to a principal appointment, and went into the Naval Academy in the same class with those to whom I had been alternate.

Wellborn #1 - 4

Q: Who was the congressman? Was it Judge Crail?

Adm. W.: No. It was Henry Z. Osborne.

It's interesting I think, maybe, to note that at the time of the competitive examinations now Vice Admiral Walter E. Moore, Retired, finished first. The second finisher was now medical doctor Albert Arkush, and I finished third. Both Moore and Arkush entered the Naval Academy and graduated, as did I, in the top half of the class of 1921.

Q: Did you come East by yourself, or did your dad accompany you?

Adm. W.: Quite fortunately he accompanied me. As I said earlier, he had great interest in seafaring things and he came along. The reason I say "fortunately" this happened is that when I went to the Naval Academy to take my physical examination, the medical officers who conducted the first one told me that I was not pjysically qualified due to color blindness.

Q: Was this news to you?

Adm. W.: It was entirely news to me because I'd never had any trouble distinguishing colors. The test seemed to involve throwing a lot of little pieces of yarn tied up in knots through a hole in a white board. When they told me to throw all the blue ones through, I threw blue and green more or less indiscriminately, and similarly with some of the roses and reds. After a number of re-examinations, which might not have been possible had my father not been with me, they decided that I had complete capability to distinguish one color from another but my education in colors was not very good. If somebody told me to pick out all the greens, I was apt to pick out all the blues and greens that were even close to it.

Q: What you needed was a special course in interior decorating!

Adm. W.: Yes. What I needed was a course in the arts of this kind. However, I probably would have been rejected if my father had not been there. After the first rejection, he and I came to Washington to call on Senator Hiram Johnson, who was then the Californian senator, and tell him about my eyes. Senator Johnson knew a good deal about the technicalities and red tape involved in getting people into the Naval Academy. He called directly to the Surgeon General of the Navy who left word at THE NAVAL HOSPITAL for several examinations, The final determination about my color blindness turned out as I have described it. So that's how I went to the Naval Academy, but this delayed my entrance several weeks while all of this red tape was being unwound.

Q: What was your first impression of the Academy and the kind of life one was called upon to lead there?

Adm. W.: I really didn't know a great deal about what to expect and the first people to whom I talked were those people who had been members of the class before me, the class of 1920, and who had failed to survive successfully their first year with that class. Their description of it was that it was practically impossible for any normal human being to get by that first year. This was understandable, because they hadn't. After a week or so there, my expectation was that I'd probably last about six months because it was a superhuman proposition to get through the Academy.

Well, after I'd gained a little experience in the place, I found that this wasn't the picture at all and the normal human being went through it without any difficulty.

Q: Did your family attempt to boost your morale in this situation?

Adm. W.: I don't believe it really needed very much boosting. I was pretty determined that I would try and make it, and it became apparent reasonably soon that this wasn't going to be something that turned out to be too difficult. So I don't think it was very much of a problem.

Q: What was it, what aspects of it were so formidable to these lads who talked with you?

Adm. W.: Primarily, I think, the academic problem. All of them had had this problem to a degree and some of them had had disciplinary problems, too. But I think most of them were concerned about the difficulty of getting grades that would pass them through the first year. After the first month of work, my grades were much better than I thought they would be.

Q: What were the courses like in those days?

Adm. W.: In those days at the Naval Academy the instruction was not very much like the current college instruction. It was a case of read your textbook, go to class, recite what you've learned and be marked each day on your recitation.

Q: This was an oral recitation, then?

Adm. W.: Yes, and in some cases something would be written on the blackboard in mathematics courses, and solve problems on the blackboard. I think it was conducted very much more on the order of current high-school education than on the order of current higher education.

Q: It was learning by rote.

Adm. W.: Pretty much, yes. Of course, in my time the instruction was somewhat different from the classes both earlier and later because I got in at just about the time the United States was becoming involved in World War I. There was a great demand for naval officers at sea and the course at the Academy was shortened from four to three years. It was compressed. They accomplished this by cutting down the time of annual leave and the time that was devoted to review and to conducting examinations. The course still included all the elements it had previously, but they were all compressed. I think my particular half of the class of 1921 was the only one that ever went through the Academy without taking either annual or semiannual examinations on any of the courses. No term examinations. We went through strictly with more or less informal tests, the normal instruction proceeding without interruption for review or examinations.

Q: Because of the time element?

Adm. W.: Yes.

Q: You say that there was a great demand, and there was, for naval officers and their services at sea. Did this mean that the teaching staff of naval officers was vastly reduced?

Adm. W.: I don't believe it was reduced. I suspect it was changed a bit, though. This is an aspect on which my knowledge is more or less hearsay, but I believe before about my time at the Naval Academy most of the instructors had been regular professional naval officers. During my stay there, the heads of departments and the superintendent along with the Commandant of midshipmen were regular professional naval officers. A great many of the instructors in the departments were reserve officers who were in for the duration of World War I, and there were a number of civilians, I think a larger number. So I think this shortage of seafaring naval officers did reflect itself in the faculty that was there in my time.

Q: How large was the student body?

Adm. W.: It of course rose during my period there -

Q: With additional appointments?

Adm. W.: Yes. I would guess that during my first year there, it was something under 2,000, and it rose to be considerably over that, by the time I left.

Q: What were the restrictions placed upon the students in terms of freedom and that kind of thing? How much leave time did you have? Give me a picture of that.

Adm. W.: Yes. During the month of September we were given just about - something less, as I recall it - one month's leave, and during this period most of us went home. Other than the one leave period in September, there was no formal leave granted to anybody at any time. My first year there, the plebes, fourth-classmen, were granted liberty to visit the city of Annapolis provided their conduct was Satisfactory, from after lunch on Saturday until just time for the evening meal formation that afternoon every other week. So we would go into the city of Annapolis for the afternoon once every two weeks. If we had conduct difficulties, this privilege wasn't granted to us. The upper classmen were given a little more opportunity to visit Annapolis. As I recall, as the first classmen we could visit Annapolis every afternoon after classes until the evening meal formation and on Saturdays and Sundays similarly we were allowed to go into the city of Annapolis. At that time, however, we were not allowed to leave the environs of Annapolis itself. We couldn't go to Washington, for instance. Our spending money was pretty drastically restricted, too. As I recall, as plebes we got something like a dollar and a half a month and as first classmen, maybe three dollars. So unless there was some outside income coming in from somewhere you wouldn't have been able to go very far anyway.

Q: Were you involved in athletics?

Adm. W.: Not to any very great extent. When I entered the Naval Academy I was about sixteen and a half years old, one of the youngest members of the class, although by no means the youngest, and I weighed something on the order of 115 pounds. So I wasn't prime athletic material. During my first class year I did manage to be not a first-string boxer but on the boxing squad, at least. I was one of those people who got himself punched around by the Number One boxer. This was a sport in which little people could participate with other little people.

Q: Bantamweights!

Adm. W.: Yes, that's just what I was. No really top-notch bantamweight but enough to enjoy the delicacies served at the training table!

Q: What about what came to be summer cruises? Did the wartime activities curtail this for you or what?

Adm. W.: Yes, the wartime did curtail our midshipman cruises very considerably. With the three-year course, we, of course, had only two midshipman cruises, one in 1918 I spent aboard the old USS *Missouri* which was a battleship about 360 feet long, as I remember.

Q: Coal-burning?

Adm. W.: Coal-burning with coal taken on every two weeks, and she operated out of the York River in Yorktown, Virginia. We did on several occasions get outside the Chesapeake Bay and this entitled all of us to wear the Atlantic Fleet ribbon of victory after World War I. We didn't get very far out.

Q: Did you see any German submarines?

Adm. W.: There were none in the vicinity at this time although it was considered a war zone. There had been at various times German submarines in the area.

Q: What was the objective of the cruise? What did you accomplish

Adm. W.: The cruise in those days took place each summer. The academic year ended in early June and all midshipmen then were embarked in ships of the fleet until about the first of September - most of June, July, and August. This part of the course was intended to give you practical experience of life aboard ship.

Q: And the application, I suppose, of some of the theories you learned?

Adm. W.: Yes. This first cruise aboard the Missouri my class took over about half the duties of the normal crew which was transferred to duty elsewhere and the midshipmen served as bluejackets temporarily on the ship, although some of the more senior ones did perofrm junior officer duties and things of this sort. Essentially, though, we were learning how to go to sea from the bottom up, and it was good experience.

Q: And on a coal-burner it was -

Adm. W.: We shoveled coal along with the professional coal-shovelers. I well recall in this instance firing a coal-fired boiler and trying to operate a slice bar. As I said earlier, I weighed about 115 pounds and I think that slice bar weighed more than I did, but we had to learn to handle one and to break clinkers off the grate bars of a coal-fired boiler. And I think this was valuable experience. You understand a lot more of the problems of a crew on board a ship having been through this.

Wellborn # 1 - 12

Q: Did it have a tendency to separate the sheep from the goats, so to speak? I mean, did it dtermine some of the lads on abandoning a naval career?

Adm. W.: I think by this time - see, we'd been in the service - a year more or less - most of those who had found a naval career wasn't for them had already departed. As I recall it, life aboard ship was sort of a lark for most of us. We were allowed half a bucket of fresh water every day whether we needed it or not and, of course, most of the time we could manage on that, but I don't recall anybody who thought that as a result of this deprivation he had to depart from the service. This didn't seem to make much difference to us. An interesting sidelight here, I believe, is that frequently in those days the midshipmen frequently fell into line alphabetically, and as we used to do this, in my class alphabetically the man just ahead of me was Robert Henry Winbourne Welch who later became founder of the John Birch Society. He left the Navy I think prior to the end of his first year because he did not like the military life. I thought he was a pretty bright, pretty interesting person in that first year during which I saw a good deal of him.

Q: Well, that was the first cruise, and the second and last one for you -

Adm. W.: The second and last one was somewhat different. By the time this came along, World War I was over. This was in 1919, and the United States had, of course, started to dismantle its

~~own~~ military esta-lishments ~~since the war was over and~~ this was true in the Navy, as it was in the other service - services, I guess, because we had the Marine Corps. The ship to which I was assigned was the battleship <u>Delaware</u>. Most of her crew had been discharged and for a good deal of that summer she wasn't able to go to sea. We spent part of this summer off Rockport, Massachusetts, where the ship was pretty much immobilized. We embarked in Annapolis, cruised down the Chesapeake Bay, and up to New England, and during a considerable part of that summer we just lay at anchor near Rockport because there weren't enough men in the ship to be safe in taking her to sea.

Q: What did they do to keep the midshipmen busy, then, and interested?

Adm. W.: Well, even though you're not at sea you can still experiment with sextants and navigation problems and they apparently had no difficulty keeping us busy. In those days there were somewhat different theories about how you maintained morale. Maintaining morale was very largely keeping people busy in those days, and all of our officers in charge had sufficient imagination to keep us well occupied and out of trouble. In that cruise, though, we served more in the capacity of junior officers than we did as bluejackets. The class of 1921 which, of course, was the incoming senior class, was divided up into small groups and limited numbers of us were sent to each one of the ships, so that when we arrived there there was a great possibility to let us act as junior officers and we did this to a large extent during that cruise, but I suspect I got more out of the original midshipman cruise in which I was essentially a bluejacket than I did out of the later one when I was more nearly a junior officer.

Q: Did your classmates ever feel in retrospect that they were deprived of some of the advantages that other midshipmen have had with more glamorous cruises abroad?

Adm. W.: I don't think so. I think we were all pretty happy to manage a shortened course and get our commissions a year earlier than we would otherwise have done. I think most of us felt that we were headed for naval careers and there was still plenty of time to get to some of the glamorous parts of the world.

Q: Who was superintendent of the Academy during your term there?

Adm. W.: At the time I entered, E. W. Eberle was the superintendent and Admiral Scales became superintendent later. I have at this point remembered the name of the congressman who appointed me, Henry Z. Osborn.

Q: The predecessor to Joe Crail.

Adm. W. I can't remember whether he was the predecessor or not.

Q: Admiral, had you determined upon any particular phase of a naval career during your years at the Academy? Had you become interested in any particular field?

Adm. W.: Not really. I simply wanted to be a seafaring line officer, so the evolvement of a specialty in my mind came along several years later.

Wellborn #1 - 15

Q: You weren't intrigued by naval aviation or anything of that sort?

Adm. W.: No. At that particular time, naval aviation was pretty much in its infancy and wasn't recognized as a field in which you could make a career.

Q: It certainly wasn't!

Adm. W.: I recall back in 1920, naval aviation didn't amount to very much. The thing to be at that time was simply a surface command-type line officer.

Q: So that's what you graduated to be, and you went to another old battleship, the New Mexico?

Adm. W.: Yes, although at that time she wasn't an old battleship. She was the very latest thing. At that particular stage of history, the means of propelling battleships was a matter of some controversy. The New Mexico was the first so-called electric-drive battleship. She was propelled by turbo generators which, in turn, operated electric induction motors which turned the propellers. This was a form of propulsion stylish at that particular moment but it didn't develop very far. The New Mexico was the very latest battleship at the time when I left her and had this electric propulsion.

Q: You say it didn't develop very much. Did it prove ineffective or what?

Adm. W.: From an engineering point of view, it was effective but I believe the weight requirements for this type of propulsion were greater than for a geared-turbine type, so this was dropped when higher speeds and higher horsepowers were needed. The weight requirement for an electric-drive ship at high speeds was out of proportion, so this system didn't progress much beyond the battleships that were contemporary with New Mexico.

Q: Were you pleased with the assignment on the New Mexico?

Adm. W.: Yes. As a matter of fact, assignment to ships was subject to degree of choice at the time. Each member of the class drew a number. Number one had first choice of the billets available, and so on down the line. Each graduate had a random choice and, as I recall, mine was somewhere along about the middle, and a dozen of us got together and decided we'd like to go to the same ship. The New Mexico turned out to be one that wasn't particularl popular with the low numbers, so she was the one that our group settled on as the one to which we could all be assigned.

Q: Did you have a good skipper?

Adm. W.: Yes. In fact, I was very much pleased with the officers in the ship. This didn't have very much bearing on our choice, but we were fortunate.

Q: But it had a bearing on your future.

Adm. W.: Yes. She was the flagship of what was then called the Pacific Fleet. Admiral Hugh Rodman was the commander-in-chief and the skipper was Arthur Lee Willard, who later became the commander of what was called the Scouting Force by that time, but had been the Atlantic Fleet. He was one of those who was destined for higher command. He was a very capable skipper, and all the staff officers and the ship's officers had, I believe, been very carefully selected for this duty in the flagship of the commander-in-chief of the Pacific Fleet. So I feel that the twelve of us were pretty lucky to land in that ship and to have the officers we did as preceptors for those formative first few years.

Q: What were your specific duties?

Adm. W.: I started out as a junior officer in the plotting room, which is the place where fire-control data was assembled and fed out to the main battery of guns. After a year of this duty, I became ship's torpedo officer after going to torpedo school at Keyport, Washington. This was fortunate, too, because it enabled me to become a division officer a little bit earlier than I would otherwise have.

Q: How long were you at this torpedo school?

Adm. W.: This was a six-month course, and very interesting it was, too. At that time, the Bremerton, Washington, area, which is where Keyport is located, was still pretty much frontier country, and it was interesting in the early stages of my career to be assigned to a naval station of this kind.

Q: Was there a variety of torpedoes?

Adm. W.: There was some variety but at this particular time there were primarily two types of torpedoes, both of them driven by compressed air and alcohol and water. One had a piston engine, a reciprocating engine, whereas the other one had a turbine and a different drive, but except for this difference in the engine, they were all very much alike. Some were 18 inches in diameter instead of 21, but they were basically pretty much the same kind of machinery.

One of the interesting aspects of this duty, though, was that all of the members of the class were required to qualify as deep-sea divers. At that time "deep sea" didn;t mean what it does now —

Q: Did it mean 50 feet or so?

Adm. W.: 75 feet, but all of us members were required to qualify at 75 feet as divers.

Q: Where was the school for this purpose?

Adm. W.: The school was at Keyport, the torpedo station.

Q: Oh, it was at the torpedo station?

Adm. W.: Yes.

Q: And what was the rationale for this, that you had to be a diver?

Adm. W.: In those days torpedoes were not completely reliable and were quite expensive.

Q: There were other days when they were, too!

Adm. W.: So when we fired torpedoes for exercise, generally we fired them in relatively shallow water and they ran erratically and you'd have to dive to recover them because you couldn't afford to waste that much money. These were pretty stringent days. So

Wellborn # 1 - 19

each torpedo officer was qualified as a diver in order to qualify him to recover the lost torpedoes that might turn up in exercise firings.

Q: When you exercised with torpedoes they didn't have the warheads, did they?

Adm. W.: No. There were things called exercise heads, which is true today. When you fire an exercise shot the torpedo always has a nonexplosive head. The ones today have means to bring the torpedo to the surface. At the end of a torpedo run compressed air is directed into the head and it achieves buoyancy that it didn't have during the run of the torpedo. That wasn't true in those days. The old exercise heads were water filled and there was no means of acquiring buoyance at the end of the run, so frequently, at the end of the run, the torpedo sank.

Q: How could you be sure when you had a live warhead that it was going to operate properly when you used dummies?

Adm. W.: You couldn't really. As a matter of fact, when World War II began, we had a good deal of trouble with this, but at this time the exploder in the warhead was tested at ordnance proving grounds, and the warhead itself, the exploder, and the booster were tested separately. The Bureau of Ordnance, which was the cognizant bureau, felt that to test each one of these segments of the over-all firing chain was adquate, though it later developed that this was not the case. They should have tested it as a system because if any of the exploders failed to function properly the warhead did not explode, but at that time we were pretty confident that the exploding mechanism functioned satisfactorily.

Q: Was this a generally accepted practice among navies? Did the Royal Navy do this also?

Adm. W.: I think other navies attempted to do a little more system testing than we did. Our method of handling this, I think, stemmed from our preoccupation with safety and not hurting anybody. There always is some hazard in firing a live surface shot, and also it's expensive. But very frequently we tended to test components in a very carefully controlled firing to keep the hazard down because in this country we couldn't afford to lose lives. The French in contrast, in the manufacture of ordnance always seemed to feel that once in every 25,000 maybe components of a certain kind of fuse, for instance, somebody was bound to get killed, and they weren't much concerned about it, so they didn't do the kind of component testing that we did. I think today we do considerably more of this kind of testing than we did in those days.

Q: This was a lesson derived from World War II.

Adm. W.: Yes, although just a few days ago we fired an atomic test shot at Amchitka in the Aleutians and there was tremendous opposition to this. A great many of the environmental people and bleeding-heart type people didn't want to see either people or animals hurt. It's always seemed to me that you must have a military establishment to be safe in this world and if you're going to have it, you'd better test your weapons.

Q: And know what you have!

Adm. W.: Yes. Of course, lots of people disagree and those people seem to be in the ascendancy.

Q: The New Mexico had torpedo tubes, hadn't she?

Adm. W.: Yes. In those days all battleships had torpedo tubes and, as I remember it, we had one tube on each side, starboard and port, and twelve torpedoes. In later battleships torpedoes were discontinued as not being worth the weight and space involved.

Q: It was a different concept on the use of a battleship wasn't it?

Adm. W.: Well, yes, and ranges were considerably shorter in the days of the New Mexico. She was originally built to shoot something on the order of 20,000 yards with her main battery guns.

Q: And they'd be what?

Adm. W.: Fourteen-inch. The torpedoes' range was something on the order of 12,000 yards and it wasn't at all inconceivable that with proper courses and speeds, the 12,000-yard torpedo could be effective within the ranges considered probable for battleship engagements. So, at that time, it made some sense to have torpedoes. Later, as speeds of ships increased and the range of the guns increased, torpedoes were pretty obviously not going to be effective weapons for battleships to carry and they weren't installed.

But we built our torpedoes when they were worth the weight and --

Q: And you were torpedo officer.

Adm. W.: I was torpedo officer so, of course, I felt that way.

Q: What other features of the New Mexico are interesting and different from what developed in later battleships?

Adm. W.: I'm trying to think now of some of the features that were more or less unique. Her class of battleships was the last one that had originally been designed with a secondary battery and located in casemates lower than the weather deck. Those guns in World War I were probably pretty ineffective. By the time the New Mexico was commissioned, all of these guns had been brought up to a higher level. But the New Mexico class still retained what we called gun sponsons, locations where guns could have been mounted. All the later ships did not have this, so she was unique in this respect and her electric drive was something new. She had in her main battery a type gun with which the Navy had a great deal of difficulty. At the time I was in her this wasn't thoroughly realized. This particular gun had been designed with a peculiar combination of rifling in the gun and a rotating band on the projectile. The projectile very rarely seated in the gun and this resulted in considerable dispersion when the guns were fired. It took many years to discover why this happened and to cure it. When I was in the New Mexico and we fired a twelve-gun salvo with the main battery, the shots were apt to go pretty much all over the ocean. None of us knew why, and we worked very hard at

Wellborn #1 - 23

trying to improve this but at this particular time we hadn't located the cause and we didn't accomplish very much improvement. I think, in most respects, though, the New Mexico was pretty much the typical American battleship.

Q: She was too early to have a catapult, wasn't she?

Adm. W.: Yes, this was installed on board later, but at that particular time when I served in her and for six or seven years battleships didn't have airplanes. The first battleship to acquire one was the Oklahoma. She was something very special with that catapult that she had on the stern of the ship. She carried a little airplane, biplane, which would fly some times, but the airplanes of that day weren't very reliable either. So it really wasn't tactically a very useful piece of gear to carry around. You couldn't count on it when you needed it.

Q: Well, the New Mexico was a part of the so-called Pacific Fleet. What did this entail, where did it take you?

Adm. W.: At that time the Pacific Fleet had pretty much of a routine. She was home-based at San Pedro in the Long Beach area in California. Round about the end of June the whole fleet started north and it stopped off in San Francisco Bay for a week or so, then went on up to Puget Sound, where we visited various ports but did some training out of mostly Port Angeles, Washington, which is on the south shore of the entrance to Puget Sound. Then along about September the fleet started south, stopped off in San Francisco Bay, spent a week or so visiting, then went back to southern California where a regular cycle of gunnery training, communications training, and some tactical training took place until roughly the first of January.

The first of January (soon after) was usually a fleet exercise. One year this would be a Pacific Fleet one and take only a month or so. We might go to the Hawaii area or we might stay right off the California coast. Alternate years, the Pacific Fleet usually went to Panama and either the Pacific Fleet went through the Canal to the Atlantic and had joint maneuvers there, or the Atlantic Fleet came through to the Pacific and we had joint maneuvers in the Pacific. This situation usually resulted in long maneuvers, as much as three months. At the end of this fleet training period, we returned to the Long Beach - San Pedro area to continue our gunnery training cycle and what you might call ship's exercising rather than fleet exercising. In those days ships operated very much more on a pre-established schedule and there were very few international emergencies, as you recall. Ships' operating schedules were established and published in the fleet as much as three months in advance, so you always knew where you were going and what you were going to be doing.

Q: Were you handicapped in any way with lack of personnel? This was a low point in recruiting, wasn't it?

Adm. W.: This was a period of stringency and none of the ships had a full wartime complement aboard. We had what was called an allowance of personnel and this was, maybe, 75 percent of the wartime complement, but this didn't restrict you very much. In your engineer force you didn't have enough to continually operate at full power, but you did have enough so that for period of forty-eight hours you could operate the ship at full power without any problem, and you could operate at lower powers indefinitely. In the gunnery department you didn't have enough men to man all of your stations and the ammunition-handling part of your turrets, but you had enough to man your gun turrets and your gun crews and things of this sort and for a gunnery exercise you borrowed men from some of the other divisions or departments. For instance, your stewards - mess attendants they were called in those days - would come into your powder-handling room and serve as ammunition men for a gunnery exercise. So there wasn't too much difficulty in operating and training the ships, although there was a shortage of personnel for warlike operations. I think that, very wisely, the Navy Department, which means the chief of naval operations, chose to keep the ships not up to full wartime complement but sufficiently well manned to be able to operate, and to limit the number of ships in commission, rather than keep the ships so short-handed that they wouldn't be able to train and operate. But we had a definite ceiling on the number of people who were in the Navy in those days.

Q: What was the state of the naval base at Pearl Harbor when you visited there?

Adm. W.: The first time I went to Pearl Harbor was in 1920 in the New Mexico, very shortly after I joined her. It is interesting to note that at that time the New Mexico did not go in to Pearl Harbor, she went in to Honolulu. There was some development, as I

Wellborn #1 - 26

recall, at Pearl Harbor but it was not a real naval base at that time. It was able to take surface and smaller ships. I can't recall clearly whether it could take deep-draft battleships such as the New Mexico through the channel. But it wasn't an important naval base at that time although the Hawaiian Islands were recognized as strategically important.

Q: Inasmuch as you had fleet exercises off Panama, would you talk a little about the defenses of the canal? Who was thought to be a potential enemy - that sort of thing?

Adm. W.: At that time, of course, aircraft hadn't developed to any great extent and there weren't any missiles, so any attack on the canal necessarily had to come overseas. It had to be waterborne. So the Navy considered itself to be the prime defenders of the Panama Canal, with the Army ashore with coast artillery guns to defend against anything that got in close. I think the most difficult aspect of the Navy's defense of the canal was reconnaissance. Without aircraft or any of the modern means of reconnaissance it was pretty difficult to know where the enemy was and when he was approaching the canal zone. So there was a good deal of attention devoted to searches by cruiser-destroyer type ships in locating them. Each year there would be at least part of the exercise devoted to this kind of thing.

At that time, being a relatively young and inexperienced person, I didn't know very much about what the Army had ashore. I did know, however, that they had some pretty big coast defense guns, 14-inch guns. They later became pretty obsolete and I don't believe they No have any part of those guns. The Panama Canal was pretty well defended at that time by this type of artillery.

I'm not sure that I answered your question very fully. Maybe you could expand on the question.

Q: I think it does. It bears out the fact that there wasn't a great deal in terms of defense.

Adm. W.: Very little in the way of fixed installations

Q: Were Mexican ports on the west coast ports of call for the Pacific Fleet?

Adm. W.: The Pacific Fleet didn't visit these very frequently, but we did have some rights along the Pacific coast of Mexico, coaling stations. I recall visiting in the New Mexico - I think this was in 1921 - at a little place called Pichilinque Bay. This was down near the tip of Lower California. I think we still had a coaling station there at that time, although it was pretty inactive. The New Mexico was an oil burner, of course. The fleet was pretty well converted to oil by this time, and that coaling station was in the process of becoming obsolete. On this particular trip, the New Mexico, as the fleet flagship, did visit several ports along the Mexican coast, but as I recall, the rest of the fleet did not enter any Mexican port, so it was rather unusual for American men-of-war to visit Mexican ports.

Q: And you were on the New Mexico for a considerable period, weren't you?

Adm. W.: Yes, I did five years continuously in the New Mexico.

Q: Wasn't that unusual?

Adm. W.: Quite unusual at that time, and then, rather strangely, I went back to her again after my first tour of shore duty. So, all told, I think I did something like seven years in that particular ship, which is highly unusual.

Q: During that time you had different jobs, however?

Adm. W.: Oh, yes. After being torpedo officer I became the second division officer, which involved turret number 2, which was the high one on the forecastle, and I later became number 1 spotter on the ship and was stationed up at the top of the foremast. I had the normal rotation of duty that was customary at that time.

Q: Why the long assignment on one ship? Was it because there were not that many ships in the fleet?

Adm. W.: Normally, an officer graduating from the Naval Academy at that time did two or three years in his first ship and then went to some other kind of ship, but each ship had something in the way of capability to protest the assignment of any of its officers at any one time, that is the re-assignment of any one time. When my three years expired, there had been a very considerable exodus of experienced officers in the New Mexico and the skipper at that time requested that he be allowed to retain several people who had some experience in the ship, and I was one of those who stayed on as something of a carryover as a good many officers left. I think this is the explanation of my five years in her. There frequently was a problem of continuity in ships, and I

Wellborn #1 - '29

provided some continuity in the New Mexico.

Q: And at the same time it wasn't proving to be a detriment to your own advancement in career?

Adm. W.: At the time, it was not considered highly favorable for your own career, because all Naval Academy graduates were expected to be generalists. They were supposed to know something of all kinds of ships, so this did tend to deprive me of any knowledge of any except battleships, but battleships were supposed to be the queens of the seas in those days, so if you had to specialize on anything, specializing on battleships was pretty good. That subsequently changed.

I finally did, when I left the New Mexico, go to a destroyer and I served for a year in a destroyer.

Q: This was something you sought?

Adm. W.: Yes. This, I think, tended to take the curse off of having stayed in a battleship as long as I did.

Q: The Gilmer was quite a modern destroyer, wasn't she?

Adm. W.: Well, for her day. She was one of the four-stack, flush-deck destroyers. She was unusual in one respect - or maybe I should say at least one respect. Whereas most of our four-stack, flush-deck, 1,100-ton destroyers had 4-inch guns, the Gilmer, along with four or five others, had 5"/51 calibre guns, which were really too big and heavy for the hulls in which they were mounted. This made her something of a heavy roller with her stability somewhat less than her sister ships with 4-inch guns, but nobody worried much about stability in those days, anyway. None of them capsized, so I guess it was all right.

Q: This made a little rough sailing then?

Adm. W.: Yes. It tended to make up for having sailed in a battleship in my previous career! The Gilmer was pretty wet and pretty lively! She had, before I joined her, done quite a lot of duty in the Mediterranean off the Turkish coast subsequent to the end of World War I. During this duty the Gilmer had acquired a full complement of bedbugs all over the ship, and during the year that I was in her we fumigated that ship frequently. Every time we got to a port that had fumigating facilities, but while I was in her we never got rid of those bugs. This made life in her somewhat disagreeable, but there were quite a number of our destroyers that had served on that Turkey assignment and had this problem.

Q: What was your particular job in the Gilmer?

Adm. W.: I did a little of everything. In those days that kind of a ship had usually six, sometimes seven, officers aboard, and the junior one was usually the supply officer, and as you moved up in seniority you got some other job considered more desirable. I started off as the first lieutenant and the supply officer and later became the gunnery officer, and, at one stage of the game, served as interim executive officer. In this kind of a small ship without very many officers, you found yourself having to deal with practica-ly every duty on board. I was never an engineer officer and I was never the skipper of that ship, but at one time or another I think I had all of the other officer assignments. This was common in destroyers at that time.

Q: What happened to the other eleven of your classmates who were with you originally in the New Mexico? Did they stay on for the five-year period?

Adm. W.: I believe I was the last surviving member of the twelve who originally went to her. They started leaving her within a year of graduation to go to various other assignments, and we pretty much scattered to the four winds, at least the four winds of the Navy, after a year of duty in the ship. Some of them are still alive and some are my very good friends.

Q: During all this time, six years, did you have any shore leave? You didn't have any shore assignment, except for the school at Bremerton.

Adm. W.: Yes. As a rule, we didn't have any prolonged leave, as such. That is, you didn't go away from the ship for more than a week or ten days at a time, but you occasionally did have this at Christmas or some other appropriate time. Shore leave as granted in those days, sometimes called liberty, was simply overnight or over a weekend — over a weekend absence from the ship and this was pretty regular and predictable in those days. You normally had a rotation of one day in three having to be on board as either a watch stander or a ship keeper or something. The other two days if the ship was in port, the officers normally were permitted to leave about 4:30 in the afternoon and had to be back by eight o'clock the next morning. In these days ships were always at anchor offshore so you had to go from the ship and return to the ship in ship's boats, so this meant that you arrived ashore somewhere along about five o'clock and you had to be on the pier ready to get into the boat to return to the ship about seven o'clock. So you would be off the ship two out of three nights, depending on your finances, from about five o'clock, say, until about seven o'clock the next morning. I bring up that financial problem because when I graduated a freshly commissioned ensign with no prior service I was paid, as I recall it, about $125 a month and even in those days $125 a month didn't go very far. So you couldn't leave the ship every time your duty section wasn't on watch. You just couldn't afford it.

Wellborn #2 - 33

Interview No. 2 with Vice Admiral Charles Wellborn, Jr., U.S. Navy
(Retired)

Place: His apartment in the Westchester, Washington, D.C.

Date: Tuesday morning, 30 November 1971

Subject: Biography

By: John T. Mason, Jr.

Q: This is the beginning of Chapter Two, Sir. It's nice to see you today. I think you're going to talk now about going to PG school, aren't you?

Adm. W.: It is very nice indeed to see you.

The PG school is the assignment that followed the <u>Gilmer</u>. The course of instruction was ordnance engineering, as it was called. This started at the Naval Academy in the building that had formerly been the Marine barracks, and we studied lots of mathematics, physics, and this sort of thing. We were a couple of years there at the Naval Academy, and then the third year of this course involved going on a tour. When I say "tour," I mean that we spent two or three weeks on temporary duty at a number of stations such as the powder factory at Indian Head, the proving ground at Dahlgren.

Q: This was the practical application?

Adm. W.: Yes, this was learning how to apply the theories that we had acquired during our two years at Annapolis. I was interrupted in this latter stay in the second year because the Bureau of Ordnance was acquiring a good deal of fire-control material from the General Electric Company in Schenectady, New York, and they needed an assistant inspector in the office there in Schenectady. So my Cook's Tour, so-called, was interrupted in midterm, and I spent the last half of that third year getting practical knowledge of how the naval inspector of ordnance operated, particularly vis-à-vis fire-control equipment.

Q: Tell me about that fire-control equipment. Was that a new type coming in?

Adm. W.: At this particular time, fire-control equipment for naval guns was advancing fairly rapidly and there were some modernizations taking place so that it did take more of the inspection operation to make sure that this somewhat different equipment - different from what we'd acquired in the past - was delivered both successful qualitywise and on time.

Q: How did it differ from what had been used previously in the Nav

Adm. W.: Well, this would require a somewhat technical discussion of fire-control equipment of that day. Previous fire-control equipment had to a considerable degree operated on a step-by-step electrical basis. The equipment we were acquiring at this stage was a synchronous one with an infinite number of steps in its operations and it was different in this respect. Also previous fire-control equipment had been, you might say, bit-by-bit fire-control equipment. The whole system for controlling one type of gun had not been well integrated. It had one system for the training of the guns, and another system for the elevation of the guns. The systems we were acquiring at that time were designed for complete control of the guns' training and elevation.

Q: Is this the equipment we went into World War II with?

Adm. W.: To a considerable extent, yes. The equipment that was available about the time we went into World War II had advanced considerably beyond the type that we were getting back there in about 1929. The 1929-type equipment sent a signal to the guns indicating what their angle of training and elevation should be, and the later equipment not only sent the signal but provided control to the power applied to the guns so that they automatically went to the angle of training and elevation without benefit of human hands. You had to train and elevate guns manually with that system that we were using in 1929, whereas in the later systms the operation became automatic.

Q: And then, I understand, during World War II there was a considerable advance, was there not?

Adm. W.: Oh, very much, yes. I would say, however, that the greatest advance in World War II fire-control equipment was in the kind of computers that we used, rather than in the kind of transmission that we used. Prior to the World War II period there hadn't been too much need for computers. Airplanes didn't fly quite so fast, and we had more time to turn knobs in the mechanical methods of solving the fire-control problem. About World War II things began to happen too fast for this to be successful and it became very largely electronic and very much more rapid and very much more automatic.

Wellborn #2 - '36

Q: Well, that was a very profitable tour of duty, I would think, for you at Schenectady?

Adm. W.: It was I think more profitable for me, probably than for the Navy or the United States government! But I did learn a good deal, not only about fire-control equipment but about how business and industry operated which was helpful- I didn't have as much opportunity to use the technical ordnance education I acquired because I only did one tour of duty subsequently with the Bureau of Ordnance, and that one turned out not to be involved with the particular kinds of engineering that I had studied, but was largely connected with explosives and ammunition.

Q: After Schenectady you did what?

Adm. W.: After that I went back to the battleship New Mexico.

Q: Did you get a degree for this postgraduate course?

Adm. W.: No. At that time, degrees were not awarded for postgraduate work. They are today, and the work I did probably would have resulted in a master's degree in possibly mathematics or possibly electrical engineering. But at that time postgraduate school, I think, was not accredited and certainly did not award degrees, so I have no degree as a result of that.

Q: You went back to the New Mexico?

Adm. W.: Yes, after finishing that tour of duty at Schenectady, I went back to the battleship New Mexico and stayed in her, I think, another two years, which was something of a record - doing seven

Wellborn #2 - 37

years in all in that one ship. During that period I had some connection with ordnance material inasmuch as I went back in the gunnery department and that kind of work, but that was gunnery duty rather than ordnance duty. There is a differentiation there. After a couple of years in the New Mexico she was sent in for modernization. She was one of our battleships that went through the process of acquiring better underwater protection and acquiring modern fire-control equipment - that is, modern for that day, and having the guns in her main battery revised so that they could elevate to a higher degree than they had originally. They were originally installed to elevate to only 15 degrees, and the modernization enabled them to go to 30 degrees.

Q: Which increased the range?

Adm. W.: Which increased the range considerably.

Q: What did they do to improve the underwater area and protect her?

Adm. W.: This was largely the installation of what were called blisters on the outside of the hull. The ships had originally been built with armor belts on the outside and the blisters were installed outboard of the armor and increased the beam of the ships somewhat, but I think the design of the blisters was such that they were streamlined and didn't reduce the speed of the ships materially. But it did improve their underwater protection against torpedoes and mines.

Q: Where did this idea originate? Was it something from the Royal

Navy?

Adm. W.: No, this, I think, came from our own Bureau of Ships, which was at that time called the Bureau of Construction and Repair. They had in their design of subsequent ships developed better techniques including the underwater subdivision of ships with the ability to withstand underwater explosions. I think it was just part of the evolution of ship design. The later ships had better protection. There were programs started sometime in the twenties, I guess, to modernize our older battleships. They started with the oldest ones and worked forward to the later ones. In about 1931 the New Mexico's turn came up, so she went into the Philadelphia navy yard for her modernization. At that time I was transferred to the battleship Nevada which had completed her modernization. She was an older battleship than the New Mexico. She came out with guns that elevated to a higher degree and with modern fire control and with the extra ~~little~~ blisters outside of her armor belt. This did an interesting thing to the Nevada. She previously had been a ship that handled rather well, but after the installation of the blisters, the Nevada's manner of turning became pretty interesting. When you put her rudder over, she was reluctant to start to swing, but when she started, she was even more reluctant to stop doing it. Keeping her in formation, as we used to operate in those days, was very tricky and you had to be really pretty alert to prevent the Nevada from wandering all over the place because she did become pretty hard to control in turns.

Q: She was erratic!

Adm. W.: Yes, she was a little erratic, but if you got her rudder shifted in a timely way you could keep her going in pretty good shape.

Q: This modernization of battleships, was this augmented somewhat because of the limited arms treaties that we agreed with?

Adm. W.: Yes. I suspect that had there been no limitation of arms treaty, no prohibition on building new ships, we might well have scrapped those older ones and started fresh, built new ones, but under the circumstances we resorted to this business of modernizing the ships. There may, in those days, have been some financial saving, too, in modernizing ships, although it was a little illusory because the cost of modernization was so great that it was almost as cheap to start with a nice fresh keel and build up from there.

Q: It's interesting to speculate a bit on what effects the limitations of arms treaties had upon various navies. The fact that we reconditioned old battleships, the Japanese apparently built ships that could be very readily converted into something else. All the subterfuges that we entered into!

Adm. W.: There were interesting subterfuges. One of them involved so-called standard tonnage. A ship's tonnage was based on the hull without ammunition, without, as I remember it, fuel - I can't recall exactly the details now of what was included in the standard tonnage and what was not. But there were a number of rather heavy items that were not.

Q: Even though they were absolutely necessary to the effective working of the ship?

Adm. W.: Yes, and the result of this was that a so-called 10,000-ton standard cruiser actually displaced something like 14,000 tons, and we always suspected the Japanese fudged a little on that because their 10,000-tonners turned out quite a lot bigger than our 10,000-tonners. But the rules did permit quite a lot of overweight ships turning up, and this was one of the important effects. Of course, another of the important effects was that the size of your ships was controlled by the international agreement rather than by desirable design characteristics. A cruiser, for instance, couldn't be more than 10,000 tons and, at that time, probably the optimum cruiser would have weighed a good deal more than that, but by various compromises as to characteristics ships were turned out within the 10,000 standard ton limitation. The battleships were similarly restricted as to total tonnage. This was all restricted, both the design of ships and the numbers of ships that each navy had. While the total tonnage was a certain amount, you could hack this up in various ways - you could have a large number of small ships or a smaller number of larger ships. All of these factors went into the determination of what ships you had.

Q: Then, in a sense, the signatories to these treaties were involved in something of a dilemma. It was idealism versus realism.

Adm. W.: Very much so, yes, and I think there isn't anything very unusual about this situation. You nearly always find world statesmen who are filled with idealism, anxious to limit armaments.

They're meeting on this today. In those days they arrived at a conclusion that was not based purely on military judgment. It was based very largely on idealism. Under the agreements that they reached, the military people had to do the best they could in the situation they had.

Q: Were there any interesting episodes that you recall from the Nevada days?

Adm. W.: I don't recall anything particularly interesting. That was a relatively brief tour of duty. I went to the Nevada in early 1931, and, as I recall it was more or less six months later that I went to the staff of the Commander of Battleships of the Battle Force that was out there in the San Diego - San Pedro - Long Beach area.

Q: Who was commander-in-chief of the battleships?

Adm. W.: The commander of the battleships was Admiral Luke McNamee.

Q: And you became his aide?

Adm. W.: Well, I became one of his aides. In those days, anybody on the staff of a flag officer was designated as an aide. Today, the chief of staff, flag secretary, and flag lieutenant are the only aides. In those days the whole staff were considered to be aides. My assignment there, nominally, was communications officer. This was because there was an allowance for a communications officer. I didn't know anything about communications other than what any naval

Wellborn #2 - 42

officer does.

Q: Did your job force you to learn about them?

Adm. W.: Yes, I learned a little communications, but primarily the work I did was not really in communications. I worked as assistant to the staff gunnery officer and as the battle force athletic officer. In those days, athletics, competition between ships, was considered something that was relatively important as a morale factor, and there was an extensive program of athletic competition between ships - basketball, baseball, football, various rowing events, and sailing events, boxing wrestling - and this program took a pretty good deal of administration to keep operating. I devoted a good deal of time to managing athletics at that time.

Q: This was a program, I would think, that could only flourish in peacetime?

Adm. W.: Yes. This couldn't operate in time of war. You couldn't operate it if the ships weren't pretty steadily at their home base, and they were in those days. The Long Beach - San Pedro area was the home base for the battleships, and this program was operated essentially in that area.

Q: Did it achieve its desired results for morale?

Adm. W.: Yes, I think it helped quite a good deal.

Q: What was the status of morale in the Navy?

Adm. W.: It was pretty high. You see, this was a period of

depression in the country and, while under executive order from Mr. Hoover, all of the military services along with all the rest of the federal employees accepted a month's leave without pay and without getting the leave, which amounted to a one-twelfth reduction in pay, this didn't seem to adversely affect morale at the time. The whole country was suffering from reduced pay and ours wasn't reduced any more than most of the other people in the country. We had very largely a professional Navy in those days and, of course, it was all volunteer, and since jobs were hard to find when people left the service, a great many of them didn't leave. When their enlistments expired, they shipped over.

Q: What percentage would re-enlist?

Adm. W.: I'm afraid I couldn't give you a worthwhile percentage, but I can say that it was considerably higher than it is today. Just what the numerical figure would be, I'd rather not guess.

Q: Tell me a little about your administrative job in terms of athletics.

Adm. W.: This involved arranging for each of the various teams to play each of the others in each of the various branches of athletics. For instance, the football teams had to go through the seasons' schedule. There were requirements for arranging the necessary fields. We operated two Navy athletic fields in the San Pedro - Long Beach area, and the schedules for the various events had to be tied in with the operating schedules of the ships, of course. So that a team of a ship's company had to be available at the right time to play another team at the right place. It was

Wellborn #2 - 44

really simply much like any other management problem. You had to consider all the various factors involved and work out the schedule. The financial arrangements for this were relatively simple. The ships paid most of the bills themselves.

Q: The individual ships?

Adm. W.: Yes. We didn't have much problem with this. The San Pedro field was a federal-controlled field and we got our labor from the ships on a "volunteer" basis - whether the laborers volunteered or not, I'm not sure, but the ships did!

Q: The word "duress" might fit in here!

Adm. W.: Yes. There might be a degree of duress involved here. The field we had at Long Beach was city-owned. I don't recall now whether they leased it to us for a dollar a year or whether they just gave it to us. At any rate, we maintained it and the city of Long Beach owned it. Those two were quite adequate for the ships.

During a subsequent period, after a year or so with Admiral McNamee as commander of battleships, he was promoted to be commander of the battle force, which included not only battleships but some destroyers and cruisers and other types. I continued with him for another year doing much the same thing, here including not only the battleships but the various other classes. During that period the ~~athletic effort for the whole~~ Battle Force organized a football team composed of individuals from various ships which played a good many of the Pacific coast college football teams, which made a good deal of money for the Navy Relief Society. For the normal intership games, no admission was charged ~~and~~

but when we organized that battle force team we got into the business of charging admission and the proceeds from the admission charges at the end of the season were turned over to the Navy Relief Society. We made a reasonable amount of money for them.

Q: We hear today much about the commercialization of athletics. Perhaps that was the beginning?

Adm. W.: Well, no. I think our effort just fit in with the rest of the picture of that day. It was interesting, though, that college teams weren't very wild to play us after the first experience. Our players, of course, were weeded out of a pretty good sized population and they generally were a little older than the college players –

Q: And consequently heavier.

Adm. W.: Yes, they were bigger. Some of our men weren't intellectual giants but they were physical giants. A college team didn't get very much glory from beating us, but they got a lot of unfavorable publicity if they were beaten by us. So after a year or so, we had a good deal of difficulty arranging the schedule if they were to be sure that they weren't going to get into something that would react unfavorably on their own gate receipts. But we did have a very good team and played quite successfully against the colleges, and then we had a final game of the season, which was played in the San Francisco Bay area, on I believe what was then known as Armistice Day, now Veterans Day. This was played against a conglomerate Army team. The Army on the Pacific coast also put together one of these teams. That was always quite an event in Pacific Coast athletic circles. The Navy's team won for several years in a row, and the series broke up much the way some of these athletic competitions do when one team seems to get quite a lot better than the other. Later the ships began to operate and weren't available as much as they had been and it became almost impossible to put one of these conglomerate teams together.

An interesting sidelight that hasn't much to do with naval history was that in those days you could put a first-class football team on the field, fully equipped, and run them through the season for a total of about $25,000. I shudder to think what it would cost to do it today.

Q: Give me a picture of Admiral McNamee.

Adm. W.: Admiral McNamee was a good, old, military man. He was the kind of an admiral that frequently would be pictured in cartoons and things. A very gruff old sailor man with a heart of gold, however. I should say that his outstanding characteristic, as I saw it, was his ability to concentrate on some particular problem, to consider all the various aspects of the problem, and to arrive at a decision, then to completely erase it from his list of things about which he had to worry. I think from him I learned the value of this characteristic about as well as it could possibly have been learned. He could be confronted with a problem of major importance, study it in an appropriate way, make his decision, and then go off to do something else completely unrelated to any worry or concern for the old problem.

Q: A tremendous asset in life!

Adm. W.: It is, indeed. I think this was probably the one characteristic that he had that made him a four-star admiral. He was otherwise normally intelligent, as I saw it. He was a very pleasant individual underneath his gruff exterior, but he was the perfect picture of "the admiral standing on the bridge issuing commands in a loud stentorian voice." He was an authoritative character.

Adm. W.:

Q: And then after that being with him all that time, you were in the California with him.

Adm. W.: Yes. She was the flagship of the battle force. He had his flag in her.

Q: How did the battle force operate in those days? Was it in both oceans?

Adm. W.: Generally speaking, the battle force was in the Pacific Ocean, and what was called the scouting force in those days was in the Atlantic Ocean. During the latter part of this period, the Scouting Force also came to the Pacific. It seemed to be the area in which the naval force was going to be required, but for a good many years the Scouting Force was in the Atlantic and the Battle Force was in the Pacific. The scouting force did not include any battleships, but was a cruiser and destroyer force. The carriers were with the battle force, and patrol planes, this type of aviation, was with the battle force. So this battle force was a part of the U.S. fleet, the part of the fleet with the greatest

Wellborn #2 - 48

striking power.

Q: Of course, at that time, there were no potential enemies, were there?

Adm. W.: Well, while there were not, I should say, immediately potential, we all regarded in those days the Japanese as our most probable enemies. Most of our thinking was directed toward possible war against Japan. At that particular time we were not as closely related to the British as we became in World War II, and we always more or less had an eye on what their navy was doing, too, but this was in a much more friendly sort of way than the way we eyed the Japanese Navy. Other navies didn't seem to give us very much concern in that way.

Q: When you left Admiral McNamee, did you ask for the Bureau of Ordnance or was this something handed to you?

Adm. W.: In those days, you took assignments that came to you more or less. You could negotiate a little bit and if you were forehanded about writing to the right people you might find that someone in some particular assignment would ask for you. But this assignment to the Bureau of Ordnance resulted rather directly from the fact that the Navy had invested a considerable amount of my postgraduate instruction in ordnance and, under these circumstances, I was normally expected after a tour of duty at sea to go back to some duty under the Bureau of Ordnance, and I did get such an assignment. So, while this wasn't something that I really opted for, it was something that I had expected and it worked out more or less in accordance with the way officers were assigned.

Q: And you were concerned primarily with ammunition?

Adm. W.: Yes. The type of instruction that we had received in postgraduate work sometimes didn't relate very directly to the billets that were open at the time we became available to fill them. While my postgraduate instruction had evolved more around ballistics and fire control than around ammunition, there wasn't any available billet in ballistics and fire control, there was one in ammunition so I landed in that. From my point of view, it was probably advantageous because it got me into a new field and more or less broadened my experience.

Q: What did it entail? Tell me about it.

Adm. W.: This section at that time handled the procurement of projectiles, fuses, bombs, and explosives, and the assembly of all these various components into finished ammunition, and the distribution of ammunition from the point of assembly to points of storage, and then the issuance of ammunition from the depots where it was stored to the ships that were expected possibly to fire it. So, you started in with the procurement of components, then went on through to distribution of the finished products to the comsumer ships. Of course, ammunition is something that has to be cared for and maintained. Explosives don't last for ever and you had to rotate ammunition into and out of ships. I was involved in this process also.

Q: Were the component parts primarily manufactured by the Navy itself, or did they come from contracts with private business?

Adm. W.: Most of them were contracted for with private manufacturers. The Navy at that time did manufacture some components. We felt it was always a pretty good idea to do a little of this manufacture ourselves in order to keep the contractors honest and to maintain our own knowledge of whether or not bidding was reasonable and our specifications also were reasonable. So we had some of our own components manufactured at the Washington Navy Yard and some components that were manufactured at some of the other navy yards. We then had a little assembly plant at Baldwin, Long Island, that put together star shells. Baldwin was a post office in those days, but I don't know whether it still exists. It was what's now Brooklyn. And we had various others - I don't recall all of them - that could manufacture various kinds of components.

Q: Was the Navy able to manufacture at lesser cost than what they contracted for?

Adm. W.: There was always quite a controversy about. How you figured costs in a navy yard, it was something that no one could ever agree upon. How much of the overhead in the navy yard you should charge off to preparedness for war and how much you should charge off to the individual component that was being manufactured, no two people could ever agree on, but my own judgment of this was that our costs were usually comparable to what we had to pay an outside contractor to make the parts. From the point of view of expenditure of money from appropriations, we frequently found that we could get components cheaper from a naval plant than we could from an outside contractor, but this really meant that some of the cost of that manufacture was being paid for by some other appropriation. I don't think that the federal government got those components at any less cost than it would have from private contractors.

Q: Did you get involved with the various manufacturers when you were in this job?

Adm. W.: Inevitably, to a certain extent, but in those days the actual contracting was not done by the material bureau involved. The Bureau of Supplies and Accounts sent the proposals for bids out to the prospective contractors, and when the bids came in the Bureau of Supplies and Accounts actually awarded the contracts, with the advice and consent, you might say, of the material bureau involved. So our relationship with the contractors was very largely one of inspecting the material and of discussing what kind of specifications were feasible before bids were called for and then in arranging for appropriate deliveries of finished material. We did not handle the actual financial arrangements.

Q: Would you say that that system, which involved another office in between you and the manufacturer, was effective? Did it permit you to maintain enough control over the product?

Adm. W.: It seemed to me that this was quite an effective system for that particular period in history. In those days, we were not in any kind of emergency situation. We had plenty of time to go through each step of transferring the information from one bureau to another, calling for bids which were quite formalized in those days - there was no negotiation of contracts. We asked respective contractors to bid on something that was quite specifically described, and there was no deviation from the product described. If any contractor proposed a deviation, why, the old bids were thrown out and you had to start all over again. So, it wasn't an effective means for wartime or emergency, and it did pretty much put you in Strait Jacket on the acquisition of the kind of material that you had specified. It didn't permit rapid advances in any particular kind of material that we required.

If one contractor came up with an improved design, well, you had to throw the whole set of bids out and start all over again, which was time-consuming. Also, it didn't encourage contractors to come up with innovating ideas, because his idea that he disclosed in his alternative bidding became the property of the government and was available to all other prospective contractors, so that he lost his advantage.

The system worked well in its day, but I don't think it would have been successful either as a wartime system or, were it operating now, in today's circumstances.

Q: With such rapidly changing situations.

Adm. W.: Yes. The technology develops pretty fast and the proprietorship of an advance in technology can be very important. But in those nice, calm, and peaceful old days, it worked pretty well.

Q: And in retrospect, I suppose, we were just as well off, weren't we?

Wellborn #2 - 53

Adm. W.: Yes. At that particular moment, we were..

Q: What about the policy of the Navy Department in that day in terms of the use of live ammunition?

Adm. W.: This, I think, was very closely related to the necessity for economy. Live ammunition was very seldom expended. The theory seemed to be that each component of ammunition went through a test, very frequently at the proving ground at Dahlgren, but this caried from component to component. Then there was generally some testing of assembled components, again at the proving ground. After this there was very little firing of service ammunition by ships of the fleet. They fired target-practice ammunition regularly. There was a competitive gunnery competition each year, but during the course of this the ammunition that was fired was not service ammunition. A propellant explosive was used for this purpose which was usually some of our older powder that was nearing the end of its life. It would be brought in from the ships, reworked from the service ammunition into target-practice ammunition, then fired. Meanwhile, the meager appropriations that we got each year for target-practice ammunition would go to buy new explosives that would go into service ammunition. Projectiles, generally speaking, were not service projectiles, which were pretty expensive things to buy. They were cast-iron slugs, essentially, made in the same shape as service projectiles but were very much less expensive than service projectiles.

Q: Taking a long-range point of view, did this policy work to the detriment of the Navy?

Adm. W.: I think in answering that question, you'd have to say yes and no. In those days of economy, it would have been extremely detrimental to our readiness to have fired any service ammunition because we couldn't replace it. We didn't have money enough to get replacement service ammunition, although we could get enough money to buy this cheaper target-practice ammunition. So, from that point of view, it was good. Then, the bad news, the result of this was that some of our components when we finally went to war didn't perform up to our expectations. Had we been firing service ammunition for target practice and other routine purposes, I think we'd have realized this and would have revised some of the components that went into the ammunition, and our performance on the outbreak of war might have been better than it was.

Q: In other words, a certain amount of experience is gained by the use of live ammunition that couldn't be gained otherwise?

Adm. W.: That's right. At the start of the war, some of the fuses in our projectiles didn't perform as well as we would have liked. Had we been firing some of it regularly, we'd have learned this earlier and by the time the war broke out, probably we'd have had other components in there. This developed in torpedoes particularly where some of the exploding mechanisms failed to perform up to expectations and had to be revised.

Q: That situation was well nigh disastrous, was it not?

Adm. W.: Yes. This pretty adversely affected the submarine

operations in the early days of the war.. They'd fire torpedoes at ships and hit the ships and nothing would happen. The warheads failed to explode. Fortunately, this was one that was fairly easy to correct.

Q: Do you recall any incidents involving manufacturers or anything of that sort?

Adm. W.: I think that one of the interesting items that developed during my period in the ammunitions section was that we began to approach automation. Up to that time, ammunition had been prepared pretty much on a manual basis. There were a few little handy tools that were used, but for the most part this was a screw-driver and monkey wrench era. During the NRA period - National Recovery Administration - when we were working out of the big depression, some money became available to the Navy and we invested some of this in getting machines designed to do some of the work that was formerly done by hand in assembling ammunition. For instance, we were at that time beginning to procure 20-mm. and other type antiaircraft machine guns that used ammunition in tremendous quantities, and it was relatively small ammunition. To put this stuff together by hand or by hand machines would have been tremendously costly. So we went out into the market and got designed for us machines that did all this work and eliminated a great deal of hand work. That was probably the greatest change that took place during my period in the ammunition section.

Q: How did we fare in terms of comparison with the Royal Navy and the Japanese Navy at that period in the ammunition field?

Adm. W.: I think that we probably were on a comparable basis with the British Navy. They had a few things that were better than ours and we had a few better than theirs, but I would have put us more or less on a par over-all. I have a feeling that at that time, although we didn't realize it, the Japanese Navy probably was ahead of us. I recall their torpedoes, for instance, which strictly aren't ammunition which we're discussing but are something that gives us a good example - their torpedoes were larger and faster and had longer range than ours. They carried a heavier warhead and had exploding mechanisms that worked. Gunwise, we adhered to the limitation of arms treaty limit of 16 inches for guns. The Japanese had more or less winked at this and although before that treaty expired they hadn't actually built ships with bigger guns, they had the designs all ready and they promptly put out ships with 18-inch guns. Their fire-control systems seemed to be at least as effective as ours. They had done quite a lot better than we did on night optics. They had concentrated a lot of energy on the development of binoculars and various other optical instruments that enabled them to do better in seeing things in the darkness than we could. This was, of course, in the days before radar had been developed. With the advent of radar, the use of radar pretty much shifted the balance in night actions and gave us a different situation.

Q: Without the presence of radar -

Adm. W.: We would have been, I think, behind them considerably because they were better at knowing what a situation was in the darkness.

Wellborn #2 - 57

Q: They obviously in the thirties went in for night training of all sorts and considered this an important aspect of their operations. Why was not our Navy impelled to do more with night operations?

Adm. W.: This is a little hard to say definitely. We didn't train at night, but I think we hadn't considered it to be an item of primary importance. We were putting our emphasis, rather, on long-range day engagements with large-calibre guns. I think we were pretty good at this, particularly with emphasis on high volume of fire. I think we could probably fire more rapidly than they could, but as a rule I think in those days, the less powerful over-all naval service contemplated night actions, hit-and-run-type actions, against the stronger power, whereas the stronger power contemplated using this greater power during an overwhelming day engagement. This may be the principal reason for their concentration on night action, and ours on day action. They were the Number Twos and they had to use some sort of deceptive means for overcoming their initial disadvantage.

Q: In the nature of a footnote - is there a maximum gun size in terms of effectiveness? You talked about the Japanese and their 18-inch guns, but not very much was heard about them. Is the 16-inch considered a maximum effective weapon?

Adm. W.: I think that it would be difficult now to say what a maximum and optimum gun is today because guns themselves have been not rendered obsolete, but their position in the hierarchy of weapons has been changed by the airplane and the bomb and the rocket, but in that day the greater the diameter of the gun, the caliber of the gun, the heavier your projectile for the gun, and this gave it longer range, so that, in this respect, the larger the gun the more effectiveness you had. You also had greater striking power with heavier projectiles. If you hit a ship with an 18-inch projectile you did greater damage than you did, say with a 14-inch gun with a lighter projectile which could not carry as much explosive. On the other hand, it introduced some problems, going to a larger caliber gun. You could carry fewer rounds of ammunition for this larger caliber gun because of the weight involved. It became very much more expensive from an economic point of view and, in some instances, it was considered quite important to get a considerable volume of fire delivered, rather than to count on too high a percentage of hits. In this respect, the smaller, lighter gun gave an advantage. You could carry more ammunition and get a higher volume of fire for a longer period of time.

So, there are some trade-offs. But, generally speaking, in that day, the larger the gun, the greater the range, the heavier projectile was considered more effective as a weapon. Of course, the limitation of arms treaty limited battleships to 16-inch guns. This was the nontechnical factor that held us to 16-inches.

Q: That implies that there had been some contemplation of buying big guns.

Adm. W.: Yes, there definitely had. We had done some experimental work with larger guns, but we never actually built a production 18-inch.

Q: Where the Navy did manufacture its ammunition in various navy yards, did we have labor problems as a result?

Adm. W.: There wasn't much of a labor problem in those days. Of course, there were always complaints that we were doing all this work in navy yards and were depriving companies and contractors of work which was rightfully theirs, and to a lesser degree there were complaints that labor in the manufacturing plants was being deprived of jobs. But labor seems to have developed power since that time. Our principal complaints came from prospective contractors, rather than from labor.

Q: You had a three-year duty at BuOrd. Did this create in you a desire to go on and specialize in ordnance, or did it do the opposite?

Adm. W.: I should say that at that time I already had motivation to specialize in ordnance. It was pretty stylish in those days as a naval officer's career and I had some years before that acquired a desire for a career in ordnance. So I don't believe my tour of duty there markedly affected this desire. This was part of the program that I hoped would work out and that I had originated some years before.

Q: Then, actually, you didn't go back to it?

Adm. W.: No, and I think this resulted from a set of circumstances. During that period Admiral Harold R. Stark became the chief of the Bureau of Ordnance, and he and I worked together, of course, quite closely while he was chief and I was the chief of the ammunition section, and this was the start of an association that continued for years thereafter, off and on, and I should say that my breaking away from an ordnance career resulted principally from my association with Admiral Stark. The next time I had shore duty, rather than going back to the Bureau of Ordnance, as I might have been expected to do, I went with him. He was ordered as chief of naval operations and could take anybody he wanted for any specialty that might have been involved and since he had a close association with me, he asked me to come with him, which I did.

Q: Well that tour of duty of his in the Bureau of Ordnance, as chief of the Bureau, was the culmination of his ordnance career, too, wasn't it?

Adm. W.: Yes. He had been previously in ordnance and had become the chief of ordnance. Subsequent to that there wasn't any place for him to go in ordnance. He had been at the top of it. Of course, he was chosen for the top job in the naval service the next time shore duty came around. After that, I more or less severed my connection with ordnance. I never went back to it.

Q: When you left Ordnance you went once again to a destroyer?

Adm. W.: Yes, I went back to the flush-deck destroyer <u>Perry</u>, Number 340.

Q: That was a great assignment, wasn't it?

Adm. W.: Yes. Of course, always a naval officer looks forward to getting his own ship as soon as he possibly can, and this gave me command of a ship, albeit a small one. I don't think there's ever anything quite as much fun as commanding one of those old four-stack, flush-deck destroyers.

Q: Where did you operate? With what fleet?

Adm. W.: She was home ported at San Diego and was part of the destroyers in the Battle Force. She was the flagship of Destroyer Division 19, I believe it was. No, wait a minute. It was not 19, it was 11. I subsequently commanded Destroyer Division 19 and that, I think, caused my confusion. We had as division commander Commander, later Admiral, Louis Denfeld. He rode in the Perry with me, so I had a very pleasant association with a very fine individual.

Q: It didn't do you any harm in later years either, did it?

Adm. W.: No. I took over command of the Perry from another officer who became chief of naval operations later, Bill Fechteler. She was a fine little ship, as four-stack destroyers went, and we had a really very happy little ship, too. The class of individual that I mentioned, Louis Denfeld, Bill Fechteler, and so forth, I was very fortunate in inheriting a good-going command.

Q: A ship without problems?

Adm. W.: Yes. Of course, all of those old destroyers were pretty well along in years at that time. We had a certain number of problems. You couldn't chip the paint in the bilges of your engineroom because it was the rust and the paint on the bottom of the ships that was keeping them afloat. Occasionally, a hole would go through the bottom and she'd have to be dry-docked for replacing a plate or two, but by and large there wasn't much of a problem making those ships run. They were, engineeringwise, relatively simple ships. Pretty good little sea boats. Ordnancewise, they didn't have very much striking power, but, as destroyers in their day went, they were about average. So I look back on that as a very happy cruise.

Q: And you were with her for –?

Adm. W.: About a year and a half, as I remember. No, I guess it was more than that, about two years.

Q: A year and a half.

Adm. W.: A year and a half, that's right. I took command of her in June or thereabouts.

Q: June of 1936 until December 1937. And you left her for a job as navigator.

Adm. W.: Yes. I went from a big frog in a little pond to a little frog in a bigger pond, the cruiser Concord. She was also in San Diego, so it was going from one ship to another ship. As far as I was concerned, I considered going from the command of my own ship to navigator of somebody else's ship as a demotion. This, in the thinking of the day, was a part of the variety of experience you were supposed to have in a generalized naval officer.

Q: Going from a lower class occasion to a higher class occasion in terms of ships.

Adm. W.: Yes, that was it. So I didn't consider this professionally to be a real demotion, although in my own heart I hated to lose my own command and go to a subordinate job in somebody else's.

Q: Who was skipper of the Concord?

Adm. W.: I was very fortunate in this one, too. The skipper was Willis Augustus Lee.

Q: Indeed, you were!

Adm. W.: He was one of the most interesting people I've ever known.

Q: Tell me about him.

Adm. W.: He was from Kentucky, I believe, and whether or not this had anything to do with his ability with a pistol I don't know. I don't believe he was ever fuedin' and fightin' in Kentucky, but he was, as a matter of fact the best pistol shot the Navy has ever had. He also had one of the keenest mathematical minds I've ever run across. He could carry in his mind the decimal figures for sines and cosines to any degree you wanted to give. He could multiply these decimals by some other number mentally and come out with the linear measures of sines and cosines.

Q: He was a human computer!

Adm. W.: Yes, he had a computer-like mind and he not only could do these mathematical operations in his head, he could apply them to practical problems. In those days ships took station in various kinds of formation on bearings and distances to guide ships and when you had to direct a change from one station to another one you had a mathematical problem of moving from one position relative to the guide ship to another position relative to the guide ship while your guide itself would move. This involved what could be a relatively simple problem for a modern computer but was normally solved graphically aboard ship in those days, but old "Ching" Lee didn't need either computers or graphics to solve his problem. He did it very quickly and very accurately without any kind of aids.

He also was an interesting person from the point of view of being very much unconcerned with normal kinds of red tape. The things he was interested in, he handled very quickly and very effectively. The things he wasn't interested in, he simply wouldn't bother with. The person in the ship who kept track of the ship's paperwork always had a great deal of trouble with him because he had a proclivity for getting a letter he wasn't interested in, putting it in his desk drawer and just letting it die. On the other hand, he was full of original ideas for fire control and gunnery and things that challenged him and things that usually utilized this computer mind he had. So working with him was an extremely interesting life, and as navigator, of course, I was on the bridge with him most of the time. It was my duty, the way things were done aboard ship in those days, to tell him what the course and the speed were to go from one position in the formation to another position. This kept me scrambling in a losing battle because he always mentally worked out the course and speed much more rapidly than I could do it with my graphics. But fortunately he was quite tolerant in this. He knew he could do it faster than I could, so he didn't really expect me to come up with an answer as quickly as he did, and my part of the job seemed to be simply to check his accuracy.

Q: That's interesting! Well, you had a basic interest in ordnance, both of you.

Adm. W.: Yes, we were both interested in much the same things, so it was a very pleasant relationship, and I was very happy on the brief cruise with him. As it turned out, he and I were almost simultaneously detached from duty in the Concord proper to duty on the staff of Admiral Stark, who came aboard as commander of that division of cruisers. So I renewed my association with Admiral Stark and continued mine with then Captain, and later Admiral, Lee. Then I left the staff in the Concord to become gunnery officer on Admiral Stark's staff.

Q: You talk about Admiral Lee's computer-like-mind - it's interesting to speculate on the evolvement of a mind like that. Would it be possible in this computer age when they don't have to exert themselves and exercise their mental agility?

Adm. W.: I doubt very much if the advent of the computer eliminates the kind of mind that Admiral Lee had. It seems to me that it may shift the location of this kind of mind, but people who could apply this capability in tactical situations are still needed in the service by those who are designing and programming computers. I think his type of mind still will be very much in demand for setting up operations that can be now done by computers. Of course, he had capability in two parts of this picture. One was to be able to visualize how to apply mathematics, the other to actually go through the process of actually multiplying and dividing mentally. The second part of it is a computer process, but the first part the computer really can't do. The fellow who designs the programs for a computer has to do that still.

Q: I suppose it was that ability which made him so good in setting up OpDevFor and carrying out that work?

Adm. W.: Yes, that I think really is correct. It was this ability to visualize how to use various kinds of capabilities that made him so effective in that billet. He was full of new ideas. Most of them worked.

Q: Do you want to go on with your tour with Admiral Stark again?

Adm. W.: Yes. This tour of duty with Admiral Stark commenced shortly before the outbreak of World War II in Europe. We started off in the Concord, which was an old cruiser, and shortly after Admiral Lee and I had taken up duty with Admiral Stark on his staff some new cruisers were completed and the admiral shifted his flag from the Concord to the Honolulu. He also was promoted in the meatime from simply division commander to commander of the whole group of cruisers, he was what was called type commander. The shift from the old Concord to the new Honolulu put us in much more modern surroundings and gave us considerably more physical room to carry on. This started off as a period during which the gunnery officer simply arranged the schedule for all the various types of practices and did administrative reporting on target practices and such thing as this, but along about 1937 or 1938 Hitler started in Europe to be a little aggressive and this resulted in some of our ships being moved from the Pacific coast to the Atlantic coast, and just before we left the Concord, that division of cruisers was shifted from the Pacific to the Atlantic. We left San Diego in pretty much of a hurry and went down through the canal to Guantanamo Bay, then shortly after that shifted to the Honolulu

This move was related to the power politics of Europe and to our shifting of the center of gravity of our naval force to the eastward. After that the scheduling of gunnery exercises became somewhat secondary to the schedule of operations of the ships, which was related very much more to the political situation than it was to gunnery competitions.

Q: You began thinking more in terms of antisubmarine warfare?

Adm. W.: At this time, while we were concerned with antisubmarines generally in the Navy, our concern in the cruisers had more to do with surface-type raiders. As you recall, the Germans operated quite a number of surface raiders. At this early stage they hadn't enough long-range submarines to do very much submarine operating very far away from home bases. So our concern here had more to do with surface raiders, both converted merchant raiders and actual men-of-war. First the potential operators and later actual operators in the Atlantic.

Q: At the outbreak of war, were there many of these German raiders in existence?

Adm. W.: The men-of-war, of course, were in existence and some of those had been designed rather specifically with this purpose in mind, and some of their ships had a combination of turbo and diesel propulsion to enable them to cruise on their diesels for long periods of time and develop high speed with their turbo propulsion.

Q: As units they certainly enjoyed a formidable reputation, didn't they?

Adm. W.: Yes, they did.

Q: Whether they were tried or not, they still had this.

Adm. W.: Actually, they didn't accomplish a great deal during World War II but they did require quite a lot of naval effort to track them down and eliminate them.

Q: And standby naval effort.

Adm. W.: Yes. Of course, at this time, we were in that category of standby. This country didn't get into the war until somewhat later, but in the period that I'm talking about now we were doing a good deal of thinking about that and the naval effort that we had was being disposed in the proper parts of the world so that it could, if necessary, cope with this raider effort. Of course, in those days, too, international politicians seemed to put a good deal of reliance in the shifting of military power from one place to another. This was one of the means of applying pressure or presumably impressing another power with the concern a nation felt for a particular situation. So our transfer of ships from the Pacific to the Atlantic and then the disposition of ships in the

Atlantic was all pointed at impressing the Hitler regime with the fact that we considered this involved our interests and we just might do something about it. At that time, of course, this country was taking the position that his efforts should not contemplate anything in the western hemisphere. The Monroe Doctrine was strong in those days. So, most of these moves seemed to me to be related to creating a very strong impression that we didn't intend to forget the Monroe Doctrine.

Q: At Admiral Stark's level, in command of these cruisers, what relationship did he have and you as a part of his staff with the Royal Navy and the French Navy?

Adm. W.: Very little, at that time. In fact, I don't recall having any contact with either the French or the Royal Navy. We, I don't believe, ever fell in with any of their ships during that period. Of course, these movements of ours were correlated with those of the British and the French navies up above our heads. I'm sure that the chief of naval operations and the commander-in-chief of the U.S. Fleet -

Q: Who was C-in-C of the U.S. Fleet?

Adm. W.: At that time I think it was Admiral C. C. Block. I wouldn't be absolutely sure of that, but I think he was the one who was commander-in-chief at that time. The chief of naval operations, of course, was Admiral Leahy. Admiral Leahy and Mr. Roosevelt, of course, were quite close and I'm sure at Admiral Leahy's level there was an amount of consideration given to coordination between the British, the French, and the American naval operations, although I didn't see that firsthand.

Q: How did your segment of the fleet view the hostilities in Europe?

Adm. W.: I would guess that among the military people of the fleet generally there was about the same degree of concern over what was happening in Europe as there was in the population of the country at large. We all felt that the Germans were posing a potential threat to us. It hadn't quite reached us yet, but if they were successful in acquiring complete domination of the continent of Europe, the next step would be the British Isles and inevitably the western hemisphere was next. I think Navy people for the most part felt the sooner this was stopped the easier it would be to stop it.

Q: Then the Navy, on the whole, was less isolationist than the populace in the country?

Adm. W.: Yes. When I said we had the same reaction as the rest of the country, I really was referring to the reaction in disagreement with what the Germans were trying to do. I don't think the Navy had any very strong feelings as regards the anti-semitism of Hitler and his regime, although if there was a feeling there it would probably have been to deplore it. I think the Navy's strong feeling had to do with the fact that if he were granted domination on the continent of Europe, this domination would probably spread and we were certainly in his mind and his plans ultimately.

So the sooner something was done to stop it, the easier it would be to accomplish that. The Navy was probably less isolationist than the country at large. I think the Navy still looked upon the Pacific as its principal hazard that had to be overcome. You recall, of course, about this same time the Japanese were aggressively expansionist, and I believe the Navy felt that its principal responsibility probably would develop in the Pacific because in the Atlantic at that particular time there was still the Royal Navy to shoulder the principal responsibility, and, at that time in history, the German hazard was largely a land-based one - one that seemed to involve armies rather than navies in bringing it to heel.

So, while we were interested in the political situation and the hazards that resulted from it in the Atlantic, I think it was secondary to our thinking about Pacific problems.

Q: Where did you operate largely in the Atlantic? Out of Norfolk?

Adm. W.: At that particular time, Guantanamo Bay was pretty much the home base. This seemed to be a pretty good location from which to operate should we be called upon to do anything about surface raiders in the Atlantic because that relatively short piece of ocean between the eastern part of Brazil and the western part of Africa seemed to need some protection, and then from Guantanamo Bay you could get up into the Azores which was a good point for the protection of trade routes in and out of the Mediterranean. This was about as close as any place we had to most of the ports of the Atlantic from which raiders might operate. But we did come for liberty and recreation, as we called it in those days, to various ports on the Atlantic coast. In the <u>Honolulu</u> we came to New York City, but various ships came to various other ports.

Q: And during this period there was no need to defend the Munroe Doctrine, was there? I mean there were no raiders making an appearance in our waters?

Adm. W.: That is correct. I'm trying to recall dates and precise times that various things happened. As I remember it, World War II only commenced - Hitler went into Poland in 1939, and this was pre-1939. This was 1937 or 1938, and at that time, as I recall it, Hitler had acquired domination over Czechoslovakia and Austria and he was expanding on the continent, so that the hazard was apparent, but he hadn't yet started any actual aggressive actions in the Atlantic. The thinking at that time was directed at things that might happen, rather than at things that were happening.

Q: Admiral Stark's performance in this particular command must have had some bearing on his next tour of duty as CNO. Can you talk a little bit about him in this command?

Adm. W.: I'm sure it did have very considerable bearing on his being selected. He was one of those people of whom I was and I am very fond. He was a magnificent gentleman with a very fine mind, and a great deal of courage which didn't become apparent until you knew him well. I'm sure that those who had known him previously understood this and his performance during this period reflected his qualities, although that particular assignment was not one in which there was a very great opportunity to shine and have his light very readily apparent. It was pretty much of a routine job that had to be done and he did it well. I think one of the things that may have been in his favor was in an earlier assignment to duty somewhere he had gotten well acquainted with Claude Swanson who first was a senator from Virginia and later became Secretary of the Navy. Secretary Swanson knew his capability very well indeed, so that in spite of the fact that this cruiser assignment was not one where he could shine particularly, the Secretary of the Navy from previous association knew his capabilities and with that knowledge and his fine performance in the cruiser division, considered him to be a leading candidate to relieve Admiral Leahy as chief of naval operations when Admiral Leahy reached retirement.

Q: How obvious was the President's effort to build up the strength of the Navy in the face of much opposition in Congress and among the people at large in this period?

Adm. W.: This had become pretty clear to the Navy in earlier days than this period, really. You recall, when he first took office we were in the midst of a pretty deep depression. One of his first acts was to close banks and to set up a lot of recovery administrations and things, and during the early stages of the administration's recovery operation, economic recovery, Mr. Roosevelt channeled a considerable amount of money into the Navy. He had been assistant secretary of the Navy in the early part of his career, he had been a yachtsman, a longtime student of sea power, and I think he understood it very well indeed. So during that period when I was in the Bureau of Ordnance it was quite apparent to us that he had a great understanding of the importance of sea power and that he intended to improve our capabilities in this direction. I think the Navy understood this pretty well. During the period when I was in the cruisers we all had a pretty good understanding of his interest in and understanding of naval problems and how they fit into world strategy. I think we probably understood him in the Navy a good deal better than the country at large.

Q: And maybe better than the Congress?

Adm. W.: Yes, well, I think the Congress generally pretty accurately reflects the thinking of the country. Of course, in Congress at that time there were certain individuals who also had a very clear understanding of the problems. I'm thinking primarily of Carl Vinson of Georgia, the chairman of what was then the House Naval Affairs Committee. He'd been around for a long time and had conducted hearings on all kinds of naval problems. He tried to exude the atmosphere of a good Georgia farmer, but Mr. Vinson knew about as much about naval power as anyone around. He was one of a relatively small number of people in the Congress who had a very fine understanding of the problem. He also had a very clear understanding of the House of Representatives' politics, what was feasible to get passed on the floor of the House. In the Senate, as I recall it, there were fewer people who had very much of an understanding of the use of sea power.

The Congress generally was extremely isolationist in those days. At one stage of this period, I recall, the House of Representatives passed a draft bill by one vote. Everybody was in the way of military preparedness and it required a tremendous effort to get it through Congress.

Interview No. 3 with Vice Admiral Charles Wellborn, Jr., U. S. Navy
(Retired)

Place: His apartment in the Westchester Apartments, Washington, D.

Date: Wednesday morning, 15 December 1971.

Subject: Biography

By: John T. Mason, Jr.

Q: Well, Sir, the last chapter was most interesting. You were talking about your assignment with Admiral Stark, who was in command of the Cruisers of the Atlantic.

Adm. W.: He was in the <u>Honolulu</u> - his flag was in the <u>Honolulu</u> - but he was in command of what was called the Cruisers of the Battle Force.

Q: Yes, and when you concluded, I think you had actually finished with that tour of duty and were preparing for the assignment in Washington, unless you have something else to add to that period.

Adm. W.: I don't believe so. I think we covered that one pretty extensively.

Q: You did tell me something about the nature of Admiral Stark's appointment as chief of naval operations, and the fact that Secretary Swanson was well aware of his abilities, and this seemed to be a key factor in the selection of Admiral Stark.

Adm. W.: Maybe I shouldn't have said a key factor, but a factor at any rate.

Q: So, will you resume from there.

Adm. W.: From there, Admiral Stark and I moved from Honolulu, the cruiser *Honolulu*, to Washington and, as I remember, this was in 1939.

Q: In June 1939.

Adm. W.: Yes, well, we left the cruisers in June but it seems to me that he did not relieve Admiral Leahy as chief of naval operations until somewhat later than that. Maybe, on the order of September. Admiral Leahy had reached the statutory retirement age and my recollection is that he retired and Admiral Stark took over from him on the normal date that his age required him to retire - that is, required Admiral Leahy to retire.

Q: Did Admiral Leahy go immediately to the White House after his retirement?

Adm. W.: No, he did not. My memory may not serve me well on this one, but it seems to me he had two assignments - nonmilitary, if you will - between the time of his retirement as chief of naval operations and his becoming chief of staff to President Roosevelt. He for a time served as governor of Puerto Rico and he also served as ambassador to France. These assignments were, I think, related to his naval experience and his capabilities that President Roosevelt knew very well, but he did not immediately become chief of staff to the President.

Q: As a matter of fact, in France, he was there during the Petain government, wasn't he?

Adm. W.: Yes.

Wellborn #3 - 78

Q: And was probably a very successful military figure with a military figure.

Adm. W.: Yes, and there were some rather important naval considerations at this time, too. You may recall that at the fall of France there were some French ships in the West Indies -

Q: Under our dear friend Admiral Robert!

Adm. W.: Yes, and ensuring that these French ships did not fall into the hands of the Germans was, I think, quite an important item in Mr. Roosevelt's mind and he felt that Admiral Leahy was particularly well qualified to be in France at that time in this connection. My recollection is that Admiral Leahy first went as governor of Puerto Rico, and this also had some naval aspects because the Caribbean and the West Indies were rather key locations in maintaining the freedom of the seas in the Atlantic.

Q: So you had a breaking-in period, then?

Adm. W.: Yes. There was a period of I would guess, maybe a month or so, maybe more, maybe less, during which Admiral Stark worked with Admiral Leahy and those of us who were aides also with our counterparts. I remained with, I think he was captain then, Louis Denfeld who had been administrative aide to Admiral Leahy and now Vice Admiral Smedberg relieved then Lieutenant Commander Freseman as personal aide, respectively, to Admiral Stark and to Admiral Leahy.

Q: As the administrative aide, what were your duties, your job sheet?

Adm. W.: They corresponded roughly to those of a flag secretary of a normal admiral at sea. I was the paper work man in his office, and Smedberg was the man who took care of the quarters, all of the personal aspects of the life of the chief of naval operations. Of course, there was some interchange between us. Each one of us had to be ready to relieve the other, but basically he was the flag lieutenant and I was the flag secretary.

Q: And what did taking care of the paper work entail?

Adm. W.: Primarily, going through all the incoming mail for the admiral and that that had been prepared for his signature by somebody else, reading it over carefully for both correctness as to form and conformity as to what I knew to be his general policy, and then preparing myself to brief him on each piece of correspondence later in the day. Our routine quite frequently involved his being busy seeing and talking with people during most of the day, having appointments with various people, and then, after working hours, when everybody had departed, he and I would sit down and go over the mail, that is, the official correspondence. This involved my being able to present to him the essence of what was in a great mass of paper and to have weeded out before we began to go over it all those things which were not in conformity with what I knew to be his policy, and getting them gone over with the author of the letter to bring them into conformity.

Q: Then he digested all of this information and the next day dictated to his yeoman?

Adm. W.: Yes, as a rule.

Q: Or did you write his letters for him?

Adm. W.: No, he dictated most of his own personal correspondence, but the way the office of the chief of naval operations is managed, the chief doesn't prepare personally a great deal of his correspondence. Papers normally start down at a working level somewhere, then work their way up through the chain of command in the office, and they arrive on his desk ready for signature. They probably have been based on discussion with one of the division heads before the letter was prepared, but the actual dictating and typing of the letter has probably been done somewhere else. There's always a certain amount of personal correspondence that the chief does himself, but by and large most of the official correspondence is prepared by someone else, based on the thoughts that have been given to him by the chief of naval operations.

Q: With such a procedure in that particular office it made an exceedingly long day, didn't it?

Adm. W.: Yes, it was a pretty long day but never a dull one. There were always interesting things going on, and in that day the chief of naval operations was pretty much the boss of what went on in the Navy Department. There was, of course, no Department of Defense, and at the time that Admiral Stark relieved Admiral Leahy there was a Secretary of the Navy and one Assistant Secretary of the Navy in the civilian hierarchy that, you might say, was superior to the chief of naval operations. So that there was much less supervision between the chief of naval operations and the president than there is today.

Q: And a great deal more depended on the individual initiative of the man?

Adm. W.: Yes. At that time, of course, the Joint Chiefs of Staff had not been formally organized. Admiral Stark and General Marshall, who became the chief of staff of the Army about that time, used to see one another very frequently and there was something - I believe it was called the Joint Board - that was formally organized, but it had no real authority comparable to what the Joint Chiefs of Staff have today.

Q: A kind of an unofficial organization -

Adm. W.: Yes.

Q: Does that mean that he and General Marshall - well not officially -

Adm. W.: Yes, they were official in that this Joint Board had official recognition, but decisions were not made officially and promulgated by the Joint Board, but the decisions were made there by the two individuals, the chief of naval operations and the chief of staff of the Army. But the orders that were promulgated as a result of these decisions to the Army went from the chief of staff of the Army, and to the Navy went from the chief of naval operations - not from the Joint Board.

Q: I suppose, then, there was a much more direct relationship between the chief of naval operations and the president, too, wasn't there?

Adm. W.: Yes, there was. Very much more direct. At the time Admiral Stark first became chief of naval operations, the Secretary of the Navy was not in very good health - this was Claude Swanson - and quite frequently, as a result of his bad health, he was not available and, at that time, the assistant secretary of the Navy was pretty generally a specialist on shore establishments of the Navy. He supervised naval ship yards and the plants and things that we had ashore, and had little to do with the operations of the fleet and of the real effective seagoing power of the Navy. So, during this period, Mr. Roosevelt and Admiral Stark dealt pretty directly with one another.

Q: Had Admiral Stark known him very well before he became chief of naval operations?

Adm. W.: He had known him - I think not very intimately, but to a certain degree. Of course, Mr. Roosevelt had been assistant secretary of the Navy, and I believe Admiral Stark had been in the Navy Department somewhere during that period. They hadn't had an intimate relationship before that, but they had known one another.

Q: Well, your task to have the background on all of these matters and then to brief the admiral entailed immediate and hot contacts with all parts of the Department?

Adm. W.: Yes. I had to maintain pretty good contacts with all the various people who were preparing correspondence and acting on various things that came up. This called for some care in avoiding my wearing the admiral's stars. I had no authority. All I had was a liaison position, you might say. I was kind of the bridge between the letter-writers and the admiral. But it did give me contact with a lot of people.

Q: Who were the ranking people? Was Admiral Ingersoll there then?

Adm. W.: He came somewhat later than this. At the time Admiral Stark first became chief of naval operations, Admiral Ghormley was what was then called the assistant chief.

Q: I'm just trying to get the complexion of the Navy Department at that time.

Adm. W.: Some of the other heads of the various offices I'm trying to recall. As I remember it, at that time the head of the war plans division was Admiral Kelly Turner. Captain, later Admiral, W. A. Lee was head of what was called the fleet training division, and that was a very important one at that time. Lee Noyes was the head of communications. Walter S. Anderson, I believe, was the head of intelligence. This may give enough of a feel for the kind of officers who were there.

Q: Yes, and there was some conflict within the department, wasn't there? Kelly Turner was a very abrasive person!

Adm. W.: Oh, inevitably. However, I never had the feeling that the conflict was out of hand at all. These were all pretty strong characters. Now, Kelly Turner, as you know, was a very positive and decided individual. Walter Anderson also was. Those two, I should say, were probably the most positive of all of those characters, but this didn't generate any difficulty in getting the business done. They were all reasonable men. Whenever you get people of that kind together, you have friction and they get annoyed with one another a little bit, but I didn't think this got out of hand.

Q: I sense the fact, especially in talking with people who were in ONI at that time, that there was a kind of conflict of interests between Kelly Turner and War PLans and ONI and what belonged under the aegis of ONI and what belonged in War Plans, and even what belonged under the aegis of communications and Admiral Noyes.

Adm. W.: This is quite true, but I don't recall any real problem in that connection. Of course, the people in War Plans felt that the only reason for intelligence was so that they could make their plans properly and so they felt they should be able to dominate the fields in which intelligence was putting forth the greatest effort. I don't think that's unnatural! Any strong-minded person who is in War Plans I think would normally feel this way. I expect if you had shifted those individuals from one desk to the other, you'd have had much the same situation. This was the way it appeared to me at that time.

Q: Sometime later, a little bit later, I guess it was in 1941, ONI was ordered to desist from the interpretation of intelligence, apparently at the behest of War PLans, and this was done. Do you have any recollection of that?

Adm. W.: Yes. This, as I recall it, wasn't quite as positive as you have indicated. The order didn't, as I remember it, tell them to desist from interpreting intelligence. It left with them the possibility that they could draw their own conclusions, but it also left with the war plans division the right to draw its own conclusions and use the conclusions that it drew rather than those that intelligence had drawn, if it saw fit. Now, my recollection may not be accurate. This was a number of years ago. But this was the feeling that I have carried with me all the time.

Q: Would this not create a dilemma, though, for the chief of naval operations? I mean he had two interpretations of the mass of intelligence coming to him. Which one would he select?

Adm. W.: Yes, this occasionally did happen. However, I believe that his feeling on this was that he would rather face this kind of a dilemma and decide for himself which one to take, as long as it didn't happen too frequently, than to get a canned solution on which there was not complete agreement. This presented to him all the various points of view and he could make his choice. I think he preferred it that way. Of course, this could get out of hand if people were disagreeing on everything. All the various details would come to him and he couldn't handle that volume. But it didn't happen in any very great quantity.

Q: What was your role when something like this did happen? I mean you had to brief him on things.

Adm. W.: My role in this connection was simply to understand the point of view of each side of a controversy and give him both of them. As a rule when this kind of situation developed, he'd call both of them in and get it directly from them. My part was giving the background on it, to explain to him what these two positions seemed to me to be, and more or less prepare him for a direct discussion with the individuals involved.

Q: I recall late in 1941 when there was a real conflict in interpretation when ONI felt strongly that the Japanese were preparing to attack in the Philippines and elsewhere, and Admiral Kelly Turner felt that they were preparing for an attack on Siberia, which was quite a different kettle of fish.

Adm. W.: Their views here weren't as far apart in my memory as you've indicated. Kelly Turner, I think, was never quite as sure as was ONI that the Japanese were going to move to the south where Malaya or the Philippines would be the target. I think he felt that there was a possibility, as you've indicated, that they might go somewhere else, but I think even he recognized the fact there was a possibility of going south, in fact, maybe even a probability. But this divergence of views was really not a fundamental one. I think the fundamental difficulty here was a couple of strong characters, rather than a basic difference in views.

Q: And then ONI and Communications had some differences, too, in terms of the codes and so forth.

Adm. W.: Yes, there was some difference here as to after the intercepts had been made whose responsibility it was to do the various parts of the operation. Here again, once a code has been broken and a message decoded, then who translates it and interprets it - that was part of the controversy. But here again, it never seemed to me to be out of hand. It always seemed to me to be just a natural result of some strong minds each of whom thought he could do it better than anybody else and wanted to! As long as we had people like that around, I thought we were in pretty good hands.

Q: Admiral Ghormley was the deputy CNO?

Adm. W.: Well, he would today be called the vice chief, but at that time he was called the assistant chief. He was what amounted to a chief of staff to the chief of naval operations.

Q: He left there and went to London, did he not?

Adm. W.: Yes. He first went to London and Admiral Ingersoll took over from him at that time.

Q: What was Ghormley's mission to London? He was not the NA. Alan Kirk was NA.

Adm. W.: I can't recall just what title he was given, but there had been a decision made that the United States and Great Britain should conduct some joint planning. The British had sent a delegation to Washington, and there was some of this going on at that time. I believe he was called SPENAVO, London (Special Naval Officer.)

Q: I suppose this was a decision at the highest level?

Adm. W.: Yes, the decision was made at the summit, and Admiral Ghormley went to London to be the U.S. Navy's representative in this kind of combined planning work that was going on both in London and in Washington.

Q: Did this pertain to the Pacific, or did it pertain to the Atlantic, or was it -

Adm. W.: It was worldwide, as I recall it. Of course, we weren't in a war either in the Pacific or the Atlantic -

Q: We were in a state of neutrality!

Adm. W.: Yes, and while we couldn't confess that we really expected to get in, we could confess that it was a possibility and that it was prudent to be ready for this contingency. So this joint planning was going on on that basis.

Q: Did Ghormley's mission have any bearing on that's called the Rainbow Plan? It was such a highly secret thing.

Adm. W.: Yes. As I recall this one, it had a bearing on it but the Rainbow planning was being done in Washington, rather than in London, so that Admiral Ghormley's mission, it seems to me, was not directly in charge of this. My recollection could be a little scrambled here, but there were a lot of aspects of this, such as the deal between the U.S. and the British government on bases and destroyers. These were all interrelated subjects and my recollection is that Admiral Ghormley was more involved in the type problem that involved the bases and the destroyers than in the Rainbow planning.

Q: One man with whom I talked who was in the war plans makes mention of the Rainbow Plan, but said it was so terribly secret that they never saw it, and when it had to be amended and brought up to date, they were somewhat handicapped because they couldn't see the plan itself.

Adm. W.: This was pretty closely held at that time, all right. I think that it's a matter of public knowledge now. But at that time it was very closely held and for quite obvious reasons. Our official position was neutrality and as you have indicated we couldn't admit that we were preparing to enter the war on either side. So this one had to be very closely held. And when I say "preparing to enter the war" I've overstated that one. We were looking into the contingency, the possibility that we might. But we really weren't at that stage fully preparing for it.

Q: Well, the President was doing what he could within the latitude that he had.

Adm. W.: Yes, exactly. My understanding of his views was that he felt it was possible and maybe even probable that we would have to get into this one eventually, and he was doing his best to be as well prepared as possible for it if and when it happened. I had never been able to agree with some of the writers who have insisted that Mr. Roosevelt was consciously pushing this country into the war from a very early date.

Q: But there certainly is that school of thought.

Adm. W.: Yes, there is that school of thought and I don't belong to it. But I do think he was doing what a prudent man should do. He was getting ready for a contingency that might possibly come about.

Q: The Rainbow Plan was almost, in effect, a treaty, wasn't it? It involved the Dutch and the British.

Adm. W.: It didn't seem to me to have quite that force. It simply was a plan which might or might not be carried out, but it did give us something which we could act in unison on, rather than every nation going off on its own and doing things that might or might not be in conflict with what the others were doing. I never quite regarded it as a treaty. It didn't commit us to anything. It more nearly, I think, illuminated for us the thinking of the other nations and for them our thinking.

Q: And, of course, it couldn't go as far as a treaty anyway without submitting it to the Senate.

Adm. W.: Yes, I never thought it had any kind of a mandatory status. It was something that was rather an interchange of thoughts and served to be a basis for actions that wouldn't be in conflict with one another.

Q: Some report I read - its authorship escapes me - was to the effect that even as an agreement President Roosevelt would not sign it.

Adm. W.: No. I think this is probably correct. I don't recall to my knowledge that he was ever asked to sign anything like this. He was aware I think of the fact that this planning was going on and very probably aware -

Q: He didn't instigate it himself?

Adm. W.: I'm hazy on this but my recollection would be that it was not his instigation. The instigation came rather from the military people. I can't tell you just exactly which one here.

It was more or less a consensus relfecting the thinking of the Department of the Army and the Navy that this was a desirable thing.

Q: Did this plan develop entirely during Admiral Stark's regime, or was it before that?

Adm. W.: No, I don't believe any of this planning had been done before Admiral Stark came into office. You see, he came in just about the time that war broke out in Europe. I was going to say the time that Hitler went into Poland. I think that's right.

Q: That was September of 1939, yes.

Adm. W.: So, this kind of planning was hardly in order before actual warfare broke out in Europe, but it became apparent somewhat later that it was a prudent thing to do.

Q: How closely were the commanders in the field drawn into this planning, or did they have any knowledge of it?

Adm. W.: They did have knowledge of it, yes. Their participation in it, as I recall it, was not very great. Their thoughts were worked into it through a number of means. Their participation was not direct, but there was a continual interchange of thoughts between the fleet commanders and Admiral Stark in personal correspondence which was, of course, very highly classified. There were relatively frequent visits to the Department by fleet commanders, and there were staff interchanges - people from Washington would go out and talk to the staff people in the field and vice versa, so that while the fleet commanders didn't participate directly in this kind of planning, they were aware of the general thrust of it and their thoughts on the matter were considered in basing the plan.

Q: Their experience and knowledge in the field was drawn upon?

Adm. W.: Yes.

Q: I was thinking of Admiral Hart in particular out in the Far East on a kind of a hot spot and whether his ideas were incorporated and whether those of General MacArthur were incorporated?

Adm. W.: I can say definitely that Admiral Hart's thoughts were a part of the planning. The question of General MacArthur I'm less sure of. I feel reasonably certain they were. How close communications General Marshall had with General MacArthur, I'm not sure, but I would think that he had certainly some communications with General MacArthur and that the interchange was at least comparable to what went on in the Navy.

Q: Admiral Hart told me once about his correspondence with Admiral Stark, being in the form of personal letters.

Adm. W.: Yes, it was to a great extent in the form of personal letters. Not entirely so. There was a certain amount of interchange of official correspondence and, I think, personal consultation every now and then, too. As I remember it, Admiral Hart, being as far away as he was and transportation from the Philippines to Washington being in that day not what it is today, didn't show up in Washington very frequently. In fact, I can't remember any visit that he made to Washington. But there were people going back and forth periodically.

Q: Couriers?

Adm. W.: Yes, courier type things, so I think there wasn't any lack of communication here. Admiral Hart and Admiral Stark had been good personal friends for a good many years. I think they communicated with one another on quite a free basis.

Q: They should have had confidence in one another.

Adm. W.: Yes.

Q: I got the impression from Hart one time talking about the Rainbow that he thought this sort of general alliance had the sanction of President Roosevelt.

Adm. W.: I think maybe the way you put it, I could agree with. It had his sanction but not his official approval - if I can differentiate in that way. He knew that the planning was going on and I believe he knew what the plans involved but, to the best of my knowledge, he never put an official FDR on it and at no time was he ever put in the position, that I can remember, of being asked to officially approve one of these things. My recollection would be that the planners at that time recognized that this would put him in an untenable position and I don't believe he was ever asked to.

Q: I would think Hart would have appreciated that.

Adm. W.: Yes, I should think so. I don't know whether he ever gave you an impression contrary to this, whether he gave you the feeling that this was an officially approved plan. But my recollection would be that it never quite advanced to that state. It was one of which the President was aware and with which he agreed, but my recollections could be faulty, but it is that he was never asked to put his signature or initials or anything on it. This was always rather carefully avoided.

Q: As a historian, this is kind of a footnote, do you know whether this correspondence between the two admirals, Stark and Hart, was ever preserved, the personal part of it? That remains unanswered?

Adm. W.: Yes.

Q: When we got into the European conflict in 1940, I think it was, in November of 1940, the British made an air attack on the Italian Navy as it was at Taranto, the naval base, and a great deal of damage resulted. I think some of the battleships were sunk. This, I'm told, made a great impression on Admiral Stark but didn't seem to make much of an impress on some of the other people around Washington.

Adm. W.: I think this highlighted in his mind the fact that such attacks were possible. Of course, in fleet exercises we had been practicing staging air attacks on harbors for a long time, and I think there was general knowledge that this kind of thing was possible. And that, of course, did, as I say, highlight this possibility. As I remember that, he recognized this as a possible contingency, but he wasn't unduly concerned about it.

Q: Did he ask War Plans to make a study of it?

Adm. W.: Yes, he did and in fact a study was made. It seems to me it was about a year or so before the attack on Pearl Harbor.

Q: Yes, it was.

Adm. W.: That a letter, an official letter now, not one of the personal correspondence type letters, was sent out to the commander-in-chief of the Pacific pointing out the possibility of this and calling for study on his part of action to be taken in that connection. I don't recall any undue pressure on this kind of a letter. It was one of a great many preparations that were being considered for things that might happen in the future. My recollection is that at this time Admiral Turner was probably more concerned about this than most of the other high ranking people in the Navy Department, and that this, to him, appeared considerably more probable than it did to most.

Q: But why, when there was this thought of a probability, why then was the fleet continued to be based on Pearl? I mean, who was back of that? Admiral Richardson certainly was not.

Adm. W.: No, he was not, as you say. This, I think, came about after consideration of quite a number of factors. While there was general recognition of the possibility of such an attack, I think the existence of a good many thousands of miles of water between the Japanese and Pearl Harbor made this kind of an attack appear not highly probable, and I believe this was a generally held view. Nobody thought - when I say nobody, very few people thought - that Pearl Harbor would be the object of the first Japanese attack. It was thought that this was just a long ways away and that they would be pretty vulnerable going and coming and that the high degree of probability wasn't attached to this particular attack. Also, I think there were political and military considerations involved in the basing of the fleet at Pearl Harbor rather than, say, in San Francisco or San Pedro. I'm not really an expert on this kind of political and military application of pressure, but I think that this was very definitely a part of the thinking that led to keeping the fleet in Pearl Harbor, that in Pearl Harbor it was applying more military pressure on the Japanese than it would be if it were in San Francisco orSan Pedro. Of course, as a matter of fact, it was 2,500 miles nearer. So I think that the decision to keep the fleet at Pearl Harbor was based on quite a complex array of factors, and that the principal one wasn't the vulnerability of the fleet there.

Q: I suppose this was the reason for sacrificing Richardson. Why was he dismissed so abruptly when he understood that he was going to stay on for another year? (No direct answer was given by Adm. W. to this)

I did have another question in mind, having examined all the sources that are available - I mean some of these things that some out, I'm not sure of the date for this, but Admiral Ingersoll made a trip to London sometime in this period and, again, the purpose of his trip seems to be somewhat obscure. There are different schools of thought, one being that he merely went to implement a British arrangement if we got into the war in the Atlantic. And another was pertaining to the Pacific.

Adm. W.: My recollection of this is a little hazy now, but it would tend to be on the side of those who have said that his visit had to do more with the Atlantic than the Pacific. I'm not completely clear on this, but I think it had to do with Atlantic bases, with destroyers, with our cooperation in connection with the escort of convoys, with an effort to determine just what the western hemisphere was, this kind of problem, rather than to Pacific planning. Though, as I say, my testimony on this particular point probably is not as good as some others that you might get.

Q: Will you talk about that area, the British bases which were made available to us and the fifty destroyers that were turned over? This has been written about and perhaps you could add some light to the whole thing.

Adm. W.: It seems to me that move was covered with a good deal of forthrightness in the public press at that time. There wasn't a great deal of secret dealing and thinking. The fact that the British were hard-pressed and needed destroyers for the escort of ships to keep the British Isles alive was pretty well known, and the agreements as to the leases on those bases, I think, were made public very shortly after the agreements were arrived at.

Q: It never has struck me as a very equal kind of deal, in that the destroyers were old cans and not worth a great deal, and the bases were very valuable. It doesn't seem that it equalized itself and so therefore it always made me think that there might have been more to it than the press reported.

Adm. W.: My impression is that there wasn't really a great deal more to it. I think that this question of equality might be a compound proposition. You multiply what you get by your need for it at the time and you come out with a pretty high value on those destroyers that the British got. On the other hand, you multiply what we got in the way of bases by the degree of need that we felt for them and you don't come out with what Mr. McNamara used to call a quantification that is so tremendously large. So I don't feel that that was so completely unequal a deal. Besides, the destroyers were quite definitely a permanent transaction. They were turned over to the British for keeps, even though they might not last very long. The bases - the rights to the bases given to us for my recollection is 99 years, and most of the bases didn't last that long. The base rights were relinquished - a good many of them - pretty promptly. So from this point of view, too, it wasn't as unequal as it might otherwise seem.

Q: Didn;t we have any more modern destroyers that we could have turned over?

Adm. W.: We had a few, but not a great many modern destroyers, but those were kind of the backbone of our own escort forces for our men-of-war, our combatant ships, and I don't think there was any serious consideration given to turning over to them our limited supply of more modern destroyers. Rather, the approach seemed to be that we should assist them in the building of new ships, though I think most of this came later, and also in the overhaul and repair of their existing ships that were damaged and that were overloading their own shipyards. As you recall, we did a good deal of repair work -

Q: Especially along the Atlantic coast.

Adm. W.: Yes. I think our approach was to help in these ways rather than by giving them our most modern destroyers.

Q: Did Admiral Stark get any flack from this deal, the turning over of the destroyers? I know there was some in the country at large.

Adm. W.: Yes, there was a reasonable amount of this, but I don't think that bothered him very much. I think he felt that this was basically a good deal from the point of view of the United States and, that being the case, let the chips fall where they might. He approached his problems very much in this light. This kind of a deal I think he felt was for the over-all good of the country, so let's do it.

Q: What were his dealings with the congressional committees at this point, and what was your role in this? This was before we actually got into the conflict.

Adm. W.: At that point Carl Vinson was chairman of what was the Naval Affairs Committee of the House. He had very long experience and was a very astute person, and Admiral Stark had very close relations with Mr. Vinson. Mr. Vinson discussed the possibilities of congressional action with the admiral a great deal and, while they didn't always see eye to eye, more frequently than not, they did. Mr. Vinson was thoroughly aware of public opinion and of congressional opinion and a master of the art of the possible. So, frequently the admiral and Mr. Vinson would discuss possible congressional action, and the conclusion of Mr. Vinson was to press for some kind of enactment. It might not necessarily be exactly what Admiral Stark would have liked - maybe not even what Mr. Vinson would have liked had he felt what he wanted was possible - but it was almost invariably something that could be overwhelmingly enacted by the House. So they worked very closely together and always in the direction of being prepared to a greater degree than we were at that particular moment.

The admiral's relationships on the Senate side, as I recall it, were good, but not as effective as they were with Mr. Vinson.

Q: David Walsh was not a Carl Vinson!

Adm. W.: No, by no means, and most of the legislation that resulted in improving our readiness was initiated in the House anyway, so that by the time this had been planned and put through the House, generally by a vote of something like 450 to 1, the Senate would simply go along with it without a great deal of controversy. So while the admiral had good relationships, legislatively speaking, with Senator Walsh, they were never the kind that he had with Mr. Vinson. As you have said, Senator Walsh was no Carl Vinson in many respects!

Q: What was the admiral's working relationship with the State Department and with Secretary Hull? How closely did you people work with the State Department, especially in terms of the Pacific?

Adm. W.: In the earliest days of the admiral's incumbency as chief of naval operations, there was in existence a committee - I'm trying to recall its title, something like the Joint Liaison Committee - which consisted of the chief of naval operations, the chief of staff of the Army, and the undersecretary of State, who at that time was Mr. Welles. Each one of these used to bring one aide along with him when the committee met, and they met I think something on the order of once every couple of weeks, with Sumner Welles in the chair. His interest was not in the Pacific, really. His primary interest at that time seemed to me to be in Latin American projects, so very frequently these joint meetings revolved around the American hemisphere's problems and there wasn't a great deal of attention, at that time, given to the Pacific.

Q: Did Hornbeck play any role in this?

Adm. W.: Yes. The meetings I'm describing were the ones that took place in the early days of Admiral Stark's tenure as CNO. Now, later, as our relationships with Japan got more involved, there were various other means of communication with the State Department setup —

Q: There were special liaison people?

Adm. W.: Yes, there were.

Q: I know ONI had one. Dr. Sam Hunter.

Adm. W.: Yes, that's right. There was a lot of cross fertilization established and in due course Admiral Stark and the Secretary of State had a good deal to do with one another.

Going back now to what I said earlier about there being little civilian hierarchy between the chief of naval operations and the President, I think that would apply also to communications between the chief of naval operations and the State Department. The admiral dealt quite directly with Mr. Hull, and there were relatively frequent meetings with the President, with Mr. Hull present at those meetings, so that during the later stages the admiral had really very close connections with Mr. Hull.

Q: When Secretary Knox came in, how did he fit into this picture?

Adm. W.: He was kept informed on all of this. The admiral was very meticulous in keeping Mr. Knox abreast of any of this kind of meeting in which he participated, and occasionally, particularly when there were internal political considerations involved, Mr. Knox would be brought directly in to it. But, as I recall the situation, Mr. Knox was the political expert of the Navy Department rather than the strategic one. In matters of strategy, he pretty generally left it in the hands of the chief of naval operations and the professional uniformed people. He wanted to be aware of what was going on and he was kept informed, but he didn't try to handle this kind of matter directly. I think this was quite a different situation fromthe one that has developed recently in which all the various secretaries and assistant secretaries do try to be strategists, rather than political experts. But at that time it was pretty clearly a direct relationship between the commander-in-chief of the armed forces, that is the President, and his officers who were commanding the Navy and the Army, the CNO and the chief of staff of the Army.

Q: From what you said before, when we were talking about Pearl Harbor and the basing of the fleet on Pearl Harbor, the political considerations then were filtered in through Secretary Hull in this whole picture?

Adm. W.: Yes.

Q: Did the State Department feel strongly that the fleet should remain at Pearl?

Adm. W.: My recollection on this one is that they thought it should but this wasn't either a very strong or a very unanimous opinion in the State Department. I think, if I were to guess, I'd say that the State Department wouldn't have objected very strenuously had there been a decision made to bring the fleet back to the Pacific coast, and I'm sure that there were certain individuals over in the State Department who would have applauded that. Although I can't document this, I have the feeling that among the various people in the State Department with whom we had some kind of either direct or vicarious contact there wasn't unanimity. This is usually the case in the State Department. Mr. Hull and Mr. Hornbeck, for instance, didn't invariably see eye to eye on various problems in the Pacific. I think Admiral Stark was aware of this from both direct contacts with them and from the little bits of information that had come back as a result of some of the contacts between ONI and the State Department and of various other individuals with the State Department.

Q: Hornbeck was more a Pacific man, wasn't he?

Adm. W.: Yes, he was considered, I think, to be the State Department's expert on the Far East at that time. His views and the Navy Department's views seemed to me to be more or less frequently in conflict. I think Mr. Hull and Admiral Stark saw things more or less eye to eye most of the time.

Q: What was Admiral Stark's relationship with Admiral Nomura, the

Japanese ambassador?

Adm. W.: Admiral Nomura came to this country as ambassador in sort of the last stages of the negotiations with the Japanese and, of course, as an old professional sailor, he got into contact with Admiral Stark and I think he did his best to give Admiral Stark the Japanese position as ably as he could. They never had been very close during this period, as I recall it. As ambassador, of course, his correct protocol point of contact was the State Department rather than either of the military departments, and this was pretty well adhered to with some reasonable exceptions.

At the time of Admiral Nomura's mission to Washington, I think it's a matter of public record that our codebreakers were reading a good deal of the Japanese dispatch traffic back and forth -

Q: Their diplomatic codes?

Adm. W.: Yes, they particularly were readable - and during the early stages of his mission in Washington, Admiral Nomura sent back to the government in Japan a message which was highly critical of Admiral Stark. Of course, this one was decoded very promptly -

Q: And rushed to Admiral Stark!

Adm. W.: Yes, and did nothing to improve their relationship, and had there been a possibility of the establishment at the inception of closer relationship and a channel of communication through Admiral Nomura to Admiral Stark to the President, I think that message rather effectively cut off any possibility of a close relationship between them. So, while it was always a perfectly proper relationship, it was never a close or warm one.

Q: Would you say, in retrospect, that Admiral Nomura was completely informed as to the intentions of the military in his home land?

Adm. W.: At that time, I thought in all probability he was. It seemed inconceivable to me that there could be an ambassador in Washington trying to represent his country without being fully informed about what his country thought. In the light of the knowledge that I've acquired since then, it appears that he was not, because he definitely didn't know what was going on in the minds of the people who were controlling the course of events in Japan.

Q: Would that not, then, explain adequately the appearance of a special emissary, Kurusu?

Adm. W.: Probably, yes. I never quite understood even in the light of present knowledge why the Japanese sent these emissaries as they did. I guess, maybe, this is due to my lack of understanding of the operation of the oriental mind, but it still isn't clear to me just why they sent those two ambassadors, as they did, to supplement their normal representation in Washington. It could be that this was completely a camouflage operation, but I still don't think that that's the whole truth. There were some perfectly straightforward objectives in the sending of those two people, but why they thought they'd succeed is a little beyond me.

Interview No. 4 with Vice Admiral Charles Wellborn, Jr., U. S. Navy
(Retired)

Place: His apartment in the Westchester Apartments, Washington, D.C.
Date: Tuesday morning, 4 January 1972.
Subject: Biography
By: John T. Mason, Jr.

Q: It's indeed a pleasure to see you so early in the new year, Sir. I'm looking forward to a resumption of this series. Last time, you talked in some detail about various aspects of pre-Pearl Harbor conditions in the Navy Department and in Washington. I wonder if you'd resume your story today, plus telling me something more about the sequence of events in the year 1941 because so much happened in that year.

Adm. W.: There was indeed a great deal during that year and, thinking about this during the past couple of weeks, it seems to me that the one thing that stood out in my mind as dominant was that during this period although the country wasn't ready by any means to go to war, Admiral Stark accomplished a very great deal in getting our Navy much more nearly ready to go to war. At the start of this period, we didn't have very much in the way of naval capabilities beyond the combatant ships of the fleet - that is, the carriers, the battleships, the cruisers, the destroyers, a few oilers, a few tenders, but in pretty small numbers. We had few of those things that round out a naval capability - minesweepers, fleet tugs, provision ships, all of the base facilities that are really pretty necessary to conduct continuous naval operations. The admiral recognized this. He also was aware of the difficulties of doing things about it. The country definitely wasn't war-minded and appropriations had to be obtained from Congress, which was pretty conscious of the public reaction to this kind of thing. Also, the President himself was, of course, in terms of recent usage, a political being and had to keep pretty close tabs on what the country was thinking. But it seemed to me that Admiral Stark really did a masterful job of working through the President and the Congress to obtain the various things that were necessary to get us into a much better state of readiness than we had been in before. Transports, minesweepers, patrol craft - coastal patrol craft - and small things of this kind, all of which add up to quite a total.

Q: I take it that many of these were nonessential in peacetime and that's why we didn't have them?

Adm. W.: Yes, and, of course, during peacetime when military appropriations are always hard to come by, the available money goes for first things first, and the first things were the combatant ships so these things, these support units, were pretty much neglected. I think this is always true in peacetime. But there was a great deal done without much fanfare, and it was done in spite of a, you might say, hostile reaction from the public. I might mention in this connection, too, that Admiral Ben Morrell, who was the chief of the Bureau of Yards and Docks, did just a magnificent job of getting ready for the base development part of this job. He always seemed to be a jump or two ahead of everybody else in the construction industry, and at that time I remember they used to kid Admiral Morrell quite a good deal about having a corner on all the constructional steel available in the United States. I doubt if he actually had it all cornered, but he had his share of it all right, there was no question about that.

Q: How large an operation did Admiral Stark and the others envision once we got into this conflict? What was their estimate of the probabilities in the Pacific?

Adm. W.: I have difficulty answering that one very precisely. I would guess, however, that they hadn't at that time envisaged an operation of the size of let's say the invasion of Okinawa, which came late in the war, but very clearly did have in mind the fact that amphibious forces would be required to land on hostile beaches and among the things that were being acquired were transports that could be combat-loaded and used for that purpose, and it was recognized that after this was done - or maybe during the course of this kind of an operation - we'd probably encounter mines and we just had no capability to deal with them, so we acquired some capability. As I say, I suspect that they didn't at that time - the admiral didn't at that time - envisage the magnitude of the operations ultimately reached, but he definitely had in mind the fact that this type operation would have to be conducted, that we didn't have the necessary things with which to conduct them, and he set out to get them. During that year we achieved at least a nucleus of this type of craft and ships.

Q: This anticipatory effort on his part, was it done in conjunctio with the Army? Were they also doing similar things?

Adm. W.: To a certain extent, yes. At that time, of course, the things that the Army wanted to do were a little different from what the Navy wanted to do, and there was a certain amount of competition for the available money and for the available manufacturing capability. For instance, at that time the Air Force, of course, was a part of the Army, and the Army's Air Corps wanted airplanes in tremendous numbers, planes of all kinds, and the Navy wanted them, too. And the production of airplanes at that time was something for which this country had a relatively limited capability, so when this was expanded it impinged to a certain extent on our capability to manufacture other things. So the Army and the Navy did have to coordinate what they were doing.

Q: Did General Marshall share Admiral Stark's point of view about the Pacific?

Adm. W.: Yes. I think General Marshall's approach to this problem - and I saw this at somewhat of a distance, so I'm not as sure about what he did as I am about what Admiral Stark did - he seemed, though, to be interested primarily in the acquisition of airplanes and then next to that the various kinds of things that were needed simply to expand the existing Army, rather than to fill out a lot of nonexistent types of forces. He wanted more tanks and more artillery and more of this and that. But my impression was that the Army's problem was one rather of expansion of what they had than of filling in the gaps.

Q: How did the needs of Great Britain fit into this whole picture?

She was already in desperate need.

Adm. W.: Yes, and this was definitely worked into the production program. My memory is a little vague on just when the War Production Board's activities came into being and just when the Combined Chiefs of Staff began to operate, but as I recall it in 1941 these were not actually in operation. But the British requirements were being considered. The mechanism, I think, at that time was what was called the Munitions Board. It consisted of the assistant secretary of the Navy, and the assistant secretary of war, I believe, plus various professional uniformed people, and it was their job to coordinate production and to match it up with capacity. We were having sent in at this time British requirements and in this connection, of course, Mr. Churchill and Mr. Roosevelt had a close personal relationship and the President was definitely kept aware of British needs through this channel, along with the more regular channels for introducing British requirements.

Q: One gathers that the President was less cautious about fulfilling British demands and much more anxious to do it, perhaps, than our own people.

Adm. W.: I think this is correct, yes. Our own people, of course, had an axe to grind in this. They all wanted production of various kinds to meet their own definite needs and were somewhat less sympathetic to meeting somebody else's needs. I think the President saw this globally to a greater extent than the people in the Department of War or the Department of the Navy.

Q: How did Admiral Stark himself feel about this?

Adm. W.: I thought he had a really very judicious approach to it. He recognized that if Britain went down before we could become an active participant in the war, that we were in very deep trouble and that it was of very great importance to this country to keep Britain alive and fighting. I think he always, however, felt that our prime reliance must be on our own forces, so while it was important to keep Britain alive at the time, it was paramount in the event Britain went down that we were in shape to pick the chips up wherever they lay and to work toward a successful conclusion of the war. My thinking was that ADmiral Stark balanced this off very well indeed.

Q: In this effort to develop a more rounded fleet in preparation for combat activities, did Admiral Stark give attention to the ordnance problems? I'm thinking of the difficulties we had immediately after the outbreak of the war with our torpedoes, for instance.. Was any attention given in this area to the needs and to the readiness?

Adm. W.: I believe that the problem of design of torpedo exploders, which I think you refer to, was one that Admiral Stark at that time considered to be a detail that the chief of the Bureau of Ordnance, as it was called in those days, should handle, and that while he, Admiral Stark, as chief of naval operations, was interested in exploders that would explode, their design was something for which he had to rely on the chief of the Bureau of Ordnance. So my recollection is that he did not specifically delve into whether or not the torpedo exploders were proper or the particular fuses that were put in bombs were exactly what they should be. He was interested in the larger picture of do we have enough bombs to do the things we ought to do and do we have enough fuses to fuse them. The technical details of how the fuses worked, as I recall it, he depended on his bureau chiefs to solve for him.

Q: When one looks back, the enemy's signing of the tripartite pact in 1940 was a definite signal that war was coming and I suppose knowing that now, maybe it's interesting, maybe it would be valuable to speculate what Admiral Stark and the others might have been able to accomplish in terms of readiness if public opinion had not held them back.

Adm. W. I would guess that things would have moved along much more rapidly than they did. I think that among the people around the Navy Department, the War Department, the State Department, there was pretty general recognition that if war wasn't inevitable it was awfully close to it, the way the situation had moved during late 1940 and 1941. I think most of the military people, having recognized that this was pretty nearly inevitable, wanted to hold it off as long as they could in order to have more time to improve readiness for it. It is interesting to speculate on what acceleration of this kind of production might have resulted from a change in the public attitude, but certainly the attitude right up to Pearl Harbor was one that didn't support very much in the way of preparations for active wartime operations.

Q: There are those who say the public knows best, but this may have refuted that idea!

Adm. W.: Yes. I'm more or less of a supporter of that view, but

I think we have to realize that when we say that we shouldn't apply that to all the decisions in all situations. I think that's a good general rule for maybe the direction that we should head for the next fifty years or something of this sort. But if you apply it to a decision whether or not we need six more cruisers right now, then I don't believe the public does know best!

Q: I wonder if you'd focus on the problem of supplies? Japan had been purchasing scrap iron from us and oil and what have you, weapons of war, for a considerable period of time. What was Admiral Stark's attitude toward this? What did the Navy - what did we think about it, what did we do?

Adm. W.: Well, there were here some conflicting points of view. There was general realization that Japan was getting from this country the sinews of war, scrap steel and oil, these things. There was one school of thought that we should forthwith shut off any flow of scrap steel or petroleum to Japan. There was another one that felt, for a couple of reasons, that this shouldn't be done. One line of reasoning was that if we shut it off before we got into a position of imminent hostilities, this would give the Japanese time to develop alternate sources, and that until we were quite sure we were going to get in, we shouldn't do this. There was another group who felt that any curtailment of this kind of thing would arouse a high degree of antagonism in the Japanese and make them even more difficult to deal with than they already were, and that, in effect, this would destroy any chance of a diplomatic solution to our problems with Japan. So, this problem was bounced back and forth and I believe it's a matter of record that we ultimately did cut these things off, some of the people thought too soon and others thought we held off too long.

Q: What was the Navy's position?

Adm. W.: I think the Navy's position generally was one of, well, we'd better cut it off and these other considerations were a little esoteric and there isn't anything quite like having the things you need and we were giving them to them, and maybe we'd better be practical and say we're not going to give them any more. Then, if they developed alternate supply sources, all right. I think most of the Navy felt that way. As I recall it, Admiral Stark generally felt that way, although he had to listen to a lot of these other arguments frequently.

Q: Does this imply, then, that the Navy was less optimistic about diplomatic negotiations than some of the other branches of government?

Adm. W.: Yes, I think that's probably a correct statement. I think the Navy felt that it was improbable that the Japanese would ever come around to a position that would be acceptable to this country. It was just at the start of 1941 a question of time before we did have to fight the Japanese.

Q: And in this same vein, I think it was in April of 1941 when the so-called ABC big powers out in the Far East had their great powwow out in Singapore, wasn't it?

Adm. W.: I don't recall exactly when that was, but that would seem about right.

Q: That was largely a Navy effort, wasn't it, on our part?

Adm. W.: I would say that that's probably correct, although all the services participated. I would say it was probably one that the navies pushed harder than any of the others, because the whole Pacific war was more of a sea-power war than the Atlantic one was.

Q: What about those discussions? I mean, what was our Navy - our - view of this whole thing?

Adm. W.: Right from the early days - and when I say early days I think it goes back earlier than 1941, probably 1940 - Admiral Stark had written up a piece of paper which never had any formal status, it was simply his thoughts on what the grand strategy for the war should be, and in very broad outline it was that the first thing we had to do, if we got into it, was to win the war in Europe in the Atlantic, and during the time we were doing this hold in the Pacific - not lose any more than was absolutely necessary, but not really conduct a high-powered offensive in the Pacific. And at such time as either we had built up our capabilities or could spare them from ensuring that we won first in Europe, then go out and clean up the Pacific. That's a very broad outline of his early thinking on how the war should be conducted. As a matter of fact, I think that's the way it was conducted. I think that paper of his really turned out to form the basis of grand strategy for World War II.

Q: That wasn't just put in a safe. Did the White House see it?

Adm. W.: Yes, the White House had seen this. When you say White

House, of course in those days the White House was the President - there weren't a lot of Kissingers and things around.

Q: That's what I meant.

Adm. W.: He had seen it and he was in general agreement with it. There were some officers in the military departments who wouldn't have wholeheartedly agree with it. There were some Pacific-consciou people and there were various shades of thinking, but I think this was pretty generally accepted in the Navy and the War Department, too.

Q: How did our potential allies in the Far East feel about this?

Adm. W.: To the best of my knowledge, they were never told in quite such blunt terms that this was the situation, but I think they recognized that this was what was going to be done. In those days the alliances were not as strong as they are now. They have NATO councils and things today and in those days such things didn't exist, so really the U.S. position became pretty much the Allied position because none of the others had enough strength to really be felt very much.

Q: As part and parcel of that, the British were urging that the U.S. fleet send units to help out at Singapore because they were engaged elsewhere. How did Admiral Stark feel about this and how did he deal with it?

Adm. W.: I have to rack my memory a little bit on this one. I remember the time it came up and it seems to me that, at that time, this was a problem that pretty much solved itself. The force that we had remaining in the Pacific after Pearl Harbor ready for action was such that we couldn't spare much to help anybody.

Q: No, I meant prior to Pearl Harbor.

Adm. W.: Oh, prior to Pearl Harbor.

Q: Yes, considerably before Pearl Harbor, the British brought this up.

Adm. W.: Oh, yes, now I get what you're talking about. I believe that at that time this would not have been looked upon favorably either in the Navy Department or in the White House because the strong effort in the Navy Department at that time was to improve our readiness for entry into the war, and any dispatch of forces out into that area would have been definitely in conflict with that. It would have interrupted training cycles and made it very difficult to pull nuclei of men off operating ships to commission new ships. I think the professional naval officers would not have looked upon that with much favor, and in the political circles this one, while it had some favorable points and it might hold the Japanese back from making moves they might otherwise make, I think the political people felt that this was a little too hazardous a thing to go into under the existing situation. We were indulging in pretty precarious negotiations with the Japanese, as it was, and the dispatch of some of our naval force to Singapore, the general feeling was, would have possibly pushed the Japanese into taking some overt action much sooner than they did.

Q: You said a moment ago that the interruption of training cycles and the like - Admiral Morison in his book deals at some length with this whole situation and makes the point that Admiral Stark was loath to ever interrupt the training cycles and, therefore, did not take to the idea of President Roosevelt to send helping forces various places in the Pacific to show the flag.

Adm. W.: Oh, I think that's right.

Q: Do you recall anything specific about that?

Adm. W.: I don't recall anything really specific. As I recall it, though, the President himself wasn't too anxious to do this. My recollection is admittedly a little dim over this, but it seems to me that he recognized the limitations of this kind of activity and the Navy didn't get pushed very hard to do this. If Sam Morison puts if differently, maybe Sam knows better than I do.

Q: Quoting from Morison, he says the President alarmed the chief of naval operations by announcing that he wished to send more ships to keep them popping up here and there and keep the Japs guessing. Admiral Stark regarded this suggestion, which he attributed to the State Department, as childish. Accordingly he drew a plan to send a carrier force northwestward from Hawaii, which he hoped would give the State Department a shock and might make them haul back, and it did!

Adm. W.: Sam may have better knowledge on this than I have, but I don't recall that.

Q: It brought up a question in my mind as I read it. Last time you said that, generally speaking, Admiral Stark and Secretary Hull were in agreement on things. Now, if the State Department was proposing something like this, he couldn't have been in agreement.

Adm. W.: No, not on this, and when you refer to the State Department, I suspect that we should differentiate a bit between Mr. Hull and a lot of the other amorphous group! I think there were some in the State Department who might well have felt as Sam Morison indicates here. Mr. Hull, so far as I could observe, from where I was, was a pretty practical individual about military affairs and I don't recall his going off on many of this kind of project that from a military point of view didn't make much sense. From what observation of him I had, I felt that he listened to reason and made pretty judicious decisions and recommendations. I couldn't say that for some of the other papers that came out of the State Department. So, maybe this is the difference. Sam is talking about the State Department as an organization, whereas I'm talking about the Secretary of State.

Q: How did Admiral Stark generally deal with some of these less than sound ideas which sometimes emanated from the White House, less than sound in naval terms? How did he deal with them?

Adm. W.: Usually, this kind of thing had to be dealt with through direct negotiations between him and the President, and it seemed to me that he was really a master of the art of preventing the President from doing anything impulsive and, you might say, playing for time until he could muster the necessary arguments to shoot down any scheme that was a little on the wild-eyed side. He got along very well with the President and when something of this kind came up, if he could get the President to delay action on it for a while, he usually could convince the President of his point of view.

This wasn't invariably the case, but my recollection generally is that he more frequently than not was able to present a sound military position to the President, and when it was so presented the President accepted it.

Q: I can think of several instances as to these ideas which emanated from the White House and I assume they were ideas that Churchill and President Roosevelt hatched out together?

Adm. W.: This happened pretty frequently. They were both men of great imagination and they did come up with some ideas and not all of these got shot down. A good many of them were tried. I recall, for instance, somebody came up with the idea that we should build some things called "sea otters," and we did build one or two of them. They were basically steel barges with a lot of great big outboard motors, down in the water through holes all over the barge.

Q: What were they for?

Adm. W.: They were to augment our dwindling supply of merchant shipping which Britain and our various other allies supplied. Somebody came up with this idea, and most of the military people felt that this would just waste our scarce production capacity, but some of these things were built and tested. There were quite a number of ideas of this kind that were never shot down right off, but were proved impracticable and I think most of them were more or less a minimum of waste of productive capacity.

Q: Somebody told me once they felt that President Roosevelt was very often influenced by some of his yachting friends who also had all kinds of theories.

Adm. W.: I wouldn't be able to comment directly on this, but if that were the case it wouldn't have surprised me. He, of course, had a great many friends of that kind, and lots of these people had a record of pretty high achievement. Some of the most important industrialists and bankers and this sort of thing in the country and my impression was, without having ever been very close to it, that Mr. Roosevelt thought these fellows had pretty good judgment. So it wouldn't have surprised me a bit if he had accepted thoughts that came in from them, but I haven't any firsthand knowledge of that.

Q: If the thought at the Navy Department was that war was so almost inevitable, why was not some ffort made, then, to build up the Asiatic fleet? It was in a sorry state, wasn't it?

Adm. W.: It was in not much of a state. As I remember it, there were nineteen old flush-deck destroyers, the four-stack type, a few submarines, and I think one cruiser, maybe. It wasn't much of a force...

Q: I like to think of Admiral Tommy Hart's oft-quoted statement that all his ships were old enough to vote!

Adm. W.: Well, I think they were! I think most of them would have voted for Tommy, too! But I believe that in line generally with the over-all strategy of winning in Europe and holding in the Pacific, then after Europe was under control cleaning the Pacific up, any assignment of additional forces in the Asiatic would have been somewhat wasted. I think the feeling was that such forces as we could produce could be used to much greater advantage even with the main body of the Pacific Fleet or in the Atlantic, and that by sending a lot of stuff out to the Asiatic Fleet we'd simply be dividing our forces and letting them be defeated piecemeal.

Q: Was it thought that they could withstand any initial Japanese thrust?

Adm. W.: My recollection of the planning at this time was that they should do exactly what Admiral Hart did do. They weren't expected to be able to withstand a Japanese thrust in force. They would retire, saving themselves as well as they could and inflicting such damage as they could, and there wasn't really an expectation that the small force we had out there was really going to be able to exercise any control of the sea out there against overwhelming Japanese strength.

Q: Was that something that Admiral Hart acquiesced in?

Adm. W.: Maybe, "acquiesced" is a little too strong. My recollection of his position was, I wish I had more to do the job properly, but since it's impossible to get I'll do what I can with what I have. He seemed to me to be, from all of the communications from him that I saw, fully aware of what the situation was, and while he didn't like it any better than anyone else would have, he recognized it and carried out the orders that he had very loyally and, I think very effectively.

Q: I know that he - and I think again Morison is the source for this - in January 1941 Ambassador Grew made an entry in his diary to the effect that rumors were going round Tokyo that the Japanese when hostilities broke out were going to make a surprise attack on Pearl Harbor, and he said in his diary that this was passed on to Washington.

Adm. W.: I believe this is correct, and I don't recall getting that in Washington at the time, although it's conceivable that it did come over from the State Department. This has appeared in a number of the histories of the Pearl Harbor days, and, as I recall it, the sources of this rumor, which I think Mr. Grew said it was, was a Latin American diplomat.

Q: Somebody out of Berne!

Adm. W.: Yes. The source of it and the fact that there really wasn't any corroboration, I think probably tended to just let this particular rumor slide down between the cracks. In Barbara Wohlstetter's book - I believe it's called <u>Pearl Harbor</u> - she covers this question of the fact that there was a tremendous amount of background intelligence coming in all the time and that it was very difficult for the people in Washington to winnow out from this great volume of stuff coming in from all kinds of sources, that which was important and believable. I'm sure you've read that book -

Q: I read many of those dispatches, too!

Adm. W.: I think she correctly assessed this situation, and that report from Mr. Grew just didn't seem to be one that should be given very much credence, and it wasn't. No one paid much attention to it. If I remember correctly, and I'm not sure on this point, in the light of hindsight, that rumor that was sent in by Mr. Grew was actually sent in before the Japanese developed their plan and really got to work on the preparation for the attack on Pearl Harbor. So, while it was in the nature of being prophetic, I don't believe it was in the nature of solid intelligence.

Q: Will you, Sir, focus on all those events leading up to Pearl Harbor itself, since this is of very great importance historically?

Adm. W.: Well, that's been written about at very great length.

Q: I know. Various people have written about it, but your own version, your own inside view is of real importance historically.

Adm. W.: This is a very complicated proposition, and the best over-all summary of this one that w available, I think, is this book of Barbara Wohlstetter's, to which I referred a moment ago. That's 300 or 400 pages' worth, but I found in that very little with which I couldn't agree. I wouldn't agree with every sentence, but that one seemed to me to catch the general situation about as accurately as anything that I have read or heard on the subject.

Q: Had you talked with her in advance?

Adm. W.: No, I've never met the lady.

Q: Did she talk with Admiral Stark?

Adm. W.: I don't believe so. I don't think she ever talked to him. Right after the attack, there was something called the Roberts

Commission that was appointed by the President to investigate the Pearl Harbor attack. I think it was pretty accurate in its assessment of the situation that existed at the time. There was a general belief on the part of practically everybody that the Japanese were on the point of doing something and everybody thought it was going to be possibly the Philippines but more possibly the Malay Peninsula that they would strike. There may have been a few voices in the wilderness who were saying, no, Pearl Harbor, but they weren't very loud voices and nobody really thought that it could happen there. I mean, nobody of real consequence. And when it did happen, I think most of the military people were just as surprised as the general citizenry were. I think that comes out quite well in both the Roberts Commission report and the Wohlstetter book. I'm not sure I'm being responsive to the question you asked me, but maybe I've shed some light on my thinking of it.

Q: I recall one bit of information I read emanating from Admiral Standley, who disagreed pretty violently with the Robert report or felt that it was only a half report and didn;t cover the situation.

Adm. W.: Well, of course, Admiral Standley was a member of the Roberts Commission.

Q: I know he was.

Adm. W.: Justice Roberts, Admiral Standley and Admiral Reeves, and General McCoy and General McNarney. In my book all five of those are very able people. I think they came up with a good report. I don;t recall what Admiral Standley's objections to the report were.

Q: In general, I believe he felt that it was something of a whitewash.

Adm. W.: Well, this is a view that a number of people have held, all right. Needless to say, I don't agree with it. I saw all those messages that went out from the departments, both the War Department and the Navy Department. They were sent to Admiral Hart in the Asiatic, and they were sent to Admiral Kimmel in Pearl Harbor. Similar messages were sent to a lot of other people, too. I think it's worthy of note that Admiral Hart very accurately interpreted the intent of all those messages and what he did I think was exactly what was expected of him. On the other hand, at Pearl Harbor the intent seemed to have been missed, and this is essentially what the Roberts Commission says — that Washington did give adequate information and warning to the commanders in the field and the responsibility lies with those commanders. This was my view. Of course, I'm a little biased because I was sitting there in Washington. But to me it was inescapable, and I think what Admiral Hart did is something in the way of proof of the view I've just stated.

Q: The gist of the messages were clear — if you wanted to read them thoroughly!

Adm. W.: Yes, and how in the world you could interpret a message that starts off, "This is a war warning," to be just kind of a mild innocuous message I don't know. To me that says — this is it, be ready any time.

Q: Were the commanders, that is Hart and Kimmel, also informed of the ONI effort on the 3rd of December, when they sent out messages to all their people, the watchers on the Chinese coast and so forth, to burn their codes and to send back an acknowledgment of the fact that they had done so?

Adm. W.: My recollection of the precise details here is a little vague, but I'm sure that could be dug out of the records and the voluminous reports that have been made on it. My own feeling on this is that there were a good many things in the line of burning codes and ciphers and making detailed preparations for hostilities that may not have been sent to the commander-in-chief Pacific specifically, but I have the feeling that he was being kept broadly aware of all the things that were being done, and my feeling at that time was and I think it still is that to have sent him information copies of all of this stuff would have cluttered his communications system and added to what Barbara Wohlstetter calls "the background of noise." It really wouldn't have materially improved the intelligence position. It simply would have cluttered up the communications circuits and the intelligence files. It was my belief that they had all of the basic information that they needed, and it was a matter of feeling, as the rest of the country felt, that we may get into war sometime but surely not today, and if a war starts surely it won't start in Hawaii or on the Pacific coast. It will start somewhere, maybe in the Philippines or in Southeast Asia but not here. I really believe it was this kind of an attitude and this kind of thinking that resulted in the people in Pearl Harbor failing to recognize the warnings that were sent

I think they had adequate information, although this of course was the heart of that great controversy - did Washington keep the commander-in-chief adequately informed?

Q: Was there telephonic communication between Washington and Hawaii in those days?

Adm. W.: There was telephone communication, but it was wholly insecure communication, and no scrambling or coding in any way of the voice communication, some of which was by radio. At any rate, it was considered insecure, and although I very definitely recollec Admiral Stark talking in the clear to Admiral Block in Pearl Harbor after the attack, it is my recollection that the telephone until the attack occurred was not used for matters of importance involvir security because it simply wasn't secure. There was rapid secure radio telegraphic communication back and forth. The Army had its circuits and the Navy had its, and this went pretty fast. Of cours it's not like voice communication.

Q: One person with whom I've talked, an ONI source, said that Admiral Wilkinson, who was then DNI, actually asked Admiral Stark on the morning of Pearl Harbor in Washington - to telephone Admiral Kimmel and impart to him the information which was gotten from the broken - through the codebreaking - that this was imminent, that Admiral Stark had not done so, and the surmise was that he had not done so because he felt all the necessary preparations had been tak all the precautions.

Adm. W.: This would fit very well in my recollection of that situa tion. I was not actually in the office the morning of December 7th,

I can't say definitely whether Admiral Wilkinson did come in and make such a suggestion. I would guess, though, had he done so, Admiral Stark's reaction would have been we've given you all the warning that we can and another warning over an insecure line of communication might be more dangerous than helpful.

Q: The assumption was also made in ONI apparently that the basic responsibility rested with the Army, rather than the Navy.

Adm. W.: This is quite true. At that time, the Army was assigned the responsibility for the defense of a U.S. base. Now, I think neither the Army nor the Navy interpreted this one too entirely literally. It was recognized that the Army didn't have enough aircraft in Hawaii to conduct appropriate searches over the ocean around Hawaii, and there was always recognition that the Navy would use such forces as it had whenever it could to augment the Army's capability in the various plans for the defense of Hawaii. The antiaircraft guns of the ships in Pearl Harbor were always expected to contribute to the antiaircraft defense. So, technically certainly, it is correct that the Army was assigned the responsibility for the defense of the base. The Army now really had the necessary assets to have accomplished this and the Navy with what assets it had recognized that it should assist as it could. That was something that I think in the minds of the public of the country never came out. I think the people of the country always thought it was a great failure of the Navy to carry out its responsibility and never seemed to realize that the Army was involved in this responsibility, too.

Q: I suppose that was natural because the end result was the Navy suffered.

Adm. W.: Yes, it was a naval disaster. But that, I think, is a more or less technical question. It certainly was up to whatever force there was there to help in the defense.

Q: Here's a point which I believe you can clear up quite effectively. This also is ONI source. They had a number of directors in 1941. I know Alan Kirk was there and didn't like it and didn't want to stay, but Wilkinson was finally there and, according to ONI sources, he appointed Sam Moore, Nobre Moore, as head of foreign intelligence in the thought that ONI would have more direct access to Admiral Stark than it had had before. Apparently there was some difficulty in this direct access - War Plans got in the way or something.

Adm. W.: From where I sat, I always thought that that controversy was a little spurious. If I've ever seen anybody that was available, Admiral Stark was. In fact, I used to do my best to get him to cut down on his proclivity to let people come in and waste his time, but he was, I thought, overly conscientious in letting anybody who thought he had a piece of information that the admiral ought to get come in and give it to him. Now, I think it's quite true that he had really very great confidence in his war planners, Kelly Turner and Savvy Cooke were the principal ones I remember. He had a very high regard for both of those two and their capabilities. But I don't think he let this exclude any one of the several intelligence directors. It's probably correct that they didn't have equal time, but I think they had adequate time. What's adequate is I think still a controversy between the Democratic and Republican parties! But it may have been a situation of this kind. The director of intelligence would have liked to spend more time telling the admiral his views on things, but there are just so many hours in the day. From my point of view, I can't recall any instance when the director of intelligence didn't have an adequate crack at him.

Q: I didn't quite understand the reference to Nobre Moore, how he got into the picture. Was he close to Stark?

Adm. W.: I can't recall that he was particularly close. He was a very pleasant individual, an effective one.

Q: He was my boss!

Adm. W.: Yes. I'm sure the admiral thought highly of him, but I can't find anywhere in my recollection a situation there that he had a particular access to the admiral that somebody else didn't have.

Q: When did you come on the scene that day, the day of Pearl Harbor?

Adm. W.: I got in the office I guess maybe about two o'clock. I heard the fact that Pearl Harbor had been attacked at my home in Chevy Chase. I didn't actually hear the radio. I wasn't listening to it, to the news broadcast when it came on, but I was very promptly informed by somebody and my immediate reaction was, I'd better get down to the Navy Department right away, and I jumped in the car and went down. It was about half an hour ro so, and I guess that would have made it something like two o'clock.

Q: Admiral Stark had been there all morning?

Adm. W.: Yes, he'd been there all day, since early that morning. When I got into the office none of us left for two or three days! But unfortunately I was not there when it happened.

Q: Can you describe some of the things that took place immediately after you arrived? I mean, what did you get involved in doing?

Adm. W.: I don't recall it now. It was a period of some confusion because the place wasn't completely manned and all of the top heads of various divisions and branches and things weren't necessarily in their offices. They all appeared pretty promptly, though. A number of them were on leave and weren't there on this particular Sunday, and getting hold of the people you wanted was fairly difficult. I devoted a good deal of time to hunting down the right person to talk to on the right subject. The admiral himself, as I recall it, was pretty busy trying to get the secretary of the navy, Mr. Knox, and the President read in on what was going on. As I said earlier, he talked to Admiral Block over the telephone I recall very definitely -

Q: To get a picture of it?

Adm. W.: Yes, to get a picture of what was happening and what had happened. It was one of those periods of trying to assess what the situation was and then trying to decide what to do about it.

That was the order of the day, and this involved communicating with people who had firsthand information and then those who could work out the orders on what to do, as I recall it. There was a good deal of running in and out of the office of operational and intelligence people.

Q: Did they have their own sources of information on what actually took place, or did it all have to funnel through Admiral Stark?

Adm. W.: You mean did the President and -

Q: Yes. Were other people in communication by voice with Hawaii?

Adm. W.: To the best of my knowledge, they were not. They may have later talked to people in Hawaii but during that afternoon I believe the admiral was the only one who talked directly. There was a continuing flow of radio messages coming in, and getting these things all sorted out and presented in a way that gave you a real picture of what was happening was pretty much of an undertaking. I think that afternoon in my memory stands out as the best example I've ever experienced of the fog of war. We knew that there's been an attack on Pearl Harbor and, at this point, there were various rumors, some of which made the dispatches that came in to Washington, as to what was happening. There was one, for instance of a landing on the west coast of Oahu by hostile forces. I recall having to run that one down and find that it wasn't the case. Then sorting out all of the welter of messages and the information that the admiral had been able to get by telephone and putting together an accurate picture of what really had happened was very difficult. I think this is the way it usually is in war,

Wellborn #4 - 134

particularly in a surprise situation. You never have adequate information either of the enemy forces or your own forces and what's happened to them.

Q: How was the admiral reacting to all this?

Adm. W.: Well, it's sort of difficult to say. I think he was as much surprised that it happened at Pearl Harbor as were all the rest of us. I don't think he expected it to happen, and I think it required his collecting his thoughts and adjusting his thinking to this new situation. His thinking up to this point had been one of the most important things to do and proceed with getting ourselves into a better state of readiness and any actual assault very probably was going to be in the Southeast Asia area, and even after hostilities commenced we still would be proceeding in a way not too different from the one that we had been using up to that time. Here, all at once, the situation was radically changed and it called for a lot of very quick re-assessment and re-thinking of the whole problem. I think he recognized the magnitude of this problem right away.

Q: Did he make any attempt to reach Admiral Kimmel?

Adm. W.: I can't remember definitely. I'm not sure on this but it seems to me - and I'm not very sure of this - that during the course of the conversation with Admiral Block, who got through to Admiral Stark -

Q: Oh, it was in that direction?

Adm. W.: Yes - as I recall it, there was something in that conversation that indicated that he was speaking for Admiral Kimmel and that this call could be considered as one covering what Kimmel would normally be expected to report, and which he did report by dispatch, but I can't recall any specific conversation with Admiral Kimmel, nor can I recall any specific effort to get him on the telephone.

Q: Was there anything coming in from the Asiatic Fleet?

Adm. W.: Not by telephone. Of course, really quite prompt and complete reports were coming in from the commander-in-chief of the Asiatic Fleet as to what was developing there. As you recall, at that time, most of the action didn't involve the Navy, it involved the Army's forces out there, so most of the reports that came from that area were Army reports. We did have some activity in Subic Bay, I believe it was.

Q: Did the President step into the picture that afternoon and call for Admiral Stark and General Marshall to go to the White House?

Adm. W.: They talked on the telephone a number of times, and I believe he did go to the White House, but I can't say specifically whether he left the Navy Department and went over there, or whether they continued to talk by telephone. They were in definite communication right along.

Q: You say you didn't get home for three days?

Adm. W.: It was something like that, yes. We just stayed in the office. Things kept coming in so rapidly, and there just didn't seem to be any opportunity to get away. You must recall that whereas includes a good many thousands of people. At that time it was something on the order of a hundred officers to do the whole job. So, when a situation of this kind burst upon us, there weren't enough people to stand watches and we just couldn't spare anybody. Everybody stayed around pretty steadily. We'd take a little time off and take a nap right there in the office. There were a great many people who didn't leave their offices, essentially.

Q: When was the decision made to send Admiral Nimitz out?

Adm. W.: This was in a matter of days, but this, as I remember it, was not made on December the 7th. I'm sure that's a matter of record that I could look up in the various literature that is available and find out that date exactly.

Q: How did the selection fall on Admiral Nimitz? Can you recall those circumstances?

Adm. W.: This kind of selection, I think at that time, was handled pretty well by maybe a half dozen of the senior people. Of course, the President had the final either veto or approval of this and the nomination of a person to the President would come up after discussion with the assistant chief of naval operations and the chief. The secretary of the navy may have been involved in the discussion. It seems to me that at that time those three were the ones who came up with that recommendation and sent it over to the President and he agreed on it. The secretary of the navy didn't normally get into technical details of the management of the Navy at that time, but when it came to the appointment of commanders-in-chief and such, he was definitely interested and my recollection is that he had a part in this, but I think probably that the spark of the idea originated with Admiral Stark and the vice chief, and at that time, that was Admiral Ingersoll. Of course, Admiral Nimitz himself was the chief of Navigation - I've forgotten when it became Personnel. Normally, in the assignment of people he would have been consulted but since he was being assigned I suspect that he didn't get very actively into that choice.

Q: Can you recall Secretary Knox that day?

Adm. W.: Yes. My recollection of him was that he was superbly calm and collected, whereas a lot of the rest of us were running around in circles yelling and shouting - and this is an exaggeration - Secretary Knox seemed to be able to do it with considerable detachment and to take quite a philosophical and just practical approach to it all. I had great admiration for him in those few days. He seemed to be not panicked at all and proceeding along good sound lines.

Q: I was wondering when the decision was made and who made the decision to replace Admiral Kimmel, because he was replaced almost immediately, and Admiral Pye took over as an interim thing?

Adm. W.: Yes. My recollection on this would be that Secretary Knox probably was the instrumental force in pushing this. As I recall it, with his rather calm and collected over-all view of this situation he seemed to feel that, for a number of reasons, the commander-in-chief out there should be replaced at this point, that there had been a disaster, and that whether or not, from a strictly professional military point of view, this required replacement, from the point of view of public confidence, if nothing else, and it did.

Q: It didn't necessarily mean that he looked upon him as guilty of -

Adm. W.: I think not at that point. I suspect that as subsequent events developed - the Roberts Commission report came out quite a long while later - but I think in due course, after a chance to reflect on it a little bit, Mr. Knox probably felt that the people in Pearl Harbor were the ones who should bear the greatest responsibility for this. But my feeling at the time was that he felt after something like this you've just got to have a new boss, and that that was probably the prime consideration. There may have been, too, some feeling of the current staff out there being - when I say staff I mean commander-in-chief and staff - being somewhat overwhelmed by this catastrophe, whereas before it happened they might have been highly competent and thoroughly capable of doing the job, after it had happened there was a sufficient psychological effect on them to render them something less than completely effective in the job at that time. But this was kind of an intangible thing, but I suspect that that kind of consideration entered into it. It's a little hard to judge what somebody's psychological reaction to a disaster of this kind is when you're 6,000 miles away, but you get impressions from reading dispatches and things of this sort.

Q: This was probably the reaction of the civilian head of the Navy, but how did professional officers react to the whole thing immediately thereafter?

Adm. W.: As I recall it, there was some feeling in the minds of the professionals, too, that maybe psychologically the commanders in Pearl Harbor had been affected by this catastrophe, and maybe some brand-new thinking on the subject would be better than the old people trying to pick up the pieces.

Q: That raises a question in my mind. Why, then, name as an interim C-in-C Admiral Pye, who was also there when this happened?

Adm. W.: He was there but he didn't bear the brunt of the responsibility, as Admiral Kimmel had. I think possibly, too, in this connection, personalities might have entered into it. Admiral Pye was considered one of the deeper thinkers in the Navy at that time, and it may be that this fact entered into his being chosen as the interim appointee because the existing situation then did call for some re-thinking of strategy and new planning. I suspect that his being named may have had some relationship to that, but primarily I think he was one of those senior people who was in Pearl Harbor and available until a permanent successor could be sent out. I don't recall any intention to make him permanently the commander-in-chief out there.

Q: No, because his interim period of command was very brief.

Adm. W.: Very brief and I believe in the case of the Pye—they call him the "caretaker." He was a caretaker commander-in-chief quite definitely.

Q: Well, Admiral Nimitz was named very shortly thereafter and he must have had some briefing from the CNO?

Adm. W.: Oh, yes. Of course, he had been in more or less constant touch with the CNO. Personnel problems, which were primarily the ones he was working on before Pearl Harbor, had been pretty difficult, as the Navy was expanding and developing new forces. So Admiral Nimitz had been in communication with Admiral Stark and with the various other people constantly during the year or so before Pearl Harbor, and he was well aware of the situation as it developed. Maybe not in the detail of Admiral Turner or Admiral Wilkinson, the planning and the intelligence chiefs, but certainly in broad outline he knew all that was going on.

Q: And he wasn't at all reluctant to assume this command, was he?

Adm. W.: No, indeed. He, I think, recognized this was a pretty tough job but if his bosses saw fit to give it to him he'd take it. He, of course, in the light of hindsight was a magnificent choice for that job. I think all those who had a part in selecting him have all recognized that he was somebody who had this high degree of capability and competence.

Interview No. 5 with Vice Admiral Charles Wellborn, U.S. Navy
(Retired)

Place: His apartment in the Westchester, Washington, D.C.

Date: Tuesday morning, 8 February 1972

Subject: Biography

By: John T. Mason, Jr.

Q: It's a great delight to see you this morning, Admiral, and to know that you had a pleasant visit out in the Middle West, even though the snow was deep! Last time, you dealt with the Pearl Harbor attack and its repercussions in Washington. I wonder if you'd resume this story at that point?

Adm. W.: Yes, I would be delighted to. There was one point in connection with this story that I think I did not bring out in our previous discussion. This had to do with the matter in which Admiral King became the commander-in-chief of the Atlantic Fleet.

Q: Yes.

Adm. W.: Admiral King, after having had a good number of good and normal rear admiral assignments of that day, was ordered to duty on the General Board, which was at that time regarded pretty generally as more or less of a graveyard for senior admirals —

Q: A shelflike assignment?

Adm. W.: Yes. This was one in which normally a senior rear admiral would serve out his declining years with a reasonable degree of dignity, then gracefully retire when he reached the age of sixty-four, which at that time was the statutory retirement age. Before Admiral Stark became the chief of naval operations, Admiral King had been assigned to the General Board. Admiral Stark felt that Admiral King's capabilities were such that he should not be relegated to this shelf, and he was alert to openings in various commands in which Admiral King's great capabilities might be successfully used. And it was, I would guess, within a year of the time of Pearl Harbor - prior to Pearl Harbor - that the Atlantic Fleet was being somewhat reorganized and upgraded, and this appeared to be the ideal opportunity, and Admiral Stark embraced this opportunity by having Admiral King taken from the General Board and put in command of the revitalized Atlantic Fleet. This got Admiral King off the shelf and back into the flow of those who were exercising important high commands.

Q: King, as an activist, must have welcomed this.

Adm. W.: Oh, he did, indeed, yes. He, of course, was always ready to hop into anything that was important and difficult.

Q: Would you say something about the General Board as it was then constituted and its effectiveness as a unit in the naval administrative setup?

Adm. W.: The General Board was a statutory board, as I recall it. It had been established a great many years ago as a group of senior people with vast experience and presumably seasoned judgment, who could study objectively various kinds of naval problems, strategic ones, primarily, but also those having to do with design of ships, and even tactical problems on occasion. They were not encumbered with the responsibilities of command so that these people, presumably, should have ample time and no distractions and would be able to devote themselves to pure thinking on problems that needed solving. This was a fine concept and, to a degree, the General Board served this way, but there was a considerable tendency to assign to the General Board people who were otherwise unassignable. So it had become something of a shelf on which people could be put. It still was given certain problems to work on, but generally speaking the people who had the responsibility for acting on things tended to do their own problem-solving, rather than to send the question to the General Board, so that frequently, although they might come up with a proposed solution to a certain problem, the individual who had the responsibility for taking action on those problems might more or less disregard the General Board's solution and use his own.

Q: Did the General Board have the authority to initiate problems and deal with them?

Adm. W.: Yes, it could originate a study on its own.

Q: They simply didn't have to wait for something —

Adm. W.: No, they didn't have to wait for something to be referred to them, but the tendency was for the bureau chiefs or the fleet commanders, individuals who were in positions of responsibility, to have their problems solved in their own staff and with their own facilities rather than to refer things to the General Board. And even in the areas where the General Board initiated its own studies, frequently its solutions might not agree completely with those of the responsible officers, so their solutions just might be ignored.

Q: Can you recall any instances of an effective use of the talents of the General Board during the time we're dealing with?

Adm. W.: At this late date, going back twenty-five years or so, it's hard to recall any specific instance, but I believe that there were some instances in which the General Board was given problems of studying what kinds of ships in what numbers the Navy needed to have a balanced fleet that could operate in either the Pacific or the Atlantic. I must confess my memory is not very good on this particular point. But this would be the kind of problem, anyway, that might have been referred to them.

Q: Well, reverting to Admiral King, he was snatched, through the good offices of Admiral Stark from this kind of oblivion and put back in the main stream so that he became available after Pearl Harbor?

Adm. W.: Yes. During the period of his incumbency in command of the Atlantic Fleet, which was from the time he was assigned there until Pearl Harbor, he, of course, did an outstanding job of making it a real fighting navy rather than a group of showboats visiting and showing the flag, and I think his talents were seen pretty clearly during this period by Mr. Knox, the Secretary of the Navy, and by the president, too.

Q: This was the time of armed neutrality, so to speak?

Adm. W.: Yes. It was quite an active period in the Atlantic Fleet, and Admiral King's aggressive, activist characteristics were quite apparent-

Q: Then, what were the circumstances governing his appointment as ComInch?

Adm. W.: I think what I just said about his capabilities having become apparent bears on this, but at that time it seemed to me that the Secretary of the Navy, particularly, felt that what was required in the Navy Department to direct the operation of the Navy was an activist of the type of Admiral King.

Q: The Secretary himself being one?

Adm. W.: Yes, exactly, and the characteristics that Admiral Stark had may not have completely fitted into this picture. Admiral Stark, I think, was a much more considerate individual than Admiral King. He had shown a great deal of patience and a great deal of - maybe empathy is the word, in trying to understand what congressional views might be and to convince the members of Congress that they should go along with his thoughts of building up the Navy and readiness for a possible war.

I think the Secretary of the Navy felt that the time had now passed for this kind of action and what we needed was the Admiral King type.

Q: Well, there was a complete change in the whole atmosphere as a result of Pearl Harbor.

Adm. W.: There was indeed.

Q: Drastic!

Adm. W.: This change, I think, was countrywide. The whole country was aroused by the Pearl Harbor attack — what was it Mr. Roosevelt called it, "a day of infamy."

Q: "A day of infamy," and it served to galvanize everybody.

Adm. W.: Yes, and the feeling in Congress was the same as the feeling across the country. It was a day of infamy and it changed the situation so that from thereon all military people had to do was to name what they wanted and the Congress gave it to them. I think Mr. Knox assessed this situation and decided that he wanted an activist running the fleet operations.

Q: So, Admiral King was called to the high command. Just when?

Adm. W.: I can't give you a precise date on that, but it was within a month or so of Pearl Harbor. It was very shortly after the attack. At first, Admiral King came in as ComInch, a name which he personally selected. Previously the commander-in-chief of the U.S. fleet had been called CinCUS, and Admiral King thought that this was an utterly inappropriate name.

Q: And so he chose ComInch?

Adm. W.: He chose that title, ComInch, which was just a different abbreviation of the same title.

Q: Wouldn't you imagine Tokyo Rose would have taken "CincUS" and used it?

Adm. W.: I'm sure this would have been used, all right, as you say, propaganda-wise. However, originally, Admiral King's responsibilities were to be simply the direction of the operations of the Navy, and the logistic side of the Navy was left with the chief of naval operations. The old office of the chief of naval operations was separated into two offices, one of which became ComInch and the other one remained the Chief of Naval Operations.

Q: Was it thought that Admiral Stark would remain as chief of naval operations?

Adm. W.: He did in fact remain for some months as chief of naval opeations and, surprisingly, the chief of naval operations had nothing to do with operations. He was purely a logistician.

Q: How did this work out, with Admiral King being the activist?

Adm. W.: This had some disadvantages. There were real problems in having two people of quite different types trying to do each his own part of this job that had at one time been all in one individual. Eventually it was decided that Admiral Stark should go to London, where there was a need for a very senior officer to coordinate our activities with those of the British, and that Admiral King should become both ComInch and CNO.

Q: How long did it take before this developed?

Adm. W.: This was probably, I would guess, a matter of three or four months. I didn't stay in Washington myself long enough to see the detachment of Admiral Stark. When Pearl Harbor developed, of course all regular naval officers were trying to get themselves out of Washington and off to a sea command somewhere, and the Bureau of Personnel itself was trying to accomplish that and to put into administrative jobs ashore reserve officers or others who hadn't actual seagoing experience. So, I managed, I think it was in January or February of 1942 to get myself ordered to sea. So I was not actually present in Washington when Admiral Stark departed, but I do recall that it was probably about three or four months, something of that sort, before he left, and at this time Admiral Horne became, I believe they called him, DEputy CNO. Admiral King was actually the chief of naval operations and Admiral Horne was his deputy chief of naval operations and actually handled for Admiral King all of the logistic side of the job of being chief of naval operations.

Q: He took over what Admiral Stark had been doing in the interim period?

Adm. W.: Yes, but without the actual title. This gave Admiral King very clear-cut authority over this part of the operation of the Navy Department.

Q: Was this by executive order, or did it require some legislation to achieve this dual title in one person?

Adm. W.: At this stage of the game it was all done by executive order. Nobody was very fussy at this particular point about the niceties and the legality of what was being done. Get it done was the objective. So this was done without benefit of legislation. Later, and as I recall it was after the war was over, there was some new legislation enacted which brought back the job of CNO as it had been originally and specified in some detail what its authorities and responsibilities were. But in the early stages of the war, as I recall it, nobody bothered about legislation, it was simply done by executive order.

Q: Did this arrangement with Admiral King coming back - was this anticipated by Admiral Stark? Did he think this might happen?

Adm. W.: No, he did not. This evolved and I don't believe anybody had expected this kind of thing to happen. I don't think Mr. Knox had this in mind when he decided he needed an activist like Admiral King to manage the operations of the Navy in wartime. I think that this all was an evolutionary process that the needs for getting the war under way developed.

Q: And when we talk about Admiral King as an activist coming in, there's a publicized story about him. Is it apocryphal or was it actually true that he said what he said?

Adm. W.: I didn't actually hear him say this, but I believe it's actually true and it's certainly in character! You have the story so I don't have to repeat it here.

Q: No. It was colorful.

Adm. W.: Yes, it was. Admiral King was colorful and I'm sure you have in your interviews with people who knew him much better than I did some background on his character. He was a tough taskmaster but he also was an equally vigorous player and relaxer when he was doing that.

Wellborn #5 - 150

Q: He was not a half-measure man?

Adm. W.: No. In both situations he was colorful and active.

Q: Perhaps this is the point to ask you if you have any personal recollections of him?

Adm. W.: Nothing that I think would really be worthwhile. I knew Admiral King, but always at some distance.

Q: You never actually served under him?

Adm. W.: No, I never actually served under him and my relationship with him always was as an aide to Admiral Stark, so that I'm sure in his mind I was one of Admiral Stark's boys! He and I never were close, although we knew one another and I think got along very nicely so far as our contact brought us together.

Q: You departed from the Washington scene very quickly then?

Adm. W.: Yes, I left I would guess about two months after Pearl Harbor.

Q: If I may be permitted an observation, it seems to me that if all the regular Navy - naval officers who wanted to leave Washington had been permitted to do so at that moment, the Navy would have been quite hamstrung!

Adm. W.: This certainly is quite true and I think the Bureau of Navigation, as I guess it was at that time rather than the Bureau of Personnel, recognized that they couldn't move everybody simultaneously out of positions in Washington into ones at sea. But they handled this one, I think, pretty effectively. They managed to get those who had seagoing experience out to sea as rapidly as they could, and the job I had there was one which I think involved the confidence of the particular admiral who was serving there and just a reasonable knowledge of the whole Navy Department and how it works certainly was one that was well within the capability of a nonseafaring person.

Q: Shall we go on to your career, and will you tell me about your new assignment?

Adm. W.: My new assignment was commander of a destroyer division. It was Destroyer Division 19 which comprised four of the 1,700-ton destroyers at that time. The Hambleton was my flagship, and these four ships were just commissioned, brand-new and not really very well shaken down, although they had finished their shaking-down period. We operated first simply off the Atlantic coast. You recall at that time the German submarines were having quite a field day against our coastal seagoing traffic.

Q: Oil tankers!

Adm. W.: They were particularly vulnerable and we worked rather ineffectively against the submarines along the Atlantic coast. At that time our merchant ships were operating pretty much at will up and down the coast.

Q: Not in convoys?

Adm. W.: No convoys and not even shipping lanes at that time. They were all going where they wanted to go, and our assignment originally was simply to go out and patrol against submarines that were working on this coastal traffic. Well, it was a pretty impossible task. There was just too much ocean for a very limited number of antisubmarine vessels to cover. Submarines could spot you very easily and evade you, so I don't think we accomplished very much at that period.

Q: That much-touted system of locating submarines and broadcasting this to the fleet units was not in being yet?

Adm. W.: No, none of this had come about. We were just beginning to get the plans made for antisubmarine work. We adopted coastal convoys later and there were certain shipping lanes that were used later, so that patrolling could be somewhat more effective in maintaining a submarine-free lane up and down the coast.

Q: Did you have any contacts with - your four destroyers, did you have any luck with submarines?

Adm. W.: No. During that period we never actually got close enough to attack a submarine that was there. We dropped depth charges on false contacts, but the closest we ever got, I think, was to see over the horizon an explosion of a torpedo hitting a tanker. We got there within probably an hour but that gave the submarine plenty of chance to get away.

Q: Did you go down into the Gulf of Mexico?

Adm. W.: We did not, although I believe there were some destroyers that did.

Q: Were you tied in in any way with Admiral Hoover's setup in

Puerto Rico, or had that been established?

Adm. W.: I can't recall definitely whether he had been established there at this stage. I think he had not. We did have a command up in Argentia which was actually based on a ship that was assisting in the operation of transatlantic convoys. The United States was escorting these convoys a certain distance across the Atlantic, presumably that part of it that is in the western hemisphere -

Q: Then there was the Chop line?

Adm. W.: Then there was the Chop line and the convoys were turned over to British control and escorts. But as I recall, at this time there was nothing in the Caribbean that corresponded to this and I think we operated out of Norfolk at that time under the command-in-chief of the Atlantic Fleet. Here, again, my memory is a little vague.

Q: Who was that? Ingersoll? Had he taken over?

Adm. W.: Yes, Admiral Ingersoll. But he had just arrived and this whole situation was pretty vague. We may possibly have been under the commander Eastern Sea Frontier at that time, but my own memory is a little vague about just what our command situation was. It was evolving like a lot of other things.

Q: How long did this last?

Adm. W.: This lasted only a short time. Then several ships were sent from our Atlantic Fleet up to join and reinforce the British Home Fleet which was based at Scapa Flow. This was at the time when we were starting to run the convoys up into Murmansk area to give assistance to the Russians somewhat as a token but also to provide a certain amount of reinforcement to the British forces in that area. There were some cruisers and destroyers sent from the Atlantic Fleet to join the Home Fleet and my division of destroyers went temporarily to Scapa Flow and became a unit of the Home Fleet.

Q: Tell me about that. How did it work? Did you escort a convoy across the Atlantic in order to arrive at Scapa Flow?

Adm. W.: No, we did not take a convoy. At that time, normally, a group of strictly naval ships, a military task force, did not operate with a merchant convoy. Merchant convoys ran at pretty low speed. The slow ones, as I remember, averaged seven knots speed at the best and the high-speed ones up like ten, and a group of men-of-war normally proceeded a little faster than that, and we proceeded with the cruisers. I think going over we had two cruisers again, I'm a little vague about this. We went at rather high speed and shook down a little bit in operating together. None of the ships had ever operated together before, so we got a little experience at this in our crossing and went directly to Scapa Flow. My division became part of the destroyer force of the British fleet and we were overwhelmed with a tremendous lot of British fleet regulations, signal books, and things. I recall arriving in Scapa Flow and being told, well, here are all your books and papers, you go home and study them, and when you're ready we'll have you go out and operate with us.

Q: This is in the nature of a footnote that occurs to me. As you became a part of the Royal Navy, operating with them, were you allowed to have grog on board?

Adm. W.: No. Our own regulations still pertained in this respect. We had no grog but we could visit their ships where they did have grog, which was very pleasant. However, in spite of the fact that we were told to go home and study these at our leisure, about, I guess, nine or ten o'clock that evening a message came over from the C-in-C Home Fleet that we would be prepared to get under way at, I think it was, 6:30 the next morning - anyway, about daylight, and proceed to sea as escorts for the commander-in-chief's flagship, the Prince of Wales, I believe it was at that time. It was one of that class of battleships. Well, this didn't encourage us very much, not having really learned how to use their signal books or their tactical instructions, to be sent out to escort the commander-in-chief's flagship nonplussed us a little bit, but we studied our books all night and, fortunately, we had been provided with an old chief signalman as a liaison with the Home Fleet and he was a remarkable individual. He knew the signals without consulting the signal book and he knew the tactics pretty nearly equally well. So whenever a signal went out he could tell us what to do, so we managed successfully to get in and we later found that the commander-in-chief wasn't taking very great chances because that particular part of the ocean had never had any submarines in it and the Germans apparently recognized this as an area in which the water was pretty well infested with British antisubmarine efforts. They stayed away from it.

Q: What was the occasion of this sortie?

Adm. W.: The flagship was going out for some routine gunnery training, antiaircraft fire, and they duly conducted their antiaircraft fire and we came back again and, presumably, since there'd been no collision and we hadn't had any real difficulties with them, after that we operated just as normal units of the destroyer force of the HOme Fleet as long as we were there.

Q: Were there any threats of the <u>Tirpitz</u> appearing on the horizon during the time you were with them?

Adm. W.: There were no serious threats, but of course, this was something that they had their eyes on all the time, but during our rather brief stay there was nothing that was really emergency in that connection.

Q: Did you get involved with any of the Murmansk convoys?

Adm. W.: No, we did not. Some of our cruisers had actually been on the run to Murmansk, but we didn't make that. We did make a run back and forth to Iceland, as I remember it.

Q: Well, there were convoys running back and forth there?

Adm. W.: Yes, they were running back and forth there, but we didn't get in on any of the Murmansk business. There had been one in particular that involved a great deal of action with the Germans just before we arrived.

Q: Was that Number 13?

Adm. W.: Yes, and they lost a great many ships. During that particular period that we were with the Home Fleet, I don't believe

Wellborn - 157

there was a Murmansk convoy run. They later, of course -

Q: It was in the summer of that year, wasn't it, when they were discontinued because of the light?

Adm. W.: Yes, it was, and I think it wasn't only because of the light that they were discontinued. I think the British restudied that whole problem of conducting convoys and when they were re-instituted their protection was a great deal better and the coordination of the various forces involved had been improved. They had their troubles just as we did in evolving the right kind of command setups to ensure that operations of various kinds were well coordinated.

Q: Were there other foreign units operating out of Scapa Flow? The Free French, or Dutch or any other?

Adm. W.: I don't recall that any - either of those, although we did have some Polish destroyers. These ships were British Town-class ships that had been renamed with Polish names and manned with Polish refugees as crews. There were several of those operating up there, and they were very good units of the Home Fleet, too. The Poles had the reputation in the Home Fleet of being the most avid fighters of all. They'd lost their homeland and they were mad about it! I think there were two of those Polish destroyers, but there may have been more than that. I think they were the only ones other than the U.S. ships that were not British operating at that time in the Home Fleet.

Q: Your destroyers left before the Murmansk group was reconstituted?

Adm. W.: Yes, apparently as a result of some kind of intergovernmental agreement, the U. S. ships within the Home Fleet were sent back to our U. S. Atlantic Fleet, and there preparations were under way for the North African operations. Being a little destroyer division commander at sea you didn't know how high-level agreements were reached! But I inferred that there had been an agreement between the U. S. and British governments that our units would come back and become a part of the planning and later the operations in North Africa, and they, the British, would take over their parts not only of the North Atlantic series of operations, but also the North African. At any rate, after a fairly brief time with the Home Fleet, my unit came back to the United States along with - I think there was only one U. S. cruiser left by that time. We rejoined our own Atlantic Fleet.

Q: And you went to join Admiral Hewitt's group down in Norfolk?

Adm. W.: We actually then took over the escort of one of the converted oil tanker carriers and we proceeded out to Bermuda, were we did some training. We didn't know what we were training for, but it was for the North African operations.

Q: Your training off Bermuda, did it involve amphibious - ?

Adm. W.: No. Our particular part of this one involved the escort of the carrier and the anti-submarine screening of the carrier which was there in support of the amphibious operation. So at this particular stage of the game I had nothing to do with the amphibious part of that operation. We did join the training for the Torch operation at that time.

Q: But that code name wasn't even breathed?

Adm. W.: No, nobody knew that code name. We didn't even know we were training for North Africa. The first I knew of the North African operation was after we had sailed from Bermuda to join the rest of Admiral Hewitt's full task force at sea, and then we were all briefed on where we were going and what we were going to do.

I hope now that I have the chronology properly in mind.

When my division 19 came back from Iceland, we did in the division go into the training for the North African operation. It was with Division 19 that we trained with the carrier and then participated in the North African operation. We were not a part of the amphibious force at this time. We were a part of the carrier screen, and when we arrived off North Africa —

Q: You went independently then, you didn't go as part of the great flotilla?

Adm. W.: We weren't a part of the amphibious convoy, but we were part of the over-all overseas formation that went from the United States over to the North African coast, not actually with the transports but in their vicinity and flying aircraft as antisubmarine protection for the whole fleet movement.

Q: Was there any particular submarine activity at that moment?

Adm. W.: No. There were always a lot of false contacts, but I don't believe there were any actual submarine contacts during the the course of that movement from our coast over to North Africa.

Q: Does this imply that the Germans hadn't gotten wind of this operation, or any operation of its scope?

Adm. W.: I suspect that they knew such an operation was envisaged, but I suspect they didn't know exactly the time and they didn't know just the route we were going to follow. They didn't have very good luck on where they had placed submarines. So without having had access to the high-level intelligence that was available at that time, I think probably the Germans knew it was going on but didn't know exactly when and where, so weren't very effective in using their submarines against it.

Q: I have heard about the ultra stringent clampdown on Admiral King's part on the knowledge -

Adm. W.: Yes. There was really a higher degree of security on this one than any other operation I've ever had anything to do with.

As I say, I was at sea on the way before I knew where we were going, and I think this was pretty general.

Q: Tell me about your participation in Torch.

Adm. W.: We stayed with the carrier for several days and then the destroyers got fairly low on fuel. By that time, the amphibious operation had been pretty well completed and, while we hadn't actually got firm control, our forces were in Casablanca and we had tankers lying off Fedala that were providing fuel for destroyers when they needed it, so I went in with, I think two of my division to get fuel. We arrived there after dark and since the screen for that night around the anchorage had already been set up, the screen commander told us to proceed into the anchorage area and anchor near the tanker and be prepared to commence fueling at daylight. In those days we hadn't quite developed to the extent we did later the proposition of fueling at sea and at night. We did proceed into the harbor and anchored near the tanker, and that night was the only night that there were submarine attacks against the fleet anchorage. One submarine got through the screen around the anchorage and fired what they used to call "Browning shots" -- six torpedoes, as I remember it - just at random into the anchorage. Of course, there were a lot of ships in there and you could hardly miss if you were fairly close. Anything you fired at the anchorage was bound to hit something and, as I recall it, there were three hits - three effective shots. One of them was seen running on the surface and finally exploded without hitting anything, and what happened to the others I don't recall, but there were three hits. One transport was sunk. The oil tanker which we were to go alongside next day was hit amidships, and my flagship, lying quietly at anchor, was hit right in the middle.

Q: Did she sink?

Adm. W.: No. She had an interesting history after that. Her back was pretty well broken and you could see her working her bow and her stern were no longer rigidly attached. They were attached, however. The midships fireroom and engineroom were both flooded, but the forward fireroom and the after engineroom were relatively intact, so she stayed together although she lost power completely. We arranged to have the salvage tug that was along for the operation tow the Hambleton from the anchorage at Fedala down 25 or 30 miles to Casablanca. They towed her into the harbor and she was the first U.S. ship dry-docked in the French floating dry dock there in Casablanca. I left her just as she was starting off on her tow to Casablanca and went aboard another ship in my division, but the Hambleton stayed in Casablanca while the repair force that was organized there cut out a section that had involved her midships fireroom and engineroom, floated her out of the dry dock, and put her back together about sixty feet shorter than she had been, welded her up, and she went back with the forward fireroom and the after engineroom operating. They put her into the New York Navy Yard, cut her open in the middle again, lengthened her once more, rebuilt her another engineroom and another fireroom, and by the end of the war she was once again operating on two firerooms and two enginerooms.

Q: A rather ingenious repair job!

Adm. W.: It was indeed. This, of course, was after I had left her, but I was following her career with some interest.

Q: Were there casualties on board the night she was torpedoed?

Adm. W.: A few, but not a great many. There was a watch in each one of these - in the fireroom and the engineroom that were damaged - and no one escaped alive from those particular compartments, but the casualties were limited to those two compartments, and this involved, as I remember it, ten men or something of that sort. It was a loss but not a very great one.

Q: Was the tanker set on fire?

Adm. W.: No. Remarkably enough, she was hit in tanks that were loaded with the heavy black oil, which really isn't explosive. It's hard to ignite. There was a lot of oil on the surface of the water there, but there was no fire. The tankers that had the fire problems, as a rule, were the ones that were carrying gasoline or some of the more volatile forms of petroleum products. Fortunately, this particular one had nothing but black oil.

Q: You mentioned a few moments ago the "Browning shots", the German torpedoes, is that the rifle that inspired that term, or what?

Adm. W.: I think probably the derivation of this was that when you used an old Browning machine gun, you more or less sprayed the area of your target with your projectiles. The submarine, in effect, is doing the same thing when she fired more or less randomly at the formation of ships. This kind of torpedo fire in that day was known as "Browning shots."

Q: What was the specific mission of the carrier you were escorting?

Adm. W.: While we were en route it was to provide antisubmarine reconnaissance around the whole fleet that was in transit from our coast to North Africa. Once we arrived at the objective, it became one of first providing some fighter protection over the amphibious formation, then also providing air support for the amphibious operation, that is, the bomber types were being used and, to a certain extent, fighter types in support of the troops that were landing, and the other fighters were being used to fly a combat air patrol over the formation. Of course there was a destroyer antisubmarine escort for these carriers. We weren't directly involved in the air operations. We were providing them antisubmarine protection and providing them with the plane guard that was required when any one of these planes landed in the water. In those days, of course, helicopters weren't available and it was up to the destroyer plane guard to pick up all fallen aviators that were in trouble either taking off or returning to the carrier.

Q: Well, having had your ship shot out from under you, you had to have a new flagship?

Adm. W.: I simply joined one of the others in my division. In this case it was the Macomb, and we came back with the transport formation after the operation.

Q: In the empty ?

Adm. W.: Yes. Destroyers were always in short supply in those days and they were continually being shifted around from one assignment to another. When we needed fuel and had to leave the carrier, some other destroyers came out and relieved us of that particular assignment, and after we refueled and got our torpedo problems resolved we were sent off to join the escorters and transports. And this was rather typical of the way destroyers operated in those days.

Q: And were those particular destroyers long-legged enough to come back across the Atlantic without refueling?

Adm. W.: No. We refueled once on the way home. The weather was pretty bad. We had some trouble doing it but we managed to get fuel and to get back to Norfolk without any serious difficulty. That, as I remember it, was a winter operation. It was November or something of this kind, and coming back the weather was not very good, but nothing serious.

It was after this operation, then, that I left Destroyer Division 19 and went to Destroyer Squadron 8, and in Destroyer Squadron 8 our first assignment was the escort of a slow convoy. I guess they didn't call them slow convoys at that time, though. At any rate, one that was moving at a speed of advance of about nine knots from New York to Casablanca. Here again, destroyers were assigned more or less in accordance with their availability. A destroyer squadron commander would usually go out with about the right number of ships, but very frequently he wouldn't have very many of his own squadron with him. He'd have a group of whatever could be put together at the time.

Q: A convoy of that sort going over to North Africa would be a fairly large one, wouldn't it?

Adm. W.: Yes, the convoys that ran on that run usually were somewhere between forty and fifty ships, merchant ships, and you would have probably seven or eight escorts.

Q: All destroyers, or were there corvettes with you? We didn't have corvettes, did we?

Adm. W.: At that time we didn't have any corvettes or destroyer escorts. They were all destroyers, but they would be a heterogeneous group. Some of them might be the old four-stackers, some would be the more recent 1,700-tonners. They'd vary, depending on what was available.

Q: And how many of those convoys did you escort with this destroyer squadron?

Adm. W.: I think two or three. I can't recall precisely how many.

Q: Just taking them over and coming right back or bringing - ?

Adm. W.: Well, you'd leave New York, the trip over would take you something on the order of a month, and when you got there, on the other side of the Atlantic, at that particular time the escorts would wait for the convoy to be unloaded. This would be a matter of a week or two before they could get enough ships unloaded to form a new convoy, and you'd go back, not necessarily with the same merchant ships but with a group of merchant ships, and you would take them back then to the United States -

Q: Did they make greater speed going back?

Adm. W.: No. Actually, going back was more difficult an operation than the one going to the eastward. The merchant ship, the old Liberty ship type, was a pretty good seaworthy ship when it was loaded, when it had deep draft, and they were, of course, all loaded going to the eastward. Also, most of the weather in the Atlantic moves from west to east, so that if you started with a storm right ahead of you, it took the next storm some days to overtake you, and you might have two or three storms during the course of your passage across the Atlantic. But coming back to the westward, all your merchant ships were light, they'd take on some ballast but their bows would be up in the air and wind affected them very badly and made them difficult to keep in a formation. Also, you were running into the storm. Now, instead of having maybe two or three in the course of your passage, you'd have six or eight in the course of your passage, and each one of these six or eight storms would scatter your convoy because those merchant ships were low power and they single screw simply couldn't steer in a high wind. So, coming back generally was a lot more difficult than going to the eastward. The submarines paid more attention, of course, to the loaded convoys than they did to the empty ones, although they didn't neglect the empty ones. So you have a little more submarine activity against you going eastward, and you had a lot more troubles with weather and other problems coming westward.

When you got back from one of these, your destroyers usually needed some repairs. They'd have some sea damage, might have lost a boat or something. So you'd usually go right to one of the shipyards on the Atlantic coast, and very seldom the same one. It was whichever one had a work load that made it possible for you to get in and get the job done. You'd go into the yard for ten days or something of this sort, get the necessary voyage repairs, and then you'd have maybe a week or so of opportunity to have a little gunner training. You always got some new members in your crew and some of your old people left you to go to newly commissioning ships. So you'd have a week or ten days to overhaul and a week or ten days as a training period before you set out on another convoy.

This whole cycle, convoy to convoy, took something like three months. I can't remember just how many of those I ran, maybe two or three, before the Mediterranean operations stepped up and, at this point, my squadron went into the Mediterranean to prepare for the operation against Sicily.

Q: During the course of these months that you were convoying to North Africa, you must have seen the rapid development of some of our techniques, didn't you?

Adm. W.: Yes, although I think prior to this we had gotten the convoy system working and by the time I got to running the convoys the system of convoy operation had been pretty well established. One of the things that was developed quite rapidly was the air cover for convoys. This was really a tremendous help. The destroyers that escorted a convoy had a limited range over which they could detect the presence of submarines. Your horizon might be out ten miles and if you could see something, either a spar sticking up over the horizon or maybe a little exhaust steam or something coming up, you might be able to spot a submarine out on the horizon or just over it. But this was the extent of your capability. Sonar didn't reach out that far. So as long as the submarine stayed over the horizon from you and just tracked you from a distance, you didn't have very much capability against him. Air cover was developing and the airplanes had a lot better chance to keep them down and to keep them away from a convoy.

Q: It was developing in what sense? We were getting more experience?

Adm. W.: Well, this was mostly shore-based aviation that was doing this job. At this point, we didn't have enough carriers to use in this function.

Q: We hadn't begun the jeep carriers, had we?

Adm. W.: We had begun, but there weren't enough of them operating yet so that they could be spared to go along with a convoy.

Q: I guess the first one was the Long Island, wasn't it?

Adm. W.: I think, yes, it was, and it, I think, was operating at this time. But they were in very short supply, and that technique of using the jeep carrier along with a convoy hadn't developed yet. We depended on long-range, shore-based aviation.

Q: So there was one area in the middle of the Atlantic where you had no planes?

Adm. W.: Yes. The planes were flying out of the Norfolk area and out of Bermuda. We didn't have the Azores at that time, but by the time I got to running them we were flying shore-based aircraft out of Port Lyautey in North Africa. So we had some air cover as we approached the African coast, but there was an area there in the vicinity of the Azores where you were without it. This was the toughest part of the Atlantic for us.

Q: Were the Germans using the Azores?

Adm. W.: No, they weren't using them, but neither were we, and what they could do was put their submarines out there in that vicinity. The Germans had a pretty good direction-finder system. They knew more or less where our convoys were and they could direct the submarines, both as individual submarines and as wolf packs, which was just beginning to develop in those days, to the vicinity of the convoy. We tried to take evasive courses and tried to avoid them, but there was an area in the vicinity of the Azores where a nine-knot convoy had pretty limited capabilities to avoid submarines that had considerably more speed than this on the surface and, once they found us, it was pretty difficult to shake them off because your destroyers couldn't locate them until they came pretty close to the convoy. And, even then, with a limited number of destroyers, you couldn't afford to have your destroyers stay away from your convoy for very long. If there was a pack of, say, four or five submarines attacking you and you only had seven destroyers to begin with, you could send a destroyer out to work on one submarine and that destroyer would keep that one submarine down. As long as he stayed submerged he couldn't catch up with the convoy, but some of his pack-mates could then operate around on the surface, get ahead of you again, and if you continued to send destroyers out, each one to hold down an individual submarine, pretty soon you ended up without any protection for your convoy. So you had some problems in trying to keep the group of submarines down while you went through the area on evasive courses. We had reasonably good success in this, but we didn't get through without some losses either.

Q: It was a zigzagging business you used always?

Adm. W.: Yes. Not only zigzagging but evasive steering. Your base course would change periodically, so that a submarine that spotted you then doped out what your base course was from the way you were zigzagging could be thrown off by a change of your base course. But, unfortunately, this didn't translate you very far off your base course at nine knots, and the submarine usually had very little difficulty in reestablishing his contact.

Q: You say you did have some losses?

Adm. W.: Yes, we had some losses. As I remember it, we started out, say, with forty-five ships - I recall on one occasion we lost two ships during the course of the passage. We got one submarine and we lost two merchant ships, and this was, I think, more or less typical of this kind of operation.

Q: You didn't include troopships in these?

Adm. W.: No. Troopships were all faster ships. They moved generally at at least fifteen knots speed of advance and they were somewhat more heavily escorted.

Q: Were the "Queens" used in this operation at all?

Adm. W.: Not in this kind of operation. ~~They were used and~~ The "Queens" always operated independently without escort at very high speed, the theory being that the best protection that could be provided to them was use of their high speed.

Q: Twenty-seven knots?

Adm. W.: Yes, and they operated independently and got through as quickly as they could with some evasive steering, too. But generally the objective for them was to get them in and out as fast as you could and hope you didn't run head-on into a submarine, and if you didn't run head-on into one you were all right.

Q: You say that on one of these escorting jobs you were in the harbor at Casablanca?

Adm. W.: Yes. On one occasion we came in and were waiting for the assembly of the convoy to return to New York, when General Patton, who was then commanding our forces in North Africa, decided he would like to bring the Sultan of Morocco and his entourage down to visit one of our ships. The Wainwright turned out to be the most modern one we had in the harbor at the time, so she was chosen to receive the Sultan and he and General Patton did come down onto the pier and, with great pomp and circumstance, General Patton and his entourage and the Sultan and his, including his son who is now the king, came aboard. I recall at that time my young officer of the deck was trying to get the names of all the important people who came aboard to put it in the log, and he had gotten from one of the U.S. aides of General Patton the names of all of the important members of the party, and then after the party was essentially all on board, up came a young U.S. Army lieutenant, who was the rear guard for the party. I remember my officer of the deck asking, who are you? And he said, "Never mind me. I'm just the contrast in all this party!" I liked that sense of humor. We never did find out what his name was.

Another interesting feature of one of our visits in Casablanca was that the Churchill and Roosevelt meeting took place while we were there. This again was a pretty well kept secret, because we didn't know what was going on. We knew that there was a British ship in Casablanca they called them command ships, I believe, in those days - a merchant ship that had been rigged up to command amphibious operations, with situation rooms and communications and things. We knew that she was in the harbor, but we didn't understand just why. And we knew that for some reason the hotel up on the hill where the conference was taking place had been put off-limits. Nobody was allowed to get up anywhere near it. But it was sometime before we discovered the reason for all of this was that the president and the prime minister were up there conferring. We did eventually find out about it, but this was a piece of pretty closely held information.

One of my convoys, too, had the questionable distinction of arriving in Casablanca on the night on which they had the only air attack that ever developed on Casablanca. It was attacked by German aircraft, bombers, just once.

Q: From France, were they?

Adm. W.: Yes. They were Ju-88s and there were a dozen or so of them. It wasn't a very heavy attack. It was one, I think, more or less just to remind us that it could happen, but we arrived there that night after dark and trying to handle a lot of unwieldy merchant ships with no good communications in the dark in close quarters there around Casablanca harbor while an air attack was going on, I remember was an interesting experience.

Q: What kind of lighting was permitted?

Adm. W.: The ships were darkened but ashore Casablanca really wasn't well blacked-out. They hadn't had an attack there before and the native quarter, the casbah, in Casablanca was one that was pretty difficult to black out. They have bonfires and things burning throughout that area, and getting ~~one of~~ those put out and the place really darkened was just an impossible task, particularly since there'd never been an attack there before. So that night Casa-lanca was not well darkened. Later they got a little better at it but never did succeed in getting it really thoroughly blacked out. The ships, though, were operating just as they always did at that time at sea, with all their lights out, except when you got into close proximity with somebody else and you felt the danger from him was greater than the danger from an airplane or submarine. That was an ineffective attack, incidentally. It didn't damage any of our ships and did very little damage ashore. The targets were ashore, of course. They didn't seem to be much interested in us. We did a little firing at them ineffectively, but, as I recall it, all those airplanes went back home.

So I had several rather interesting experiences in and around Casablanca, but nothing really historic of importance.

After these convoys, my squadron was sent over - as I remember it, we escorted a troop convoy to Oran and then we stayed -

Q: What speed did she have?

Adm. W.: I think a speed of advance of fifteen knots - something of this sort, steaming probably at eighteen. These were passenger ships that had been converted to troop transports and they were all capable of pretty good speeds. This one was an uneventful trip across, and when we got into Oran my squadron became a part of the Naval Forces, North Africa.

Q: You were under new orders then, weren't you?

Adm. W.: Yes, we were under a new boss. This was normal for a destroyer. You expected to get a new boss every now and then. We worked around the North African coast, escorted some coastal convoys back and forth between Oran and Bizerte. At that time, that was one of our bases. Of course, Algiers we got into occasionally, but for the most part U.S. effort was in Bizerte or Oran. The British generally used Algiers, rather than the U.S.. But during this period, too, we were training for support of our amphibious operations and then when the Sicilian operations finally came on, we went with part of the forces from Oran up to Sicily. This operation was nowhere nearly as secret as some of the previous ones had been.

Q: It was an expected one!

Adm. W.: Yes. Of course, the bases from which this one was launched were so close to where German aircraft could operate that we were under observation all the time. They didn't actually attack Oran while we were there, but they did attack Bizerte periodically.

Q: Then there was the question of the timing of the operation!

Adm. W.: Yes, and I think they were pretty sure of when we were going.

Q: Tell me about your training operations in preparation.

Adm. W.: These were very largely fire on targets ashore and the escort of the coastal convoys back and forth of course was good training for the escort of the amphibious ships over toward Sicily. Those were the two basics, I think - training in escort of ships back and forth, and training in fire support of forces ashore.

Q: What kind of landing ships did we have at that time?

Adm. W.: We were beginning to get pretty well equipped at this point. We not only had the big former passenger ships that had been converted to troop transports, we had quite a lot of LSTs, which carried tanks and vehicles. We had a lot of what were then known as LCIs - that was landing craft, infantry, I believe - and these carried primarily personnel. Then we had a lot of things that were called LCTs in those days. I believe they're called LSMs now. But these were medium-sized things. They carried two or three tanks but were more maneuverable and more easily beachable than the LSTs were. There was quite an array of this kind of equipment.

Q: Were we using any British equipment of this nature?

Adm. W.: The British were using some of their own, and at this time we were cooperating very closely with the British in developing these ships, but we were building most of them, turning over some of our production to the British and keeping some for our own use. So most of the LSTs and the other landing craft were U.S.-built both for the British and for us. The British generally were using their own troop transports and they had a lot of smaller ships that had been cross-Channel ferries and this kind of thing that they used for carrying troops, whereas we used larger ships that had been passenger ships for open-sea type of use.

From the base at Bizerte we, I think, launched very largely a landing-craft expedition. That's LCI, LSTs, and this type craft, but from Oran we launched our troop-transport type of troop carriers to Sicily. The part in which I was involved was the troop-transport part and as soon as we got over there the destroyers that weren't involved in actual fire support of the forces that were landing, turned around and would take something back to Oran and pick up a new convoy. The second relay, then, of ships would usually be Liberty ships, or that type, that were bringing in supplies. We'd run several trips back and forth between Sicily and Oran, or maybe Bizerte.

Q: Was it more difficult escorting convoys in the Mediterranean than it had been in the Atlantic?

Adm. W.: This reminds me of one British destroyer sailor's estimate of the difficulties involved in convoy work. He was talking about the North Atlantic and when you asked him about what the great difficulties were he would always say that the Number One difficulty was communications, getting your instructions by radio, and getting them deciphered and thoroughly understood. The Number Two problem was always weather. And your Number Three problem was German submarines. And I'm inclined to think he had something there. This was about the order of difficulty.

In the Mediterranean it was a little different from this. Down there we had a U.S. system of communications that was quite a lot better than the British, though it still offered some problems. Weather was no problem, it was delightful, although winter weather in the Mediterranean could be fairly difficult. These operations all took place in the period of the year when the weather was fine. That's a good place to fight a war from the weather point of view. Submarines were much more difficult in the Mediterranean than they were out in the Atlantic because the temperature gradients in the Mediterranean were quite unpredictable and this meant sonar was unpredictable. So in the Mediterranean in the summer time, submarines, I thought, were a much greater hazard than they were in the North Atlantic, and the weather and the communications much less of a problem.

Q: Then you had the added thing of danger from the air in the Mediterranean?

Adm. W.: Yes, although at this time the danger from the air wasn't as severe as it might have been. We had some air capability over there, although our fighters weren't long enough ranged to provide fighter escort for us all the way even if we had had command cooperation that would have permitted it. We didn't have that command cooperation. At this time, the Army Air Corps felt extremely independent and their attitude seemed to be that they would handle the air and we seagoing types should handle what went on on the surface and under the surface of the ocean and never the twain should meet.

Q: Or plan together!

Adm. W.: Yes. So we didn't get very much help from them directly, but their indirect help was considerable. They contested control of the air all right, so that at this particular stage of the game, particularly if we stayed close to the North African coast, which was at more or less extreme range for the German planes of that day, we didn't have too much trouble. When we got up close to Sicily, or later close to the Italian coast, then we had some German air attacks, but certainly there the German air was not the problem that it was at some other stages in the war.

Q: Weren't they at that point still using that little island, Pantelleria?

Adm. W.: Yes, although, as I recall it, Pantelleria was taken just before Sicily. It had folded without much of a fight.

Q: They did have airfields there didn't they?

Adm. W.: Yes, but there were actually, I think, no German aircraft operating from Pantelleria during the course of either the Sicily or the Salerno operations. I've forgotten just when Pantelleria was taken. While we had some attacks, they were not in great force compared to some of the problems we had with the Japanese in the Pacific. This kind of air effort wasn't too severe. Now, during the course of the initial landings on Sicily there were, as you recall, some problems. The Germans mounted an attack from the air while we were trying to run off an airborne landing, and both the German attackers and the U.S. - they were DC-3s converted, carrying our troops arrived over the landing area where all the ships were and about the same time. And with a lot of inexperienced antiaircraft gunners around I think we shot down more of our own planes than we did German planes.

Q: This was at dawn, was it not?

Adm. W.: Yes. But, generally speaking, the Germans didn't mount very much of an air effort against that operation and while we had some losses from it, they weren't of any real importance in the outcome of the operation.

Q: Was Admiral Hewitt very much in evidence to those of you in the escort force?

Adm. W.: I shouldn't say that he was "very much in evidence." We all knew he was in command and we got various kinds of orders and instructions from him, but this operation was an extremely well planned one and by this time the United States Navy and Army had considerable experience in running off this kind of an operation. So, as I recall this one, it didn't call for a dominant personality to be on his white charger running up and down before the troops! The thing was well planned and it rolled along and when some unexpected event came along, why, some kind of orders came out to take care of the particular situation that developed. But my recollection of it was that it was an orderly operation that had been planned ~~out~~ in advance and was carried out relatively smoothly. Of course there are always unexpected things that happen and would have to be taken care of, but this was done also pretty smoothly.

Q: Did you have any instance in your own particular command?

Adm. W.: During this stage, no. We were fired at and fired, but as I recall it, none of us got hit. Whether or not we hit anything, I doubt. We had contacts, as I recall it, with submarines, but I don't think we sank any at that stage, but we didn't lose any ships, either. This seemed to me to be, from my point of view, a pretty much routine operation. We got the ships in there and they unloaded and we got them back.

Q: The real excitement happened on shore, didn't it?

Adm. W.: Yes.

Q: With Patton's army?

Adm. W.: That's right. There were some ships damaged - landing craft, as a rule. I remember some LSTs that were beached and were hit by artillery from shore and burned. One particularly, burned for a couple of days. It was quite a landmark, a great cloud of smoke rising pretty vertically when there wasn't much wind. But losses in that landing were not very severe.

Q: Was the Italian Navy in evidence at all?

Adm. W.: Not during this operation. We saw nothing of the Italian Navy. As I recall it, it was holed up up in northern Italy or somewhere of that sort and it didn't come out at this stage of the game at all. Later, in the operation against Salerno, they did make some sorties, but they never got out effectively. I recall after the Sicilian landings I arrived on the south coast of Sicily with some ships - by this time Admiral Hewitt had left and Admiral Connoly had stayed in command on our landing beaches - and I was called over to his flagship, the Biscayne, she was a converted aircraft tender, a little ship about the size of a destroyer, and he said that General Patton was getting fairly close to Palermo, up on the north coast. The harbor of Palermo had not yet been opened, of course, but he was assigning to me some YMSs, about a dozen of them, little minesweepers, and some larger minesweepers, and I've forgotten how many destroyers - three or four destroyers - and he wrote out on a sheet of paper what the ships were and told me to take them up round the west coast of Sicily and to start sweeping that area for mines. The coast was reported as mined but we didn't know how much, and have the place ready so that we could send shipping into the harbor when General Patton took Palermo. I never had any written orders for this one. It was simply an oral directive to take these ships and go on up there and sweep the harbor.

Q: That's how fluid the whole situation was!

Adm. W.: That's the way it ran. And communications, I recall - the Biscayne was about to get under way at this time and they wanted to get me off the ship so they could proceed. I walked down the after part of the deck with his communications officer while the communications officer on a slip of paper wrote out the communications plan, the frequencies we were to use, and so forth, and I went over the side and back into my boat. The <u>Biscayne</u> went off on her business. Then we assembled the force of YMSs, the larger sweepers, and destroyers, and went up to Palermo. We got there at pretty nearly the same time that General Patton took the place and we did start sweeping the harbor. We found just one or two mines. It had been mined all right, but there were not very many and we didn't have very much trouble getting it cleared up.

Q: Were they Italian mines?

Adm. W.: Yes. Then we went on into the harbor and we began to use the harbor, I think the next day - very promptly. We reported the harbor clear and the ships didn't have very far to come. They just came right on around. *the western end of Sicily.*

Q: Does this denote cooperation from the Italian populace?

Adm. W.: No. The Italian cooperation was kind of unusual. Their hearts weren't in fighting at that particular point, and I can recall stories coming back from the Army people. I didn't see this myself, but I did see the Army people who had been involved and they said that Italians surrendered quite readily. They'd fire a few shots at a group of Italians and normally the Italians would surrender. Once they had a group of prisoners, the prisoner group, the Italians, were used as labor battalions. They'd send a group of maybe a hundred men out with a minimum number of Americans in charge, and during the course of the day's operations, if they started out with a hundred they were very apt to come back with a hundred and twenty-five. They'd picked up some volunteers. The Italians, I think, at this stage, felt about this way about the war. They wanted no part of the Germans. They weren't particularly wild about us, either, I guess, but we were the lesser of two evils anyway. So, while we didn't get active cooperation from them in getting the port open, we didn't get very much opposition, either. An example of this, for instance — we knew there must have been some kind of swept channels or directions on how ships should enter the port while they held it. We never could get any Italian who would give us those instructions. They just shrugged and said they didn't know. So what we had to do was to sweep the whole area and then establish our own swept channels into the port which we kept swept from then on. Maybe that will illustrate the degree of co-operation we were getting at that particular time from the Italians. But we did very promptly get ships into the harbor and the harbor itself was cleared. There were some ships, small ones, that were sunk in the harbor but not very many and very little damage to the harbor.

Q: Well, it hadn't been under heavy air attack?

Adm. W.: No, it hadn't. We did manage to start using the port very quickly. There was a little Italian ship yard, a small dry dock, a graving dock, that was put into use very quickly. You remember old Commodore Sullivan, the great salvage expert. Sully arrived pretty promptly there and in short order he had that port working very well.

Q: Would you comment on his activities in North Africa and later in Naples?

Adm. W.: He was a genius. I saw some of his operations in Casablanca where there was considerable damage to the harbor, and he was a master of improvisation. He could raise a ship and get it out of the way so that the pier space that it had been occupying was then available readily. If it looked like a difficult salvage job, he wouldn't bother with that, he'd just build a wooden platform over the ship and put ships alongside the hulk that was sunk at the pier. He was just full of this kind of trick. He'd look the situation over, see what the easiest way to get this harbor operating might be, and follow this path of least resistance. And in due course, if you had time, you could go back and do the major job of salvaging a badly damaged ship. But the primary object was to get the port working and he did that beautifully.

Over in Bizerte there was really a lot of sabotage in the channel. They'd sunk a number of ships to block that channel. Sully came in, had a look at them, and picked out the easiest ones to remove. I think in this case the removal method was simply plenty of explosive. He just blew them out of the channel. The channel he cleared from the point of view of the ship-handler was not an easy one. It twisted and turned round these hulks. It wasn't too well marked, but the channel was there and if you navigated your ship properly you could get in and out. He certainly had the channel open and had it open quite quickly after we got into this area.

At Palermo we had really very little problem. There wasn't much to clear up, but up in Naples we had another big problem. I wasn't present to watch that one, but I'm sure he used the same methods that he had in the other places. He was one of our very great assets at this stage in the war. Incidentally, quite a colorful character, too.

~~I've kind of lost the train of our~~

Q: Well, we had gotten into Palermo and the harbor was in use the very next day.

Adm. W.: This reminds me of an interesting yarn. At this time, General Patton, of course, started from Palermo off to the eastward to get to Messina. Meanwhile, Field Marshal Montgomery, his British counterpart, had landed down on the southeast coast of Sicily, had worked his way up to the vicinity of Mt. Etna, and some rivalry then developed as to who was going to get to Messina and take that area first, Montgomery or Patton.

Q: Was this considered a prize?

Adm. W.: Well, yes. This, you see, then gave them a bridgehead from which to jump off into the toe of the boot of Italy, and this closed out the Sicilian operation and got us ready to go into Italy. So this was quite a prize. General Patton was pretty competitive and certainly wanted to beat Montgomery into Messina, so he planned more or less on the spur of the moment ~~some~~ what he called leapfrog landings. His troops would operate ashore until they ran into some kind of a hard point of resistance, and then he wanted the Navy to pick him up and land him on the other side of this resistance so he could take it from both sides. We could provide a little gunfire support from the sea side. Then he'd move on to the next one, and during the course of the discussions in getting ready for these operations, he said he had just taken a whole field full of the German equivalent of our jeeps. They were kind of Volkswagens dressed up like jeeps. And all of us naval types who helped him in this operation, if he was successful and beat Montgomery into Messina, he would give one of these German jeeps which we could then take back to the United States in great glory.

Well, this was quite an incentive for us and we thought that was fine, so this just added to our degree of help in the leapfrog operations. We were in several of these. The first one started out with Admiral Davidson, who was in a cruiser, the Brooklyn or Philadelphia, one of that class, in command. He had two cruisers and I had quite a number of destroyers, and we had a lot of LSTs and amphibious craft, and we started off from Palermo one afternoon and headed off to the east to land at a little place called Terranova. Well, we got maybe an hour or two out from Palermo when a message came in saying that some Italian cruisers had left Genoa and were standing to the southward at high speed to attack Palermo, and that Admiral Davidson was to take his cruisers up to the northward to intercept the Italian cruisers. That left me in command of the amphibious operation that was to land on the rear side of what was then the front line along the coast of northern Sicily.

So we went on in, and this one apparently was a complete surprise to the forces ashore. It was very successful. We got our troops ashore without any difficulty and we delivered our gunfire support.

The Germans were completely surprised and the operation worked very well. Meanwhile, Admiral Davidson off to the north apparently was spotted by somebody because the Italian cruisers turned round and went home within an hour or so of the time he left our formation. This, so far as I know now, was the only time that during the course of one of these operations the Italians came down.

There was one other amusing instance when they came down that I'll tell you about in a minute. But that particular leapfrog landing worked well. After this the Germans were never caught again. They expected them all the time, and they ran in some - I think they were about 6-inch guns. There was a railroad that ran along that northern coast of Sicily and it was full of tunnels - that's a pretty rugged coast - and they put these 6-inch guns in the railroad tunnels. They'd roll them out, fire a few rounds, and then roll them back into the tunnels. We had a good deal of difficulty handling those guns. They weren't shooting at us, they were shooting at the troops ashore. But they wouldn't be exposed long enough for us to do much damage with our guns from the ships. By the time we found out where they were and got some fire directed at them, they'd pulled back in the tunnel. The Germans developed this thing for later leapfrog landings. There were two or three of those. The first one worked beautifully and the later ones weren't much of a success.

Q: This leapfrog technique was entirely new?

Adm. W.: So far as I know, it was at that time. It may have been used in other places, but it was the first experience I had had with it, and I think it was the first time it had been used in that theater.

Q: And the first experience the Germans had had!

Adm. W.: Yes, and the first one caught them, but the later ones they were pretty well ready for. Our troops had more trouble getting ashore, and when they got ashore the Germans either hadn't retired ahead of them or they had a retirement route ready. So the later ones really didn't accomplish much. But at any rate, General Patton did beat Montgomery into Messina, but by that time all of us naval types who had helped him do it had been ordered off somewhere else and we never fell in again with General Patton to collect our jeeps!

Q: Who got them?

Adm. W.: I don't know. Presumably the Italians inherited them.

Q: And are still using them!

Adm. W.: They Probably are, yes. At any rate, we never got the jeeps that General Patton had promised us. I mentioned earlier an amusing incident that happened in which some Italian ships sortied while we were in Palermo. This was after the leapfrog landings. We had sent out small ships to accept the surrender of all the outlying islands off the Sicilian coast, and there was one just north of Palermo named Ustica. Ustica had a small population but no water supply. Its water had to be provided by water barge from Palermo, and once we had taken control of the island it was up to us to provide it with water. So periodically we used to send a self-propelled water barge which is low in the water, kind of a flush-deck thing, escorted by a submarine chaser from Palermo up to Ustica, and this was a pretty slow-moving operation. It took the better part of twenty-four hours to get it up there, and one night we had the water barge escorted by a submarine chaser commanded by an ensign, U.S. Naval Reserve, on the way up to Ustica when two Italian cruisers appeared. They got this sortie accomplished without knowledge on the part of the allied forces that they were doing it, and they got pretty well down toward Palermo before we knew they were at sea. We eventually did find out about it, but the first people who found out about it were the submarine chaser commanded by a young ensign, U.S.N.R. about nineteen years old and the water barge. These two Italian cruisers came racing at them at twenty-five knots probably, and here were these poor little craft. Well, the Italians apparently saw them at about the same time they saw the Italians. The Italians seeing two ships, one, the submarine chaser, with what looked like a conning tower, and the other one with almost awash deck, apparently thought they were submarines. At any rate, a blink on the blinker gun from the submarine chaser first let the Italians know that they were there. These two Italian cruisers very promptly turned 180° and ran for home! And when this young ensign came in he was really full of mixed emotions. First he was scared to death, and second he was very proud of having won a naval victory over two Italian cruisers!

Q: With one gun! Where were they based? In Bari?

Adm. W.: I think they came out of Naples. They were somewhere up north anyway. Either Naples or possibly Livorno. Anyway up on the northern Italian coast.

Q: They had the same spirit as the people at Palermo.

Adm. W.: Yes. They weren't too anxious to get involved in fighting. Their hearts weren't in this particular war.

Wellborn #6 - 192

Interview No. 6 with Vice Admiral Charles Wellborn, Jr., U.S. Navy
(Retired)

Place: His residence in the Westchester Apartments, Washington D.C.

Date: Wednesday morning, 24 February 1972

Subject: Biography

By: John T. Mason, Jr.

Q: It's nice to see you this morning, a nice snowy morning.

Adm. W.: This is sort of a disagreeable morning, isn't it?

Q: So we're going to talk about a more pleasant clime. You were involved in the actual invasion of Italy back in 1943, and last time we dealt with the invasion of Sicily. Now I think you're going to move a little bit farther north.

Adm. W.: Yes. The next operation was a landing in the vicinity of Salerno and in that one I had part of my own destroyer squadron and some other miscellaneous destroyers as a screening group for the transports that brought in the main body of the troops for that Salerno landing. I believe that was on September the 9th 1943. At least according to my records that was the date. My group came up with the transports. Then, as was normal for destroyers in those days, we began to do all sorts of various things, screen the anchorage, provide fire support for the troops that were ashore, and some antiaircraft fire support for the anchorage, and

Q: As you came up for this operation, what did you actually anticipate? The landing on Sicily hadn't been quite as ferocious as some others. What did you anticipate in Italy proper?

Adm. W.: We were not very sure about this one because there were some political activities that happened about this time. As I recall it, just before that landing there was a very serious possibility - there appeared to be at least, a possibility that there might not be opposition. The Italians were on the point of breaking down and dropping out of the war, but the Germans were still there ashore and just who was occupying the beaches that we were going to assault we weren't very sure. We felt the Italians probably wouldn't resist but the Germans would. So there was some uncertainty about what we were going to run into and, as a matter of fact, there was I think just about the normal opposition when the landings were finally made. When I say "normal," I mean normal for that part of the world, not the kind that we encountered in the Pacific where the Japanese would defend each little island and each atoll right down to the last man.

The opposition to the landing itself at Salerno, it existed but it wasn't overwhelming. In fact, as I remember that one, the most serious difficulty that developed was maybe three or four days after D-day when one of those quick little Mediterranean storms blew up. They're very severe. They don't last very long - three or four hours and they're all over, but during the course of that time there were all sorts of landing craft and even some of those small Mediterranean freighters bringing up material that were piled up on the beach. It took a couple more days to get the beach cleared of landing craft and get the situation sorted out after that storm.

Q: Another factor was the luftwaffe, was it not?

Adm. W.: Yes, the luftwaffe bothered us some. Actually, the Salerno operation, as I recall it, was the first one in which guided missiles appeared. There was one of the Brooklyn-class cruisers - I think it was the Brooklyn, maybe the Savannah - but one of those cruisers, at any rate, that was hit by one of these things, and while she wasn't lost she was seriously damaged. It seems to me one of her turrets blew up.

Q: Had we anticipated the use of these flying bombs? Did our intelligence inform us beforehand that they were in being?

Adm. W.: They may have informed somebody, but it didn't filter down to a destroyer squadron commander, at any rate. I didn't know about it. Destroyers weren't the favorite targets for that kind of thing, so none of us got hit by that type missile. Our problem there was submarines and torpedo boats. There were some submarines in the general area, though they didn't bother us in the anchorage at Casablanca, or Fedala rather. Torpedo boats were more of a problem. We didn't lose any ships coming in to the landing area, but as we left after the transports had been unloaded and we started away from the landing area we did run into some torpedo boats and I lost one of the destroyers from the screen to a torpedo boat that night.

Q: These were Italian boats?

Adm. W.: Yes, Italian torpedo boats. We could pick up a torpedo boat that was moving at high speed from its wake on the radar screen but a torpedo boat that was lying dead in the water sometimes you got and sometimes you didn't. They were wooden boats and there wasn't much in the way of a radar reflection to be got from them. On this particular night, as we left the landing area, we did pick up some boats approaching us and, as the screen commander, I sent a destroyer out to chase them away, which she did. I don't know whether he did any damage to them or not. I suspect not, but at any rate he chased them away. Then he started back to take his place in the screen and he got about halfway back from where he had been to his position in the screen without having seen any radar reflection, nor did we see any reflection, although we saw the destroyer coming back. About that point we saw a terrific explosion and it developed later from discussions with the survivors that there was a torpedo boat lying dead in the water that they passed pretty close to without realizing it was there until it fired its torpedo. At this point, the range was so short they couldn't do much in the way of dodging and the ship was hit.

Q: The torpedo boats had only one torpedo?

Adm. W.: Apparently it only launched one from the stories that we got, but at any rate it hit the Rowan [Rowe] amidships and she went down very promptly from, I think, more from internal explosion than from the torpedo itself. We did pick up a pretty good percentage of her crew although there were some losses. Other than that, though, my own ships I think had no problems during the course of that operation. That operation, though, did bring about indirectly my next assignment because during the course of this one then-Captain

George Dyer, who was Admiral Connoly's chief of staff, was hit in the leg and his leg broken by a spent 20-mm., I think, projectile. He was standing in one of the antiaircraft machine gun tubs on the deck of the flagship - I think it was the Biscayne - and I suspect one of our own antiaircraft machine-gun bullets came down hitting this gun tub, bounced around inside of it for a while, and ultimately hit George in the leg. By that time it had lost so much velocity that it didn't do the kind of damage it might otherwise have done, but it did break his leg which put him out of commission.

Q: Put him in the hospital ship immediately!

Adm. W.: Yes. After that operation I was detached from my destroyer squadron and ordered to duty as Admiral Connoly's chief of staff to replace George Dyer. I suspect I was due for a change anyway about that time, but this triggered it off, at any rate. That took me then from the Mediterranean out to the Pacific.

Q: Did Connoly go out to the Pacific?

Adm. W.: Yes, he left the Mediterranean about that time too.

Q: Before the Italian operation was completed?

Adm. W.: No. He completed his part of that landing and immediately after that he was ordered out to the Pacific to take over command of Amphibious Group 3. He left a little before I did, and I left shortly after this Salerno operation. We joined at Oceanside, where the Fourth Marine Division had been training.

Q: California?

Adm. W.: Yes, in California. That was quite an interesting trip getting to California from North Africa, too.

Q: In what sense?

Adm. W.: Well, flying across oceans wasn't quite what it was to develop into and, as I remember it, the route I flew was from Oran to Gibraltar, from Gibraltar to Gambia, from Gambia to Trinidad, from Trinidad up to New York, I think. I've forgotten exactly, but this was the general route. You had to do it in steps and zigzag across the Atlantic at that time.

Q: Using the Azores?

Adm. W.: No. The longest hop, I think, was the one from Gambia to Trinidad, but at that point we weren't using the Azores for this kind of purpose, at any rate. I believe we had begun to fly anti-submarine patrols from there, but I'm not sure about that. At any rate, for passenger traffic this was the route that we were following. I think there was another more or less commercial one from Lisbon, but for some reason we military people didn't fly that one. We flew military airplanes on this other route.

I joined Admiral Connoly, then, out in Oceanside and there we had no ships but they were expected to appear very shortly, and they did.

Q: They were being turned out by the ship yards?

Adm. W.: Yes. We set up shop in Camp Pendleton at Oceanside and worked on the planning with the people in the Fourth Marine Division and its staff and in due course the Appalachian, one of our command ships, appeared and became our flagship, and a division of transports gradually assembled in San Diego and LSTs in reasonable numbers began to show up in San Diego. Most of these had been built somewhere up in the Great Lakes. They had come down the Mississippi River and when they got into the New Orleans vicinity they went into ship yards there and had their masts and superstructures completed, and then were sailed to Panama, and from Panama to San Diego. This was their shake-down, and when they arrived in San Diego there really was no time for any training. They got a little voyage repair there in San Diego and they unloaded the cargo that had been put in them in New Orleans to bring out to the West Coast and were reloaded with their combat cargo -

Q: What kind of a time schedule did you have? What operation were you to be involved in?

Adm. W.: We were getting ready for the operation against Kwajalein Atoll and there were two task forces involved in the assault on Kwajalein. Admiral Connoly's Group 3 was to take the northern islands of the atoll, Roi and Namur. The southern half of the atoll I believe Kelly Turner had himself. It might have been Harry Hill. At any rate, there was another task force that took the island of Kwajalein.

Q: When you were still at Oceanside where you aware of your destination and the type of terrain and so forth?

Adm. W.: Yes, we were aware of the objective and our intelligence on it was kind of meager, but it improved during the course of our planning and preparation.

Q: Had the Fourth Marines been involved in -

Adm. W.: No, it was a brand-new division. All the ships were brand-new, and this one was really a shoestring type operation.

Q: And it was a very hurry-up one!

Adm. W.: Yes, it was. It was put together in quite a hurry. As the LSTs particularly arrived, we would have a look at them and try to get them into as good shape as we could, but they had to be sailed - they were slow ships - from San Diego well in advance to get to the destination by the required time. It seems to me that assault took place was it April of the next year? Maybe it was a little earlier than that.

Q: As fresh-caught amphibious operators in the Mediterranean, did you have to relearn some of the tactics for the Pacific or did you do this as you went along?

Adm. W.: There were some differences but they weren't, I think, very radical differences. The Army in the Mediterranean seemed always to like to make their landings during darkness, just before dawn, so that by the time there was daylight they were safely ashore and ready to operate.

Q: That was typical of Sicily, wasn't it?

Adm. W.: Yes, and this was Salerno, too. I think that's also the way they had landed in North Africa. In the Pacific, however, the preference seemed to be for landing just after daylight so that you did have daylight for the preparation, the gunfire and the air operations, the bombing and machine gun strafing, to soften up your beach. I think also there was probably a little more emphasis on preparation in the Pacific. In the Atlantic the effort was - I mean in the Mediterranean the effort was toward surprise and you didn't do a lot of artillery preparing with naval gunfire. In the Pacific you didn't, apparently, pay much attention to surprise but you did pay a lot of attention to hammering your landing beaches and trying to ensure that there wouldn't be any opposition right on the beach. I think these were the principal differences. Technique were pretty much the same.

Q: The enemy himself was so drastically different!

Adm. W.: Very different, yes. In the Mediterranean distances were short and you could use LCIs and short-range landing craft to go directly from your own base to the target area. Pacific distances were too great for this. You could use LSTs and LSDs were beginning to appear as transporters of LCTs, but you had to have larger ships for long overseas journeys before you got to your target. So this was another difference. But, generally speaking, it seemed to me that as something new developed in one ocean the news of it got to the other one very promptly and they all knew and tried to use the same kinds of techniques. Of course, one thing that you had in the Pacific that you didn't have in the Mediterranean was the Marine Corps. The Marines were very much more aggressive in this type of operation than were the Army. There were two schools of thought and these were beautifully illustrated right there in that Kwajalein operation. The Marines' thinking was that you went at the landing and the subsequent clearing up and establishing yourself ashore very vigorously and very rapidly. You accepted pretty heavy losses during the brief period that you were engaged, but you got it done in a hurry. The Army's approach always was to minimize their losses and operate very much more deliberately, to require lots more artillery and air support, to ultimately achieve the same objective that the Marines did.

On Kwajalein it was an interesting comparison. The north and the south islands of the atoll were assaulted from the north by Marines and from the south by the Army and, as I recall it, it took the Marines something like two or three days to clean up their north end against opposition that compared to their strength in about the same ratio that in the south compared to the Army's strength. Though I think there were more involved in the south on both sides than there were in the north, it wasn't very different. It took the Army something like ten days to two weeks to clean up their half of the atoll. The Marines accepted much heavier losses during the few days that they were engaged, but in the end the ratio of casualties to the strength of the forces engaged turned out to be almost identical. This comparison seemed to me to work out that if you did it the way the Marines did it, you got the job done in a short time. If you did it the way the ARmy did it, it took a longer time and more ammunition. You didn't lose more men either way, and as long as you kept the two separated either one worked. But it was difficult to put the two together and have them work side by side because they didn't work in the same way. This came out later in the Smith versus Smith controversy, where

General Holland Smith relieved an Army general also named Smith, because he didn't think he was operating with sufficient vigor.

Well, I think this is an illustration of the fact that the Army method and the Marine method simply didn't mix very well. EAch one was a good method in its own way but you had difficulty putting the two together and operating them as a team because their methods were different.

Q: It has been said, and I think there's evidence to support that, that many of the naval officers involved in the European theater didn't get much of an opportunity in the Pacific. Was this one reason - that they were familiar with the Army technique rather than the Marine technique?

Adm. W.: I don't believe that had much bearing on this particular problem. I think generally people who started in the Pacific had acquired an esprit that was very good. They always felt that they were fighting the important war and that the people in the Mediterranean were fighting kind of a gentlemanly not very rugged war. So there was a tendency on the part of the people who had originally been in the Pacific to ask for other Pacific people to join them, I mean among senior ones who were in a position to ask for the ones they wanted. I think this probably had more to do with what you mentioned than the difference between the Army and Marine techniques.

Q: I see.

Adm. W.: In due course there were a lot of people who did well in the Atlantic who also did well in the Pacific. Admiral Connoly is one.

Q: Jimmy Hall is another.

Adm. W.: Yes. Jimmy Hall is another one. There were a lot of them. They had some difficulty achieving acceptance in the first instance in the Pacific, but after they got going I think they were recognized as being just as capable as - just as good fighters - as the Pacific warriors were.

Q: On the other hand, a man like Alan Kirk didn't get an opportunity and he was terribly frustrated as a result.

Adm. W.: That's quite true. I think that there may have been, too, some reaction that came down right from the top. Of course, Admiral King was always a Pacific strategist and he stressed the importance of the Pacific and usually was having a battle to get the material he wanted, whereas the president tended to stress the Atlantic. I think in the Navy the fact that Admiral King who was a very important person in the Navy in those days stressed the Pacific tended to make most ambitious naval officers also stress the Pacific. This I think resulted in most people who wanted to get ahead trying to get out to the Pacific where they would come to the attention of the boss man. It naturally tended to make them gravitate that way whenever they could.

There was a little more than this to it and I'm probably exaggerating the point. I think we all felt quite sincerely that the war in the Pacific was a naval war, whereas the war in the Atlantic was essentially a ground war. We had submarines to fight getting the material across the Atlantic, but the real naval war was in the

Pacific.

Q: And it was primarily a U.S. war.

Adm. W.: Yes, so this was, as the current expression goes "where the action was," so that was where we wanted to go. I think most -- not quite all, but most of the senior officers of that time managed eventually to get to the Pacific. There were a few like Admiral Kirk who didn't manage it, but for the most part, they did. Admiral Connoly is an example.

Q: How long were you at Oceanside in preparing for this operation and waiting for your transportation?

Adm. W.: I haven't any records here to pin that down accurately, but as I remember we got established in Oceanside somewhere along about the end of 1943 and we left there maybe in March. My recollection is just two or three months there, during which time the ships arrived in San Diego and we ran off one rehearsal landing on the Oceanside beaches. This involved only the transports. The LSTs weren't there. And this landing went very badly. The Marines were inexperienced and the naval ships weren't experienced, but I think it was a very valuable exercise because everybody got some experience in a hurry and when the final landing took place in Kwajalein, while it wasn't one of the smoothest operations I've ever seen, it went acceptably well. It approximated the plan as nearly as operations frequently do.

The LSTs had to do their part without really any rehearsal. Being slow as they were they had to leave a long time before D-day and they left San Diego without having copies of the operation orders. These had not yet been really formulated, much less reproduced and distributed. So they sailed without really knowing what the plan was and the operation orders were delivered to the LSTs for their operation by air drop while they were en route from I believe it was Pearl Harbor to Kwajalein. I thought it was pretty remarkable that a bunch of ships that had never had any real training, manned mostly by people who'd never been to sea before, arrived at an objective such as Kwajalein and successfully carried out an operation order that they hadn't seen before they got under way.

Q: Weren't there some veterans interspersed among the personnel?

Adm. W.: Oh, yes, but for the most part those LSTs were manned by young men who hadn't seen the ocean until they left New Orleans. As a rule, at that time, I believe, the commanding officers of the LSTs were officers who had been subordinates in other LSTs. They tried to move people up from subordinate jobs to command in each class of ship. I think there nearly always was somebody who had some experience in each one of the LSTs, but the average of experience was very low. But they did a very creditable job. Of course there were amusing incidents that developed.

After this operation on Kwajalein all the LSTs when they were no longer needed in the objective area were sent down to Majuro for reassembling. There was one ship that was given orders by blinker signal to proceed to Majuro. Well, he got under way and proceeded to Majuro and when he got there went into the lagoon, looked around, chose a nice anchorage, and lay there for three or four days and nobody heard anything from him. So we initiated a search for LST-whatever his number was. We had airplanes flying all over the ocean there for a couple of days and finally one of them, in more or less desperation, flew over the anchorage of Majuro and there was our LST ~~No. What's It~~ calmly anchored in the midst of a lot of others. The skipper of this particular one was asked why he did that, why didn't he [make his arrival report or at least] let somebody know he had arrived at Majuro. Well, he said, his orders told him to proceed to Majuro and he did and here he was. He didn't realize that he was supposed to report to anybody! He had assumed that sooner or later somebody would give him some more orders and he was just waiting until they did.

Of course, this story I think generally illustrates the level of inexperience we had. Here was a young fellow who was following out his orders to the best of his ability and he didn't realize that he was supposed to let somebody know that he had arrived in Majuro. "Movement reports" were something he'd never heard of and reporting to his senior officer present [was] an old naval custom that was brand new to him. So when you have ships of this kind your problems sometimes develop from inexperience, but they were usually pretty easy to sort out. I think by and large the young people without experience did a pretty magnificent job.

Q: You went first to Pearl going out to - ?

Adm. W.: Yes, but that was only for a brief stop and, as I recall it, nobody went ashore at Pearl on that trip out. It was a refueling and replenishment affair. We really did nothing there except refuel, replenish, pick up the mail, and be on our way.

Q: How large an armada was it going from Pearl to Kwajalein?

Adm. W.: It sailed in several groups, so none of the individual formations were very large. My recollection is maybe a dozen ships in the transport formation which the flagship was with. The LSTs had sailed in, I think, two or three groups and there were probably thirty or so of them, all told. Then we had an air group. Some of the converted oil tanker type carriers that were to provide us close air support at the objective, and there were some surface gunfire support ships, cruisers and destroyers, that had sailed as a unit. So it was quite an armada, all told, but it didn't sail in one formation. It was in several different dispositions. Of course, Kelly Turner had a similar group, a somewhat larger one, for his operation at the south end of the atoll. He had the same kinds of components and at the same time one of the carrier task forces was operating at sea providing what was called strategic cover for the operation. They were supposed to prevent any strong Japanese forces from interfering with the operation.

So, all told, there were really many ships involved, but each little formation was quite handy and easy to maneuver. This one was put together fairly rapidly for such an operation. It required quite a lot of coordination each little task group with each other task group, and I think this was probably our greatest difficulty after the inexperience of the people involved, because it was pretty difficult with Kelly Turner and his Marine force - Army force, I mean - in Pearl Harbor, Admiral Connoly and his Marine landing force in San Diego and Oceanside, and the over-all planning was being done by CinCPac in Pearl Harbor. But those difficulties are the kinds of things that you manage to overcome.

Q: This was expected to be a fairly formidable operation, wasn't it?

Adm. W.: Yes, reasonably so. You see, this was fairly early in the Pacific atoll-type operations. Tarawa had turned out the real tough one and we expected really a tougher job than we got at Kwajalein. There was really very heavy preparation by air and by gunfire for this landing, and there was of course overwhelming force that was landed. This one, I think, turned out to be considerably easier than everybody had expected.

After Tarawa all the planners had got the feeling that the Japs were ten feet tall, and after Kwajalein they got back to normal size again. The Tarawa experience, I think, helped a good deal in the planning for the preparation of artillery there, for Kwajalein. The method that Admiral Connoly liked to use was one that he described as punching holes in concrete bunkers with major caliber projectiles and then patting them down with thousand-pound bombs. He used that one quite successfully against the concrete that was put up on Roi and Namur. The battleships and the 8-inch cruisers stood in pretty close and fired with almost horizontal trajectories at this concrete, and that did punch them pretty full of holes. Then the thousand-pound bombs would flatten out the weakened structures. So I thought that system was pretty effective.

Between Tarawa and Kwajalein, too, there had been some new techniques, some new types of ships, produced. Small rockets came into use, I believe for the first time, in this operation, and there were some rocket ships, LCTs, with tremendous numbers of rocket launchers on their decks that were used there. And when you combined the 5-inch batteries of destroyers and cruisers with these rocket ships pouring their rockets on the beach, it really made a mess of things. Watching it offshore, you wouldn't believe that anything could be alive on a beach that had been subjected to that kind of punishment.

Q: That's what they thought at Tarawa!

Adm. W.: Yes. But it developed very definitely that people could stay alive. After one of these things, the Marines said the beach defenders seemed to be more or less shocked, but the Japs would come crawling up out of the dirt and start firing their rifles at the Marines. I think the beach preparation was much more effective at Kwajalein than it had been at Tarawa and casualties were, of course, much lighter.

Q: How far off the beach did you stand in the Appalachian?

Adm. W.: Well, originally I guess we were a couple of miles or something like this, and before the operation was complete we went in to the lagoon inside the rim of the atoll, and there we were probably three or four miles offshore. By that time, of course, there was no major caliber gun left on the island, nothing that could reach us, and there was really no air opposition to speak of. Now there was one night air attack on the north end of the island during the course of that operation - a small number of planes and I don't recall just where they came from, but a number of Japanese bombers, maybe a dozen, did get to the atoll and did drop some bombs. They set some fires ashore, they didn't cause many casualties and I don't think they slowed up the operation really appreciably. I recall the fires principally because for the first time on the staff of Admiral Connoly we had a fire marshal. He was a man from the Puget Sound area who had been involved in fighting waterfront fires as a civilian, and he was pretty good. When fires developed on Roi and Namur he went ashore and gave quite a lot of assistance to the Marines in getting the fires under control.

Q: Did you have the help of the Seabees in this operation?

Adm. W.: Yes, they went ashore with the Marines, as I remember fairly early, and they started right in putting the airfield on Roi back in commission. It was pretty well full of holes and pretty badly beaten up, but they got in with their bulldozers and scrapers and sheepsfoot rollers and things of this kind, and they had that airfield operational really in quite short order.

They told a story which I think is probably true that the Seabees there on that island operating on the airfield before the island really was secure. There were still some snipers firing from the perimeter of the field. The Seabees were reported to have developed a technique with their bulldozers. When a sniper began to fire at them, they'd turn the bulldozer in that direction and raise the bulldozer's blade and use it as armor. That sounded like Seabees, all right! I didn't actually see this one, but I suspect it took place.

Q: Tell me about the command ship itself. This was a relatively new concept, was it not, for command ships?

Adm. W.: Yes. This one was relatively new, as you say, but not completely so. This was one that I think we really borrowed from the British. They had developed this concept for some of their operations. They first used rather small ships for their commando-type operations - the hit-and-run type landings. Then they began to use larger passenger-type ships. I remember one called the Bulolo that came into Casablanca as a headquarters and communications ship for Winston Churchill when they had the Casablanca Conference. We had picked up this idea and further developed it into merchant ship hulls that were completely redone for the specific purpose of providing facilities, communications for command in this kind of operation. Of course, communications are the heart of an amphibious operation, keeping track of what's happening and directing the necessary forces to the right places.

Q: And because that is so important, I suppose a man-of-war is inadequate?

Adm. W.: Yes. In some cases where these special ships weren't available, men-of-war were used, but this interfered with their activities as men-of-war. If they were fire support ships, then their communications were interfered with and the noise and confusion of the gunfire made it difficult to communicate. So that, generally speaking, they were something less than completely satisfactory.

The command ship itself was one whose primary purpose was this exercise of command. It was built with this in mind. All communications were there. There were operations rooms, there were adequate quarters to take care of people that had to handle all this exercise of command for the commander. So they were much more satisfactory. I recall after this operation was complete, after the northern half of the atoll was secured, Admiral Connoly did shift his flag to the battleship _Maryland_, and the difference was really remarkable. The facility with which you could exercise your command from the _Appalachian_ as opposed to the difficulties you had in doing it from the _Maryland_ was something that you couldn't miss.

Q: What sort of ~~airplane~~ armorplate protection did the _Appalachian_ have?

Adm. W.: Really no armorplating. She had the usual gun tubs of light, maybe half-inch, steel, around the machine guns on deck, but the hull itself had no armor. She was no different from a normal merchant ship. I believe they call them two-compartment ships. She could flood any two compartments of the five or six that she had and she wouldn't sink, but other than that –

Q: How large a vessel?

Adm. W.: Five hundred feet long, or something of this sort, sixty-foot beam, and she drew probably twenty-five to twenty-seven feet.

Q: I would think that a ship of that sort would have been a primary target of Japanese airmen.

Adm. W.: I think they would have been, but really there weren't very many Japanese airmen around by this time. Their air power was all very much farther to the westward.

Q: But with the advant of the kamikaze a little later on, was the command ship not a prime target?

Adm. W.: Yes, it was a prime target for the kamikazes.

Q: Was it disguised in any fashion?

Adm. W.: Well, its hull was exactly the same hull as the transport hulls. It did have a lot more top hamper in the way of radar antennas, communications antennas, and this sort of thing, but I suspect in an airplane making a high-speed approach and usually at low altitude that this kind of ship would have been fairly difficult to differentiate from the normal transports. I can't recall that they had a very rough time against kamikazes. It seems to me the kamikazes tended more to go for the picket destroyers than they did for the command ships.

Q: The command ships' only protection, self-defense, was anti-aircraft — ?

Adm. W.: Really, its protection was the combat air patrol, the airplanes that were flying over the formation in the objective area. It had no real self-protection against aircraft. It had I remember a couple of 5-inch guns, one on each end, and a lot of 20-mm. machine guns scattered around, but its fire control was pretty ineffective and I don't think it could have protected itself. It had to depend for its protection on the over-all air protection of the objective area or of the formation if it was en route that was given by the combat air patrols and the other dispositions around it.

Q: What are some of your personal recollections of that particular operation?

Adm. W.: I would say probably the one that I came out with quite strong was the leadership of Admiral Connoly, and this includes the preparatory period as well as the actual operation itself. I've served with a lot of fine officers during my career, but he seemed to me to have probably the best perception of all of them of what the role of a commander was, what the role of his chief of staff was, and what the role of each one of his staff officers was. He seemed to know also better than most how you fired up a team to have them at the peak on the day of the operation. I came out of that one with tremendous admiration for Admiral Connoly. He didn't have the brightest mind of all the people I worked with, but he had an understanding of leadership that I thought was outstanding.

Q: What was his technique for peaking at the right moment?

Adm. W.: Well, you've known a lot of effervescent, outgoing Irishmen, I'm sure, and he was one of these and I think this tied in with his/ability to use his staff too. At the beginning of the day, maybe at breakfast or maybe at a quick conference, informal conversations or something, he would get his staff going on the lines that he wanted to pursue for that day. Then he'd be off to circulate around with the various people who comprised the force. He had personal contact with them. He had great enthusiasm himself and I think he transferred a lot of this enthusiasm to the various people who comprised his force. This seemed to me to be the technique he used, but I think a lot of this had to do with his own personality. He was an enthusiastic, outgoing person, and a scrapper. As a wartime leader he had the right natural equipment and knew how to use it.

Q: How did he get along with Kelly Turner?

Adm. W.: Not very well. This, I think, was more or less understandable. They were two very strong, very able leaders. I think Kelly Turner tended to, maybe subconsciously, feel that in Admiral Connoly he had a possible competitor, and I think he tended not to give Admiral Connoly any very tremendous opportunities to distinguish himself for this reason. In this respect, Admiral Connoly may also, by virtue of some of the things I've said about him previously, have tended to - antagonize is too strong a word, but tended to make Admiral Turner kind of stand off from him a little bit. They were entirely different types, although they were both strong characters and able commanders. Kelly Turner, as you know, was the austere autocrat and I think the difference in personalities and this competition that I see between the two was something that prevented them from ever being very close, although this competitiveness between them never developed to the point where it prevented them from working successfully together. In the Kwajalein operation Kelly Turner was the over-all amphibious force commander, and Admiral Connoly was his subordinate, and for my money he was a loyal subordinate and in the course of the operation Kelly Turner ably supported him. But there wasn't any very close relationship between these two.

Q: Did Connoly go on to have an extensive amphibious career in the

Pacific?

Adm. W.: I would say extensive but never one that shone very brightly. He did well in every operation he had but he never was assigned to one where there was a great deal of glamor or opportunity to make a name for himself. Maybe what I have said earlier was based somewhat on this fact.

Q: What else do you recollect about that particular operation?

Adm. W.: After the main two islands were secure I remember we had quite a lot of fun clearing the smaller islands in the north half of the atoll. There were dozens of these little islands and there were also dozens of little Japanese detachments anywhere from half a dozen up to maybe fifty posted around in various places. They had communications and in some cases they had some minor artillery, I think. We had to mount what was called in the task force Operation Shoelace to clean out all of these people, and I recall someone came up with the suggestion that maybe we really didn't have to clean these out with force. We could just drop leaflets on these islands telling them that the main islands had now fallen and that they should surrender, and that would do the job. Well, that didn't do the job against the Japanese. They didn't fight that way. They didn't surrender.

Q: You did use propaganda leaflets?

Adm. W.: They were tried, I think, around the islands to a limited extent but nobody had much confidence in them and they didn't work. It took force on every one of the little islands to clean out these little nests of Japanese.

Q: It was do or die with them!

Adm. W.: Yes. With them, at that time, the only prisoners the Marines took were people who were wounded and just couldn't help being taken prisoner.

Q: Were there any civilians on the islands?

Adm. W.: Whether or not they were civilians I think it's sort of difficult to say. There were some Korean laborers there and the difference between the civilian and the military man on that island was kind of hard to distinguish. They all did about the same things and lived in about the same way. I guess maybe technically some of the people on the islands were civilians, although from our point of view and from theirs it didn't make any difference. The civilians fought us just as hard as the military did.

Q: Since you mentioned propaganda leaflets, the Japanese had propaganda leaflets. Did they use them on our forces at this time?

Adm. W.: I don't recall them being used. I don't think so. This was a pretty long way out from the Japanese mainland and there were quite a lot of things that happened both later in the war and closer to the main islands of Japan that didn't seem to reach out as far as the Marianas.

Q: When this operation was concluded, what was your next step?

Adm. W.: After the operation we went back in the <u>Maryland</u> to Pearl Harbor. We learned very promptly that the next assignment for an

Amphibious Group 3 was to be a landing on Guam.

Q: Where did you abandon your command ship?

Adm. W.: It went over to someone else. I've forgotten who it was. At that time there was a shortage of everything, of course, and after an operation was completed a commander and his staff would have to go ashore to plan for the next operation. The ship that had been the flagship would be assigned to some other operating group and go off to participate in another operation, and that's the way we lost the Appalachian. She went to somebody else for another operation. As I remember it, that was Admiral Harry Hill who went up to another atoll just north of —

Q: Tinian?

Adm. W.: No. I'll think of it. They had some atomic tests there later, not Bikini but close to Bikini. But the flagship went over to Admiral Hill for his operation and we came back in the Maryland for planning ashore with the Marines there in Pearl Harbor. About this time I got orders to come back to BuPers. By this time Admiral Louis Denfeld, with whom I had sailed in destroyers back in 1936, 1937, had become the Number Two man in BuPers.

Q: Under Jacobs?

Adm. W.: Under Jacobs, yes. And he was assembling some people he had known before to do the job in the Bureau. Although Admiral Connoly and I both did our best to prevent this, we didn't, and I got orders to come back to the Bureau in Washington. So I did come back there in April, or so, of 1944. I spent one year then in the Bureau of Personnel in the Officer Personnel Division. There was a scheme of rotating officers in and out. When I arrived John Roper was the chief of the officer personnel branch. Slim Wooldridge was the Number Two, and I came in as the Number Three. Three or four months later, John went to sea, Slim moved up to become the chief, and I moved up to the Number Two spot. Then, three or four months after that Slim went to sea, and I became the chief. In due course - in another three or four months - I got myself out to sea.

Q: What was your particular job there in the Bureau of Personnel?

Adm. W.: It was officer personnel acquisition, distribution, and discipline problems went along with it - the whole ball of wax having to do with officer personnel.

Q: Reserves

Adm. W.: Yes. They were all put in pretty much the same pool at this time. The records would indicate who was reserve and who was regular, but so far as distribution was concerned they were all the same.

Q: What were your objectives in your officer assignments? What did you attempt to achieve in trying to match a round peg to a round hole, so to speak?

Adm. W.: Yes, of course at this time business machine records hadn't been really very well developed. We did have punch cards on which we had the qualifications of officers set forth, and we did have, to a certain degree, knowledge of what the requirements were in most if not all of the jobs to which we had to assign people. Generally speaking, though, we had to depend pretty much on monthly reports that came in from commanding officers. They would send in a monthly roster on which they would list all the officers under their command, then list the billets for which each officer was in training and those for which he was considered qualified. The distribution was divided generally into type desks - all the officers in battleships were under an individual in the bureau, all those in carriers were under another one, destroyers and small craft were at another desk. Generally, these rosters provided you with - provided the desk officers, with the information on which of their people were qualified for which billets.

Q: How did a man break out of a type?

Adm. W.: There was some of this, but generally speaking, not too much. The regular officers liked to break out of their type more than the reserves. As far as the reserves were concerned, they were in for the war anyway and it didn't make much difference to them which type they were in. But for inter-type work we had another desk that did deal with requirements that couldn't be met within a type desk and the shifting back and forth of the officers from one type to another. That operated reasonably well. Of course, occasionally, too, you would find an earlier mistake had been made and this desk would pick up mistakes in which maybe you had somebody who was educated and qualified as a dentist but had gotten in somehow as a line officer, and he was operating a landing craft instead of taking care of somebody's teeth. We would try to pick those mistakes up as they came to light and shift the individual from one specialty to another.

For the most part, though, people moved up in their own types and as new ships were commissioned, you would assemble a new outfit of officers from the ships of the type, taking officers who were qualified for particular assignments according to the rosters of the ships that were operating.

Q: In a case of that sort, a new cruiser being commissioned, the captain has been named and they often had the captain express a preference for the personnel on his ship. How much credence did you give his requests?

Adm. W.: Wherever we could we would try to meet his requests. In many cases there would be demands of various kinds that had to be met and some of these demands had higher priority than others. But all things being equal, if he wanted a certain individual rather than just take his chances with whatever came out of the hat, we'd try to give him the one he wanted. I remember particularly the Manhattan Project which got priority over everything else, and when the Manhattan Project asked for a certain individual, it got him. This was an order that came right down from Admiral King, through Admiral Jacobs.

Q: So necessarily you knew about the Manhattan Project?

Adm. W.: No, we didn't, as a matter of fact. It was a very closely held secret. We knew that there was something being done that had top-notch priority and whenever a request for this group came, even though many times we protested taking an officer who we thought was essential from some other job, we always lost. The officer always went to the Manhattan Project. We didn't know what it was but we did know that there wasn't any use protesting. In due course, after several months of futilely protesting, we realized and just sent him along.

There were others that had not quite the same high priority, and there were various cases of individuals who were untouchable for various reasons. I can remember at this particular time each one of the secretaries had a few people that he wanted put in certain places. We very quickly spotted who these people were and then there was no effort made to move them out. They were untouchables.

Q: Were they usually reserves?

Adm. W.: Yes, usually they were. There were a lot of special programs that were going on that didn't seem to be very high priority to us, but they did to somebody else. One, for instance, was the tire inspection program. To those of us who were distributing officers this one didn't seem to rate a very high priority, but to some of our superiors the tire inspection program was very important and it did get a certain number of officers that we thought could have been better used somewhere else. But for the most part we were permitted to distribute the people as seemed best to us.

Q: Was the ruling in effect at that time that you had to match commander who was a line officer per se with a chief of staff who was an aviator?

Adm. W.: This was at the top level, yes. Where you had a commander such as, well, Admiral Mitscher comes to mind, who was an aviator. His chief of staff was a non-aviator, Burke, through most of his career out in the Pacific. Admiral Halsey who was an aviator had Mick Carney as his chief of staff, although he started off with I believe an aviator, Miles Browning earlier. But, generally speaking, during this period, yes, the senior commanders, the flag officers with two or three stars and above, had to have their chiefs of staff officers who were of the other variety, that is aviator and non-aviator. This, I personally, at that time didn't think was very essential and I still don't, but this was the decree at the time.

Q: What was the reason? Why did it come to be?

Adm. W.: The reasoning behind it, I think, was that many of the aviators had spent a lot of time in airplanes but very little in ships. There had been a few instances in which officers - senior aviators who had little experience with ships, in command both of individual ships and groups of ships, had failed to recognize some of the problems involved in ship-handling. This on the one side. On the other side, there was a feeling that - among the aviators, that whenever an airplane was involved command of that should be exercised - maybe even beyond command, control of it should be exercised only by somebody who had had the experience of flying airplanes himself. And I think there was some merit in each one of these points of view, but I think it was carried too far. It was made mandatory, whereas it might well have been a matter of some discretion. There were instances in a carrier task force, for instance, where I didn't see any particular virtue in having as chief of staff a non-flyer, but it worked all right. I think there was enough competence either way to handle the situation.

Q: Did you have any cognizance over the assignment of WAVE officers?

Adm. W.: Yes, we did. We had a WAVE desk. Of course, the WAVE officers were assigned only to shore duty only within the continental United States. Late in my period of duty in BuPers we sent the first group of WAVEs as far as Pearl Harbor, but during my period there the WAVEs, both officer and enlisted, were used only in the continental United States and this one exploratory group left just about the time I left the Bureau.

Q: Did you have any contact with Captain McAfee?

Adm. W.: Yes. She was the director of the WAVEs, of course, at that time, and while we distributed the WAVE officers she was the director of the WAVEs in much the same manner that the chief of chaplains is the director of the chaplains, although we distributed the chaplains, too. The chief of chaplains advised us which chaplain was suitable for which place, and Mrs. McAfee did that for us as far as the WAVEs were concerned. We did the distributing and she did the policy determining as to how the WAVEs should be employed. She was, I thought, a great person. She came to the Navy Department from an ecclesiastical background and an educational career and she hadn't much experience with some of the seamier sides of life and I think in the early days she was really quite shocked at some of the things that she learned about. But she reacted very favorably to all these things. She set a very high tone for her WAVEs and I think her experience with the Navy probably was good for her. She'd been a maiden lady up to this time and she got married during the period that she was in the WAVEs. I have very high regard for her. She did really a marvellous job of establishing the WAVEs and handling them in a manner that kept their standards high and at the same time kept their morale high, too.

Q: Did you, at the outset, accept the idea of WAVEs in the service?

Adm. W.: Not really, no. I didn't think they served any very great purpose. There was some reasoning behind this that involved the ability to rotate officers. From the point of view of the distribution of your officer personnel, when you found an officer who'd been out at sea in a destroyer for maybe three years and through various sources of information learned that he was getting kind of tired, you'd like to bring him ashore and give him a rest for a while. Well, if the billet that you might put him in was occupied by a WAVE officer who couldn't be rotated to sea, this foreclosed that particular rotation. So, from the point of view of the distributors, the WAVEs occupied billets that otherwise would have been available for rotating some of the officers who had been at sea for a long time into a shore billet for a rest.

Q: That's a very interesting point, because this is the reverse of the coin. The WAVEs were recruited to relieve men to serve at sea.

Adm. W.: Well, they did this and from this point of view they were very effective, but I don't think that we were so short of manpower that we couldn't have produced enough men to fill these WAVE billets. But the WAVEs did some very good work.

Q: So in the end they justified themselves?

Adm. W.: I guess so, particularly in the light of current women's lib type things, they were justifiable and maybe even necessary, but from my point of view at that time and my current point of view they weren't really necessary. We could have gotten enough men to do the job and we'd have had some more flexibility in doing it had there been all people who were usable in billets afloat and in the advanced areas.

There were some interesting things that developed. The original thinking was that WAVE officers should be handled under just exactly the same sets of policies and the same manner that male officers were handled, and we started off that way. It pretty soon became apparent that WAVE officers not only were prettier than male officers but they were different in other respects, too. Their approach to wartime duty seemed to me to be the outstanding difference. I think quite understandably in a wartime situation male officers tend to feel that their primary duty was to the country, whatever the Navy ordered them to do they did, and their personal and their family considerations had to be secondary. But with the WAVE officers it very promptly became apparent to me, at any rate, that this wasn't the case and that whether we were at war or not the female officer considered that her family responsibilities were her primary ones and that within the limitations that were set up by her family responsibilities, she was delighted to do anything she could for her country. And I don't mean to impugn their patriotism by saying this, either. I think this was biological.

At any rate, we found very promptly in the game that if a WAVE officer's mother became seriously ill, the way to handle that situation was to send that WAVE officer off on leave to take care of her mother and when her mother was back in good health she'd come back and work her heart out for the Navy. But it was a losing game to expect that girl when she had a family responsibility of importance to really put her heart in doing something for the Navy. Once you understood this kind of a difference, WAVE officers were fine and no great problems in handling.

Q: There was one problem which is reported to have claimed the attention of Admiral King and Admiral Nimitz at many of their conferences out on the West Coast, the placement of high-placed officers, or replacement of high-placed officers. I've been told that they devoted a great deal of time to this whole problem. Did it have its reflections in your bailiwick?

Adm. W.: Yes, but generally speaking I kind of got the backwash of this in my office. I was about a medium senior captain and I was involved in distributing officers of captain rank and on down. Generally speaking, the flag officer distribution was handled on the level above mine. I took care of the mechanics of issuing the orders, but the determination of who went where was Admiral Jacobs' and Admiral Denfeld's for the Bureau and Admiral King, Nimitz, and so forth for the top people. So that once the determination had been made as to who went where, I went through the mechanical operations of issuing the orders and taking care of the paper work, and then the follow-on business of filling out their staffs, making the changes that resulted from the changes of the senior people. But I didn't have any discretion in ordering flag officers around. It was all done at levels beyond mine. If I had any thoughts on the subject I never hesitated to pass them orally on to Admiral Denfeld, but this was strictly just a personal thought. I had no real responsibility for the distribution of flag officers.

I think that, as you say, Admiral Nimitz particularly was very active in trying to get the right people in the right jobs and he I think was very good at it. I didn't always agree with some of Admiral King's thinking on the subject, but Admiral Nimitz I thought was really very good at picking the right person for the right job. Of course, he was operating at the flag officer level and I was operating down below that and I was about to add that this got interesting sometimes because you had to handle your own contemporaries' assignments –

Q: Your classmates!

Adm. W.: Yes. Sometimes the people you'd always held in high personal esteem turned out, when you looked at the records, not to have records that justified some top-notch assignment, and sometimes also the other way. People that personally you didn't think very much of turned out to be very good on the record at handling difficult jobs. I found I had to revise my personal thinking about people to a considerable degree after looking at their records. I think that experience brought me to the conclusion that whenever you have a record of say twenty years on somebody, you have the means of pretty accurately determining what he's like. It is almost invariable that an officer who has as an ensign right out of the Naval Academy or out of officer candidate school made some kind of a mistake in judgment, he'll make that same kind of mistake over and over again throughout his career, and over a period of twenty years or so this becomes something that's quite apparent. On the other hand, somebody who starts off with top-notch marks pretty generally continues to get them throughout his career.

Q: I thought we learned by experience!

Adm. W.: Well, this may be true, but also I think we have certain inherent capabilities and characteristics that begin to show up. Of course, there have been any number of different forms of fitness reports used over the last fifty years or so. They get revised periodically. Fitness reports generally tend to be over-marked. That is, if you have a group of, say, a hundred officers and the commanding officer is marking them and trying to separate out the top ten percent and the bottom ten percent and the middle ~~twenty~~ *eighty* percent, let's say, you'll find ninety percent of his officers are in the top ten percent. But you very quickly learn to read between the lines of a fitness report and differentiate the real top ten percent from the other eighty percent that have been marked. There are enough minor variations and differences in phraseology to make it pretty clear where almost any individual really stands in the hierarchy. The different forms that are used for fitness reports don't seem to make very much difference. They're all over-marked. Through all of them there comes this meaning between the lines that makes it fairly easy to pick out the real good ones from the less good ones or the real bad ones from the less bad ones.

Q: The rule of thumb prior to World War II for the advancement of an officer was a wide background of experience. Was this held in abeyance during World War II?

Adm. W.: Necessarily, to a certain extent. Among the regular officers there was still some effort to achieve a general experience, but even among the regulars this had to be put in abeyance pretty much. For instance, an officer, say, who was a lieutenant commander at the start of the war in command of a destroyer was very apt to continue. He would get a bigger destroyer, maybe two or three destroyers and become a division commander, then he'd make squadron commander. This was the kind of thing that was almost unavoidable in wartime if you were going to keep a degree of experience in all the various jobs.

Q: Advancement was so rapid, too, that that tended to change the old system.

Adm. W.: Yes. This certainly contributed to it. People who started off as lieutenant commanders at the start of the war ended up rear admirals, and advancement in the lower grades was even faster. This resulted in some amusing situations, I think, too. At the start of the war I personally had just become a commander and I had a permanent commission as a commander dated, I think, 1941. Then promotion became temporary and everybody moved up pretty fast. First, you got a temporary commission, then it became permanent —

Q: What was the time lag there?

Adm. W.: Varying amounts. The dates that were involved in these varying time periods were shuffled around in an effort to adjust interservice seniority. When we got to conducting joint operations, interservice seniority sometimes became important, so each one of the services was trying to keep people who were originally contemporary also contemporary in their advanced rank. In my own case, as I say, I had a commission as commander dated 1941, I think it was, and when I eventually came up with a permanent commission as a captain it was dated, as I remember, about 1938, a couple of years earlier than my commission as a permanent commander, which seemed a little unusual but that kind of thing did develop. We all got pretty well scrambled but this didn't seem to make too much difference. Nobody paid too much attention to rank. As a matter of fact, the further away from Washington you got, the less you cared about relative seniority. Whoever was the right man to take command was given it and in some cases he was given a spot promotion, in other cases his subordinates were just told, you take orders from him. And this worked, too, very well.

Q: Tell me a little about Admiral Randall Jacobs.

Adm. W.: I wish I could tell you more about him but I never really got to know Admiral Jacobs well. I knew him slightly over the years and served in his Bureau for about a year during the war, saw him frequently, but never really got to know Admiral Jacobs, whereas I had known Admiral Louis Denfeld well before this, I hadn't known Jacobs well. Admiral Denfeld always let me know why I was doing something and I always felt that he had given me a good picture of what we were trying to do and why we were trying to do it. Admiral Jacobs, on the other hand, always seemed to me simply to tell you what to do but never read you in as to why you were doing it. Maybe this will give you some understanding of why I never felt I got to know him well. He had a good mind and was very pleasant to work for, but you never knew what he was thinking, and for my money this made it a little difficult to try and do the job because you had to work by inference rather than by any clear-cut understanding of where you were going.

Interview No. 7 with Vice Admiral Charles Wellborn, Jr., U.S. Navy
(Retired)

Place: His apartment in the Westchester, Washington, D.C.

Date: Friday morning, 7 April 1972

Subject: Biography

By: John T. Mason, Jr.

Q: It's good to see you this morning. I'm sorry that you're a bit congsted, but I don't think it will hamper your singing at all!

Adm. W.: We seem to have some bad weather and that may be a greater drawback than the allergy problem.

Q: We're going to deal with your tour of duty as the skipper of the battleship Iowa. I think you went aboard her in July of 1945, leaving the Navy Department for this purpose.

Adm. W.: That is correct. I don't recall the precise date but I left Washington and headed west and as I left Washington I was ordered simply to what was known as "the large ship Pool", I believe it was, or maybe "battleship and cruiser" command pool. At this stage of the war prospective commanding officers of the large surface ships, other than carriers, were ordered out to CinCPac to a command pool —

Q: Rather exclusive!

Adm. W.: Well, yes, it was a rather small pool, and the individuals who were ordered to it, went to Pearl Harbor and at that time waited until some ship needed a new commanding officer, and were then ordered to a specific ship. So, when I left Washington I had orders only to the command pool. As I remember it, traveling by train from Washington to California, we got to about Denver or so and got a telegram delivered to the train ordering me specifically to the Iowa. Her previous commanding officer, Jimmy Holloway, who later was CincNelM and chief of Naval Personnel, was being detached for some other duty and this was the first ship that became available. So I was very fortunate in the first ship becoming available at the time I did being one of the large fast battleships. So I went on out from the point at which this telegram was delivered to the train to I believe it was San Francisco and from there flew on to Pearl, and at this point waited for just a day or two until some ship that had been in Pearl was going out to join the operating ships in the western Pacific. This turned out to be the cruiser St. Paul which had been in for some minor repairs of some kind, and I boarded her and went out with her to join I guess it was the Third Fleet that was operating at that particular time. No, wait a minute, the Fifth Fleet, because Admiral Halsey was in command and the carrier task forces were operating under Admiral Mitscher.

Q: Had Willis Lee left the Pacific by then? He had the fast battleships at one time.

Adm. W.: Yes, I believe he had left and he was now in a training command. He had come back to take charge of some of this sort of thing. I don't remember for sure just what it was but

Q: ComDevFor.

Adm. W.: Yes, he was out of the fast battleships by this time. I went on out in the St. Paul and we joined up with the Iowa which was operating with the ~~fast~~ Task group that was commanded by Admiral Radford, and I transferred from St. Paul to a destroyer then from the destroyer over to the Iowa all underway.

Q: Did Holloway turn over a happy ship to you?

Adm. W.: Oh, yes. I rode with him for a week because there was no way of getting him off the ship until we went back for another refueling. Several days later we retired from the operating area and at this point he went off by high line to a destroyer and then from the destroyer to some ship - I've forgotten which one - that was coming on back to Pearl.

So I joined the Iowa and took command entirely at sea. We didn't get to port before the change of command and, in fact, the first time that the Iowa while I was in her came to anchor was in Sagami Wan, just south of Tokyo Bay, after the surrender. We stayed under way the entire time from my taking command until we anchored off the coast of Japan. But, to be somewhat more responsive to your question whether the Iowa was a happy ship, she was indeed, well organized and a going concern. It was one of those happy situations in which really all the skipper has to do is smile and keep everybody doing what they were doing!

We had as our flag officer embarked the division commander, Admiral Oscar Badger. Arthur Radford, as I say, was the tactical commander of our particular task group. I was really very much impressed by him as a tactical commander. I've sailed with a lot of them in both peace and war time and I felt that that task group of his tactically was handled with more precision and more effectiveness than any other one I've ever sailed in.

Q: Did he have an entirely different way of operating from what most men did?

Adm. W.: I shouldn't say it was so much different as it was more alert and more responsive to whatever situation arose, and promptly responsive. He seemed to me to react correctly and promptly to whatever happened and there was a degree of decisiveness that isn't always present in officers in tactical command.

Q: Can you think of something specific to illustrate that point about him?

Adm. W.: During the course of normal air operations there's a good deal of changing of course, sometimes changing of access [axis], in the formation, ships are being moved around from one plane guard station to a screening station and things of this kind more or less constantly, and in handling these he seemed always to know precisely what he wanted to do and the directions that came from the tactical commander, usually by voice radio under these circumstances, were quite clear, the signals that directed these various movements were invariably accurate and directed what he wanted, and this isn't always the case with tactical commanders. They sometimes make mistakes. When you turned into the wind, it was into the wind, it wasn't ten degrees off the wind! Things of this

Sort. When you went in for replenishment day he always knew which ships he wanted going up to the tankers and the supply ships first, the order was clearly established, and it was always well thought out, so that you didn't end up with no operating carriers at any time and no heavy support ships available to be used if necessary, your screen always was intact during the whole operation. The whole thing was carefully thought out and -

Q: Is Admiral Radford a good chess player?

Adm. W.: I never played chess with him but I suspect he is.

Q: When you joined the Iowa were you to be part of the Coronet Operation, or what?

Adm. W.: At this particular time the heavy battleships were being used primarily as a heavy protective screen both against possible surface ships and against aircraft because they had tremendous antiaircraft fire power around the carriers and the carrier task forces. As I remember it, there were about five fast carrier task groups at that time and the available battleships and cruisers were spread around among these groups. There would be, say, four carriers, maybe two battleships, and three or four cruisers in each of these task groups with a screen of twenty or twenty-five destroyers, and occasionally the battleships and cruisers might be sent off for independent operation. I recall just before I arrived in the Iowa they had gone up to bombard some steel plants that were located on the coast of Japan. They went up there separated from the carriers, delivered this bombardment, and then rejoined the carriers. But primarily they were heavy support ships for the carriers. One of the places they bombarded was Hitachi - the names of the others escape me, but they were steel plants, as I recall, that they had bombarded on that mission. There were some more of these being planned but the surrender made them unnecessary.

Q: You were in Tokyo Bay at the time of the surrender ceremony, were you?

Adm. W.: Yes.

Q: Would you describe that?

Adm. W.: Yes. We did our normal carrier task group operation until the ceremony, and I recall that first none of us in the ships knew that the atomic bombs were to be dropped. Our introduction to this was a message that came through directing that the carrier air operations in certain areas should be restricted and we should not get in the way of those particular flights. We didn't know what those flights were involved in but we did know that we had been told to stay out of the way of certain operations. Then, very promptly after the nuclear weapons were delivered it became public knowledge as to what was going on.

Q: You are quite adept at the deductive message. When you were in personnel you were aware of something too in the background that was unmentionable. Did you begin to put these things together?

Adm. W.: Yes, these things began to fall into place when you had associated certain names with a high-priority operation that got any person that was asked for and some of the names again were mentioned when nuclear weapons finally were delivered, and it became pretty apparent that this was what had been getting the high priority. But very promptly after those weapons were delivered, the surrender process started. The first thing we got on this was a message that Admiral Halsey sent out to the fleet. He apparently had gotten one in a higher classification, a more closely held cipher, that told him what was going on. The message that he passed on down to us was that a surrender offer had been accepted and he followed this statement with a suggestion that we must continue to be just as alert as we always had been and in the event of Japanese air attack on the fleet we should shoot down the attackers in a friendly sort of way. I've always remembered that message very well - shoot down the attackers in a friendly sort of way! You probably have heard this same message quoted by other people.

After that we had really nothing to do but steam around for a little while, but very promptly after this, in a matter of a day or so, plans were formulated for taking the fleet into Japanese waters and participating in the acceptance of the surrender. This involved transferring lots of Marines from one ship to another and of course at that time each one of the heavy ships had a Marine guard on board, maybe sixty men or something of this kind. Each one of these Marine guards was transferred from the ship in which it had been serving to one - I think they had a little transport out there that took them. I don't recall just what ship finally got all these Marines, but they formed a task force of Marines who were to go in and occupy the Japanese shipyard and naval base at Yokosuka. So we spent a couple of days one ship going alongside another ship and transferring the Marines, then when they got them concentrated in the second ship it would transfer them somewhere else. This took quite a while and during this time the planning was going forward for the taking over of the Japanese base at Yokosuka. The job of commanding that operation was given to Oscar Badger whose flag was in the Iowa so the people in the Iowa had quite an active part in this particular planning. I recall that while ships had been going alongside one another for replenishment for a long, long time and had gotten pretty expert at it, normally the big heavy ships just went alongside tankers or supply ships, smaller ships. When this operation started there had been no instance of one 45,000-ton ship going alongside another 45,000-ton ship, but we did it in that particular operation. I recall spending several hours alongside the Missouri, a sister ship of the Iowa, during which we transferred our Marine guard to the Missouri and we also transferred various kinds of equipment that was to be used in the Yokosuka occupation. So there was real pioneering going on there.

Q: Did that afford you any anxious moments? Lying beside the Missouri?

Adm. W.: Not really. It was a first time, but those ships handled beautifully. They were rated as 45,000 tonners. Actually, when you went to sea they displaced 53,000. They handled like destroyers

They had lots of power and great flexibility. Of course, a lot of inertia, too. When you once got one turning, she'd turn inside of a destroyer, but it advanced something on the order of a thousand yards at, say, 15 knots before the ship really began to transfer to make its turn. You simply went sideways. Your stern would swing out when your rudder went over and you'd move sideways for 500 yards or so, then gradually you'd begin to move off into the new direction. But once you got turning, you turned beautifully if you just remembered you got a long advance before you'd begin to translate sideways, then those ships were a joy to handle and going alongside another big ship really offered no problem at all.

I left out one interesting feature of the Iowa command. While we were at sea in the period before the surrender, by this time we had scores of press representatives in the fleet, all of whom were writing thousands of words, and this verbiage had to be transmitted somehow back to the United States and the means that had been evolved was that it was all transmitted by short-wave stuff, not long-distance type radio that could be picked up other than in the immediate vicinity, to the Iowa. In the Iowa we ran an operation where this was all collected and then transmitted on a medium frequency by a very long-range, high-power radio back to San Francisco. This was an interesting operation because when you warmed up that transmitter that went on the air, it radiated enough energy to completely flood the radar screens. They were just full of trash and you couldn't see any of the pips that you normally used for a great many purposes, detection of possible air attack, keeping station in formation. All your radars were simply jammed by this press transmitter, and it transmitted maybe twelve hours a day or something of this kind. While this was, of course, something that very definitely could be used for direction finding and fixing the position of the fleet, by this time we didn't care very much about that. We had such overwhelming power there that we were pretty confident of being able to defend the fleet even if they did know exactly where we were --

Q: And there weren't very many Japanese ships extant, were there?

Adm. W.: No, there was very little that was able to mount an attack on us, so this angle didn't bother much. But the tactical one, at night particularly, steaming around at high speed in a formation of big, heavy ships without the use of radar, we'd become accustomed to by that time. It occasionally did get a little bit exciting.

Q: Were the other units of the fleet aware of your difficulty?

Adm. W.: Yes, they knew about it, but we didn't feel that that gave us any privilege of running anybody down. We managed all right. This involved your watch officers becoming quite expert at estimating distance and bearings and courses of other ships without the use of radar. We had to revert to the way we kept station pre-radar.

Q: And you were a little rusty in that area!

Adm. W.: Yes. This was something people hadn't done very much over the past two or three years, but the art was revived and the watch officer did it very well. We didn't collide with anybody.

Q: You must have had to augment your staff of communicators, didn't you, to handle all this traffic?

Adm. W.: Yes. There was some augmentation of the radio people who handled all of that type traffic. I can't recall just how large a group it was. Not very large because a good deal of this was typed on tape and fed into a machine that did the transmitting.

Q: Did this operation (added to your duties) put you in touch with Fitzhugh Lee?

Adm. W.: Not directly. He, of course, we knew about.

Q: I was thinking he had over-all supervision of this.

Adm. W.: Yes, and, you see, we spent all of this time that I was in the *Iowa* at sea and had no contact with Pearl or with Guam. We were out there and the only contact we had was by radio, so I had no real contact with Fitz Lee at that time. We would get our orders on what to do and go ahead and do it.

Q: He had to handle the headaches, dealing man to man with the press!

Adm. W.: Exactly. He had all that. Of course, we had our quota although there weren't very many press people actually in the *Iowa*. Our augmentation was largely the communicators who handled the traffic that the press people wrote.

Q: That was a rather unique assignment.

Adm. W.: Yes, I thought it was quite interesting.

Q: Who dreamed that up?

Adm. W.: I would expect that this one came about at a pretty high level. The people who were actually operating in the forward areas tended not to consider the press a very desirable adjunct, but when you get into the higher levels of military command and into the even higher political levels of national command, then public opinion and press activities assume greater importance in your mind. So I would guess that this whole scheme was evolved at a relatively high level, one that had weighed the tactical disadvantage against the psychological advantage, and it had been determined that this was the way we'd do it. But at this time I had no access to the councils in which this kind of decision was made. But I got diverted with it and probably should get back to the surrender.

Q: All right, Sir.

Adm. W.: Well, for this a tremendous armada of ships of various kinds first went into Sagami Wan, which is a little bay just south of Tokyo Bay, and the ships anchored there overnight. As I recall this, the carriers with a destroyer screen remained at sea operating just in case this surrender involved some perfidy. But the surface ships, the battleships and cruisers for the most part, went in to Sagami Wan, and anchored there overnight. We remained darkened and continued in condition of readiness watch. We were still at war insofar as the ships were concerned, but we did anchor there overnight, and then at first light in the morning this armada got underway and steamed in to Tokyo Bay. As we did this we didn't have our main battery guns actually loaded, but we had ammunition on the loading trays and we could have opened fire very quickly if necessary.

Q: We, as a military force, couldn't conceive of the power of the emperor's orders?

Adm. W.: No, and it was simply prudence. Certainly that was the way I interpreted it, and I think that was what the fleet commanders who were superior to me had thought. We hoped that the Japanese were perfectly sincere in their surrender, we didn't know and we were not going to get caught again, as we did at Pearl Harbor. If they weren't sincere, then we were going to be ready to open fire. So we went in to Tokyo Bay completely ready for action. Of course there was no action and no resistance. The Missouri, Admiral Halsey's flagship, as I recall it, led the way in with a couple of destroyers screening ahead of her. Iowa was second in the column, right behind the Missouri. It's a narrow channel, so necessarily we were in a column formation as we went in. We anchored I guess it was more or less off of Yokohama. Iowa was anchored a thousand yards south, down the bay from the Missouri, and we lay there for a day or two, I guess. General MacArthur flew up from the Philippines and a group of military people - I've forgotten what it was now, maybe the First Cavalry Division, came in - an Army unit, at any rate, as a security force to accept the preliminary surrender and to take charge on the mainland of Japan.

MacArthur came up quite early in the game, and Admiral Nimitz flew in to Tokyo from Guam. They were both ashore in the Yokohama vicinity to begin with. It seems to me the name of that airport was Haneda, but I wouldn't be too sure of that. In due course, they were brought out in a U.S. destroyer and went aboard the Missouri for the actual signing of the surrender. The Japanese signers came out in a Japanese destroyer. The American ship actually went alongside the Missouri and General MacArthur and Admiral Nimitz walked across a gangway, a brow, from the destroyer to the Missouri. The Japanese destroyer, however, we did not think should be put alongside the Missouri directly. There, again, there was a chance for perfidy that we didn't want to take, so she just lay to a thousand yards or so off the Missouri. This introduced a little bit of a problem. There was quite a good sized party to be handled and in those days, of course, ships didn't carry much in the way of ships' boats. They had all been put ashore because they were fire hazards, and it ended up by, as I recall it, they used the Missouri's little skimmer boat. We did carry one small boat maybe twenty-five feet long that was a reasonably fast boat that planes on the surface. The Missouri had one of these -

Q: A hydrofoil?

Adm. W.: Not quite a hydrofoil, but one in which the hull of the boat skims the surface rather than ploughs through the water. At any rate, the Missouri had one of these and the Iowa had one of these, so our two boats were used to transfer the Japanese party from the Japanese destroyer, the name of which I can't remember, but it's in the records, I'm sure, over to the Missouri. All my crew got quite a lift out of having provided the boat in which the Japanese surrenderers were transferred to the Missouri.

Q: I suppose there's a certain amount of symbolism involved in that, too, is there not?

Adm. W.: Yes.

Q: In the fact that they came in a lesser way?

Adm. W.: I think that there was a certain amount of this. General MacArthur, particularly, was a master of this kind of theatrics.

Q: Of the nuance.

Adm. W.: Yes. I don't say that in a derogatory way because I think that was important.

Q: It certainly turned out to be in his command of their land.

Adm. W.: Yes, and he started out having complete command of this kind of psychological effect. The party came aboard and the table at which the surrender was signed was located on the forward level just above the fo'c'sle, just about abreast the bridge, and ships were swung in such a way that I, from my bridge, with a pair of binoculars could observe it very clearly. It was all broadcast to the fleet. General MacArthur was in basic charge, with Admiral Nimitz more or less the co-chairman of the ceremony. This whole thing was broadcast by our Navy communication circuits from the Missouri to all the other ships, so we could hear it all, and I could see it through binoculars from my own bridge. So I had a good maybe not firsthand but at least second-category view of the surrender ceremony.

Q: More comfortable, perhaps, than perched on top of the turret!

Adm. W.: Possibly so, yes, and the skipper of the <u>Missouri</u>, Sunshine Murray, at that time, had some pretty heavy responsibilitie for arranging all the details of the ceremony and making sure that everything went off smoothly, whereas I was simply a spectator. I didn't really envy him his position of having it take place on his deck.

After this, the occupation progressed pretty rapidly. I don't recall now whether Admiral Badger took his occupation party ashore the minute we got into Tokyo Bay or waited till after the surrender ceremony, but I believe he went off immediately and took over the base at Yokosuka and he was actually over there at the time the surrender was signed. That operation went off quite smoothly and with no opposition. The Japanese carried out their part of it in perfectly good faith and everything seemed to go very smoothly.

One of the highlights of that surrender ceremony that I will never forget was the display of air power that was put on - this again now was psychological warfare, I think at its best. We still weren't completely sure of Japanese good faith in the surrender, so there was ordered an air review to take place immediately after the signing. All the Super Forts that the Army Air Corps could muster first flew over the Tokyo Bay area where the surrender took place, and then we had, I think it was five carrier air groups each one with about four carriers and maybe averaged eighty planes per carrier. This adds up to quite a lot. But this great mass of carrier airplanes followed the Super Forts over the bay. If there was any doubt in anybody's mind about who had the air power over Tokyo Bay at that time, it certainly must have been dispelled by that display. You've heard of ducks and geese blackening the sky, I'm sure. Believe me, those airplanes that flew over Tokyo Bay blackened the sky that day.

Q: The roar must have been —

Adm. W.: It was, and they flew at rather low level. Maybe two or three thousand feet. I always thought that was a fine example of the right way to use psychological warfare. But shortly after that, the main body of the ships that had been in Tokyo Bay started moving around to various places. There were several task groups set up to go to various parts of Japan and take charge of various naval bases and to determine where there were minefields, what sea-lane were clear, and generally get into the sweeping-up operation.

Q: What about the operational charts for all of these things? Did our intelligence make them available?

Adm. W.: Yes. The Japanese turned over pretty complete information on these things, but at this stage of the game, of course, this involved a lot of reproduction of charts to provide them to the people who needed to know. And there was also still an element of suspicion. Before we accepted a Japanese chart at face value, we felt we had to check it out and make sure that there was no deception involved in it. This was a time-consuming process, but it went forward expeditiously.

Q: One might call that a supreme illustration of the inability to understand the Eastern mind, I suppose?

Adm. W.: Well, yes, and this to a degree was, I think, proved there. I think all of us at that time had the same feeling that was developed, you recall, in the little boy whose father set him up on the dining room table and told him "jump down and I'll catch you." Then he didn't catch him, in the effort to teach him not ever to trust anybody. We felt we'd learned our lessons about the Japanese, don't ever trust 'em. It developed after the surrender that they were pretty trustworthy, but our comprehension of this hadn't yet been substantiated, hadn't developed and been substantiated so we were still checking everything out before we believed it.

Another thing that I think contributed to this was the fact that there seems to be a tendency on the part of the Japanese people to find out what answer to a question the questioner would like to receive and then give him that answer. It wasn't during this period that I had experience with this. It was later when I was the chief of staff of the Fifth Fleet and I found repeatedly when you asked a Japanese official for information he would do his best to find out what answer you'd like to get and then give you that answer rather than give you a factual one. I think that this tendency on the part of the Japanese contributed to our skepticism in accepting things that they told us. We were definitely skeptical. There wasn't any doubt about that.

Q: A very proper role for the military, wasn't it?

Adm. W.: Yes, I think it was really quite proper and I hope we never lose that kind of skepticism.

Q: One can see more readily this being the role of the diplomatic representatives to accept it for what they report it to be.

Adm. W.: Yes, and I suspect it's more appropriate for the diplomat to be somewhat more trusting than it is for the military individuals.

At any rate, in the Iowa we eventually got Admiral Badger himself back on board after the actual occupation of Yokosuka was completed and he turned over command of the base to Commodore Kessing - Scrappy Kessing, quite a well-known character in those days. Admiral Badger returned on board and in due course we sailed from Tokyo Bay with another group of ships down to Okinawa. By this time the clamor had developed in the United States to get the boys back home.

Q: It didn't take long!

Adm. W.: No, it didn't. It was a matter of days. So, we went down to Okinawa where we had a considerable force that was to be got back home. We went into Buckner Bay, which is a pretty tight little bay for a ship the size of the Iowa, incidentally, and there we picked up about fifteen hundred Seebees whose function in the war was now complete and who wanted to get back home and get demobilized. The Iowa was designed for a crew of, maybe, eighteen hundred to begin with and by the time the end of the war came we actually had something like twenty-five hundred on board, and when you put another fifteen hundred Seebees on board we were really crowded.

Q: You immediately became a part of the Magic Carpet, then?

Adm. W.: Yes, but the Magic Carpet name had not yet been dreamed up, but this was the first effort of the Magic Carpet enterprise. I recall that particular passage as being interesting when we left Buckner Bay with our Seebees and with some other ships headed back to Pearl Harbor. We had about twice as many men in the ship as she was designed to carry. Feeding them wasn't much of a problem, you could feed them in shifts. Sleeping them was a much greater problem because there weren't enough bunks to go round and we had to do what was called "hot bunking." When one man got out of a bunk, somebody else got into it.

Q: Sleeping around the clock!

Adm. W.: Yes. But the real problem with this voyage was neither eating nor sleeping. It was keeping those men occupied. The war was now over. You had no problem in discipline as long as they were fighting the war and knew that there was a certain amount of hazard involved in being out there in the Western Pacific, they'd be alert, they'd stand good watches. Now the war was over, there weren't any more hazards, they all wanted to get out of the service and get back home, particularly those Seebees who were not noted as being the best disciplined people in the world anyway. They had nothing to do. They were passengers in the ship. So our main problem became maintaining a reasonable degree of discipline in an overcrowded ship with lots of people who had no duties and nothing much to do.

Q: Too crowded for any kind of deck sports or anything like that?

Adm. W.: Yes, you couldn't do anything like this. We did arrange all sorts of things. Anybody who had an idea presented it. The term "brainstorm" hadn't been developed, but we did just that. We brainstormed for how can we keep these people busy, and we came up with lots of odd ideas. We had gymkhanas in which there were tugs-of-war on the deck and races around the weather decks - just name it and we tried it.

Q: How long a trip was this?

Adm. W.: A couple of weeks, I guess. We came back, I think, at 15 or 18 knots. It takes a long time to cross the ocean from Buckner Bay to Pearl Harbor. We didn't have any real trouble. A good many crap games interrupted and some things of this kind, a reasonable amount of insubordination which the police petty officers seemed to handle pretty well. Eventually, we got into Pearl and there the boys had a chance to go ashore and this caused a certain amount of disciplinary problems. A good many of them hadn't had anything to drink for quite a while, so they made up for it when they got ashore, but this really wasn't too severe. About what you'd expect, and we weren't there very long. We were there a day or so provisioning and fueling, and then headed for Seattle.

Q: You didn't have any miss the ship?

Adm. W.: Nobody missed the ship! Of course, there was another passage with nothing to do and we again had the problem of trying to keep people occupied, but eventually we made Seattle all right.

Coming into Seattle we had one amusing problem with the berth that had been assigned us. At low tide, right alongside the pier there were only about thirty feet of water and we were drawing about thirty-seven feet.

Q: Was it a crowded harbor? Was that the reason?

Adm. W.: No, the slips had been used. They were really intended for merchantmen and supply ships had been going in alongside and th water was adequate for them, but there had been some silting right under the foundations of the pier, so there there was only about thirty feet of water, whereas out in the middle of the dock between the two piers there was forty feet. We finally had to solve that one by bringing in some barges that were maybe forty or fifty feet wide, putting the barges up alongside the pier, then putting the Iowa alongside the barges to get her breasted out into the middle of the channel where there was adequte water to keep us afloat. But we got in alongside finally there —

Q: That's a hazard of occupation for the skipper of a ship.

Adm. W.: Well, that's what you're paid for. We finally got her moored and got our Seebees off the ship very promptly and, in fact, we got a lot of our own crew off.

Q: You mean they were demobilized also?

Adm. W.: Yes, many were demobilized the moment we hit the United States. There was a system of points very promptly established.

war so that it could be put into effect immediately the war was over. We began discharging people very promptly. Then some public relations angles developed.

We got in to Seattle somewhere about the 23rd of October, on that general order, and Navy Day was the 27th of October. So orders came for Oscar Badger to go somewhere to make a Navy Day appearance, and orders came for me to go to Davenport, Iowa, for a Navy celebration - a Navy Day celebration. So very promptly after getting the ship alongside of the pier in Seattle, I took off for Davenport, Iowa, where we had a very pleasant celebration. One amusing thing developed there. Back in the 1900s or thereabouts we had had an old battleship named the Iowa, and she was about three hundred feet long, I think, but at that time it was the custom for the state for which a battleship was named to present to the ship a complete silver service set, a punch bowl and a lot of punch cups and various kinds of platters and trays and things, and they were very ornate and, in those days, were considered very expensive. What they paid for them in those days seems ridiculously small now, but the state of Iowa had bought and presented the original battleship Iowa this ornate, typical "gay nineties" design silver service. This silver service had gone into retirement somewhere after the original Iowa had been decommissioned and, of course, my Iowa had been commissioned during wartime when ships didn't carry a silver service, but now that the war was over, the silver service originally presented to the old Iowa by the state was resurrected and part of our ceremony during Navy Day in Davenport was as a token to re-present the silver service from the state of Iowa to the new ship *Iowa*. Of course, she wasn't there so the silver service couldn't actually be delivered to her. Subsequently, there were two or three more presentation ceremonies. They eventually got the silver service and the ship matched up and re-presented the silver service to the ship. I think that was in San Pedro, California. At any rate, this silver service is probably about the most thoroughly presented token of esteem that we've ever had. It was presented a number of times. It was a beautiful outfit, although the design of it was definitely a dated design.

After this I went back to the ship. Admiral Badger didn't get back in time for our next movement, so it developed that I had to take charge of the group of ships and proceed from Seattle down to San Pedro. We went down there and lost a lot more men. It eventually got to the point where the ship operated under something of a hazard because we didn't have enough men left who were fully technically qualified.

Q: Did they have to double up in jobs?

Adm. W.: Yes, somewhat.

Q: This created an administrative headache, didn't it?

Adm. W.: Yes. Of course, at this stage of the game the ships weren't doing anything too much, so the fact that you were short-handed wasn't as important as it would have been if you'd been operating. At any rate, I left the ship very shortly after arriving in San Pedro. At this period, promotions to flag rank were handled not by formal selection boards, but by sort of an informal polling of the flag officers who were operating in the fleet.

Q: That was a wartime expedient?

Adm. W.: Yes, it was a wartime expedient. The flag officers operating in the fleet had the best contact with the captains who were coming up into range for promotion. So you never really knew when you were selected for promotion to flag rank until all at once you were, and this happened to me. After really a rather short period in command of the Iowa I was promoted out of her.

Q: Just July to October!

Adm. W.: Yes, much to my disappointment because commanding one of those beautiful big ships is something you look forward to.

Q: That was your great command, wasn't it?

Adm. W.: Yes, that was it. I was relieved by a classmate, Captain Entwistle, in San Pedro, and went out to Japan again. I was ordered to duty as chief of staff to the commander, Fifth Fleet. Meanwhile Admiral Towers, who had been the deputy commander to Admiral Nimitz, really managing the logistics of the Pacific war, had been ordered to relieve Admiral Halsey as commander of the Fifth Fleet. The Fifth Fleet was given the assignment of carrying out the Navy's part of the occupation of Japan, so my orders were to go out and relieve Admiral Ramsey who had taken the place of Admiral Carney. Carney was Halsey's Chief of Staff, then Admiral Towers came out and Admiral Ramsey relieved Carney and became Chief of Staff to Admiral Towers, but there was a new assignment for him very promptly and I turned up available at the right moment so I was sent out to be Admiral Towers' Chief of Staff in Japan. I thought I'd finished my Japan duty when I got out to Tokyo Bay. Not at all! I went right back to Tokyo Bay.

Q: This is a good example of that wartime rule that the aviators in command ...

Adm. W.: Yes, this was a fine example. One of the reasons Ramsey had to be relieved was that he also was an aviator, and they didn't want him as an aviator as chief of staff to Towers, who was another aviator.

So, back I went, and this was the point in my career at which I learned this Japanese proclivity for trying to give you the answer that the individual thought you would like to hear, rather than the factual answer. We had a great deal of trouble with this, but eventually we began to understand it and could pin people down and say - look, don't give us a pleasant answer, give us facts.

Q: Isn't it a part of their code of being courteous?

Adm. W.: Yes. It's part of Japanese courtesy to try to tell people what they want to hear.

This turned out to be an interesting experience. I had an opportunity to fly around the various parts of Japan - Kyoto and, of course, Tokyo we saw a good deal because we had to confer with our opposite numbers in the Army who were located in the area. After a reasonably short time Admiral Towers was again relieved from his job with the Fifth Fleet and ordered to be CinCPac at Pearl Harbor. Admiral Nimitz, you recall, came back to Washington and took over as chief of naval operations from Admiral King, and at this point

Admiral Towers - I believe there was a brief interlude when Admiral Spruance was CinCPac, but shortly after this Admiral Towers came back and became CinCPac, and Admiral Frederick Sherman was ordered as Commander, Fifth Fleet. At this point the job was downgraded from four stars to three stars, and Frederick Sherman took on the command of the Fifth Fleet. I stayed with him briefly, but Admiral Towers had asked me if I would like to come back and join the CinCPac staff in Pearl Harbor.

Q: Was that a combined command at that time?

Adm. W.: CinCPac was, yes. I told him I would like to do it, so I was ordered back, not as chief of staff now, which was a rather senior job. I didn't have the necessary seniority for that one, but I did come back as the deputy chief of staff for plans. I was relieved by Admiral Mac Bledsoe as chief of staff for Admiral Sherman.

Then I was around Pearl Harbor for a couple of years as the planning officer for Admiral Towers and, in due course, Admiral Towers was relieved by Admiral Denfeld as CinCPac and I continued on as planning officer for a while and then pretty soon there was a change in personnel and I fleeted up to be chief of staff to Admiral Denfeld.

Q: A kind of a musical chairs period, wasn't it?

Adm. W.: Yes, there was a great deal of changing around because there were a good many people who were retiring and there were a number of deaths. Admiral Lee died quite suddenly, Admiral Mitscher died. There were a number of people who had been under a good deal of strain during the war and when the tension was off they seemed to have problems, usually heart attacks, but various kinds of physical ailments began to develop. I remember those two, but there were a number of others, too, who died very shortly after the war, and this plus retirement and reorganizations. A lot of the commands that were set up during the war were not applicable to the demobilization and peacetime establishment, so there was a lot of changing going on.

Q: A very fluid situation. Would you revert back to that brief period when you were with Towers in Japan and tell me about your command relationships with MacArthur's set-up there?

Adm. W.: This was an interesting period. MacArthur was, of course, set up as the supreme allied commander. He was called SCAP. I think SCAP was Supreme Commander Allied Powers, at any rate he had command not only of all of the various services from the United States, but also from any other nation that was involved. There was a little British involvement here. The Russians tried to involve themselves. They very desperately wanted to get in there and be a part of this occupation, but MacArthur resisted this one very successfully. By this time, he had some knowledge of what had gone on in Europe and that the Russians were difficult to work with in an occupation of this kind. Besides, they hadn't contributed much to the Pacific war.

Q: They really hadn't earned that right.

Adm. W.: No, they hadn't. So while we had Russians around occasion as observers, there was no Russian force involved in this occupation. There were some Australians, as I recall, and Canadians and some British, but these were all more or less tokens. This was essentially a U.S. job. But MacArthur had command of the whole ball of wax, including representation of all the services in the United States. He, in effect, was the emperor. He had a headquarters which was very largely military people, but this was probably more involved with the civil administration of Japan than it was in military matters.

Our Fifth Fleet had a relatively minor role in the occupation. It was primarily an Army job - a shore-based job. We had some naval bases that we occupied and there was a certain amount of control of shipping involved, but for the most part the occupation was a U.S. Army affair.

Q: Were you there when the survey of strategic bombing was inaugurated - I mean the naval part of it?

Adm. W.: Yes. They operated pretty independently. We provided them support.

Q: You provided facilities on the Ancon, didn't you?

Adm. W.: Yes, but we really didn't have much to do with their studies or the results of their studies. We were their logistics, but not much else. I think that was the proper way to do this job, incidentally. We were there and had all the various things that they needed, but we simply provided them to them. When they needed some air transportation, we could produce it for them. This kind of thing. But they were supposed to be an independent study group and there wasn't any command influence on what they found.

Q: Well, it was a kind of play-it-by-ear operation, I gather.

Adm. W.: Yes.

Q: They discovered info and documents and so forth.

Adm. W.: Yes. Our intelligence people cooperated a little bit, but the point I was trying to make here was that we did not control how they went about their studies and, while we expressed our views to them, to various members of the committee, we didn't try to determine in advance what they were to find.

Q: That remained for when the report came to Washington!

Adm. W.: Yes. I think it was pretty objectively done.

Q: Were there any other interesting aspects of that brief tour in Japan?

Adm. W.: I'm trying to recall now - that's the reason for my hesitation - whether there was anything else. One human interest story - are you susceptible to having that kind of thing taped?

Q: Quite.

Adm. W.: During the course of the original occupation, the Marines took over a little airfield at Yokosuka - I can't remember the name of the field now, but it was a relatively small one - and Colonel, then, Munn took over command of this airfield. Well, it was, of course, manned by a lot of Japanese people who spoke no

English, and he spoke very little Japanese, but during the course of the original occupation he found a young boy, maybe twelve, thirteen years old, who had been stranded there and the Japanese had been more or less taking care of him on the base - a little Russian Jewish boy named Isaac Shapiro, whose parents were musicians. They had been in Japan with a muscial company when the Russians got into the war and I'm not sure what happened to the parents, but at any rate little Ike ended up on this airfield acting as a kind of messenger boy for the Japanese.

Well, when Toby Munn came in to take over command of the airfield, here was Isaac Shapiro who spoke fluent Japanese and fluent English, as well as Russian.

Q: Three languages!

Adm. W.: Yes, and he was a godsend in managing that little airfield and in due course they became very much attached to one another. After a certain time Colonel Munn was transferred from the airfield there at Yokosuka to Pearl Harbor and became a member of Admiral Towers' staff. By this time, he was so attached to Ike that he brought Ike along with him. At first, this was just kind of an informal arrangement, but in due course it was all regularized. I think he never formally adopted Ike but he became his guardian or something and for a couple of years Ike lived with the teen-aged children of all the rest of the officers around Pearl Harbor. When he got through the high-school stage, Toby Munn by this time a general, sent him through college and at the present time Ike is a very successful practicing lawyer in New York City. General Munn, of course now retired, is living out in California but he and Ike have maintained a close relationship through the years, and I have maintained a kind of a precarious relationship with both of them.

I don't recall anything else particularly that might be of interest during that stay in Japan.

Q: What were your impressions of Admiral Towers as you served with him in that close capacity?

Adm. W.: I thought Admiral Towers was a very able person. He was not a particularly easy person to work with, but I always had a very high respect for his capability and good, clear, logical mind. When confronted with a problem he analyzed it and came up with what to me seemed to be the right answer. Socially, he was very pleasant indeed, but I never quite knew how he was going to react to a specific problem. He was a little unpredictable, I thought. When I say "unpredictable" I mean —

Q: There was no definite pattern that —

Adm. W.: No, and this had to do with the details, his own personal reaction, whether he was angry or pleasant, whether he wanted quick action or wanted to think it over a bit. My feeling was that he always arrived at the right decisions, but I never quite knew through what process he was going to arrive at it. I'd have been very happy, though, to see him as the commander of any kind of an operation. He was highly capable. But some of the other people I have served with were easier to work with and to understand than he was.

Q: When you came back to Pearl on the planning side of his staff, what was the job chiefly?

Adm. W.: Of course, during the course of the war, you had very largely operational plans that were to be executed, and then you had to make a new operational plan. The situation after the war was somewhat different in that you had no warlike operations to conduct or plan, but what you had to do was to get out a plan that would cover the more or less administrative tasks of reducing all your great base structure to what you wanted for peacetime, to establishing the routines for all of the Western Pacific, and these plans existed only in the minds of some of the commanders. There wasn't anything on paper.

Q: No guidelines came out from Washington?

Adm. W.: Well, yes. You'd get some direction from Washington on what was wanted, but it all had to be produced and put on paper. None of it existed in the way of contingency plans that had been reduced to writing. This whole thing was a process of evolving the orders under which we were going to live during that period of demobilization and the commencement of peace.

Q: It called for quite a shifting of gears, didn't it?

Adm. W.: Yes, it did. For instance, during the wartime operations there was really no need to separate the joint command, that is, the CinCPac, as it became later known, from the strictly naval one, the one that became known as CinCPacFlt. One operation order did for the whole business. With the advent of peace, though, it became necessary to separate these two functions in the planning. You had one set of plans that had to do with the joint effort, and the joint effort really got to be minimum, and you had another set of plans that had to do with the strictly naval effort. And the strictly naval plans had to stem from your joint plans, and your joint plans had to be so drawn that they covered the mission of the Army elements that were in your command. Of course, the Air Force hadn't yet evolved, and the Marine Corps came under the Navy component plans.

So there was some technical involvement in drawing up the right plans, but this was a technical task. It wasn't a very difficult one compared to the planning for wartime operations. It was really lots easier. The principal thing that was involved in the execution of these plans was demobilization of the great big bases scattered all over the Pacific Ocean, and there were LSTs and various other kinds of craft scattered all over the Pacific Ocean. We were required to demobilize the men and if possible get the ships back, but our orders at this period definitely were when the men's points entitle them to discharge they'd leave their ships and come home. If the ship gets immobilized at anchor, leave it there. This happened to quite a number of ships. Out in the Western Pacific their crews dwindled down to the point where they couldn't be operated, and the ships were simply anchored and the few that were on board left them.

Q: What about the wisdom of such a precipitate move?

Adm. W.: My personal view as part of the executing force of this procedure was that it was most unwise. It, of course, was a bowing to public opinion at the time. The country wanted the boys back home, and we got them back home.

Q: Emotionalism!

Adm. W.: Yes, it was a highly emotional thing. The ships could have been brought back in a pretty orderly way without a great deal of delay, two or three months maybe, in the discharge of the men involved. But leaving the ships out there, they deteriorated pretty rapidly and getting them back involved then sending other ships out and either manning them or towing them in and, in some cases, disposing of them by giving them to the Japanese, the Chinese, or the Filipinos. It didn't seem to me that this was a very wise thing. We had no discretion in it. We were simply told to get the men back, and we did.

Q: It could be a situation bordering on the chaotic, couldn't it?

Adm. W.: It came very close to it. This was our greatest problem. I remember Admiral Towers used the expression in his morning conferences he didn't want to hear any more about counting LSTs. One of my jobs was to keep track of how many LSTs we had that were operable, how many we had that were inoperable, where they were, and to make some sort of provision for disposing of them one way or another. It got to be, unless you were deeply immersed in these figures, an exercise that didn't have much meaning because there were three of them here and two more there and they were scattered all over the Pacific, many of them inoperable. So the Admiral decided, don't bother me any more with counting LSTs!

Q: The waste involved in a program like this was -

Adm. W.: Oh, a horrible amount of waste.

There was another operation going on during this period of trying to salvage various materials from the bases that had been set up.

Q: The roll-up.

Adm. W.: Yes, the roll-up of the Pacific bases was an enterprise that Admiral A. J. Wellings headed up. This was another one that was pretty chaotic, trying to decide what was worth bringing back and what could be just left on the spot. If you left it, what to do with it, was something that had to be handled both judiciously and expeditiously because your people to do these things, to do the roll-up job, were disappearing very rapidly.

Q: Weren't there some prohibitions also placed on what could be brought back for commercial reasons?

Adm. W.: That's right. There was a story circulated at the time - I never did know whether it was correct - that I thought was amusing. It seems that during the course of the war, the Chinese with pretty cheap labor built a lot of airfields in China. They built them largely with hand labor, picks and shovels and bushel baskets, and there had developed a tremendous debt which the United States was supposed to owe to China for the laborers building all these airfields.

Q: The minimum wage applied?

Adm. W.: Yes, I think so. Anyway, this was known as the Yuan Debt, and the story went that the United States had no intention of paying this Yuan Debt. In the meantime, the United States had developed a tremendous amount of surplus property on all sorts of islands in the Pacific where we had bases, and, as you pointed out, some of this stuff couldn't be brought back for commercial reasons and some couldn't be brought back for the reasons that there weren't enough people left to do it, some wouldn't be brought back simply because they weren't worth bringing back. It cost more to bring it back than it was worth. So we had a lot of surplus material scattered all over islands in the Pacific. Then somebody dreamed up the brilliant idea that in return for the cancellation of the Yuan Debt, the United States Government would turn over to the Chinese government all this surplus material out on the Pacific bases, which they could salvage or not, as they saw fit. Well, with the price of Chinese labor what it was, it apparently was an economically feasible operation for the Chinese to salvage a lot of it. And the story went that we cancelled the Yuan Debt, which we had no intention of paying anyway, in return for a lot of surplus material which we had no use for. Then the Chinese Government turned it over to various Chinese contractors who made a very handsome profit out of it.

As I say, I don't know whether this whole story's true, but I think it's an amusing one and more or less illustrates the way we got the Pacific rolled-up.

Interview No. 8 with Vice Admiral Charles Wellborn, Jr., U.S. Navy
(Retired)

Place: His apartment in the Westchester, Washington, D.C.
Date: Friday morning, 14 April 1972
Subject: Biography
By: John T. Mason, Jr.

Q: We're about to begin Chapter 8 of your very interesting story, Sir. I think you have some more to say about your period as deputy to CinCPac in Pearl Harbor - chief of staff, actually.

Adm. W.: During the earlier period I was deputy chief of staff for plans and when Admiral Denfeld relieved Admiral Towers I moved up to be chief of staff. As we commented on before, at this time when you had an aviator as a commander, his Number Two always was a non-aviator and so forth, and in the hierarchy at CinCPac when Admiral Towers, an aviator, was in command his deputy commander was a non-aviator, his chief of staff an aviator, and the Number Four man, which I was, as deputy for plans, was a non-aviator. Admiral Denfeld relieved Admiral Towers. Admiral Denfeld was a non-aviator and his deputy commander, the Number Two, had to be an aviator, his chief of staff a non-aviator, and his deputy for plans had to be an aviator. So I moved up into the Number Three job from the Number Four one and became chief of staff.

This was a relatively uneventful period. We just kept on doing the things that we had been doing.

Q: No enemy!

Adm. W.: No enemy, no war, and by the time Admiral Denfeld got out there the roll-up of the bases and the Magic Carpet business was pretty well in hand, so this became pretty much of a routine operation, keeping the fleet maintained and keeping it in the places where it had to be for routine peacetime control of the Pacific Ocean.

Q: Was there any morale problem as you had to face the rapid demobilization and all of that? Did this constitute a morale problem that CinCPac dealt with?

Adm. W.: As I recall it, this really wasn't what I'd call a morale problem. There was a problem of keeping your ships effective because you had lost so many trained people that there weren't enough left to go round, and the problem became one of training up new people to man your ships effectively and to keep them going. My recollection of this period was that morale was pretty high. Everybody was pretty happy. There was no more war. The tension of wartime operations was gone and the tempo was much slower than it had been in wartime, so as I recall this period it was a pretty happy one. We thought we were going to get back to the same kind of peacetime that had prevailed in the early thirties. This didn't develop, of course. The Cold War came on. But during that early period after the war, 1946 to 1948, we seemed to be in a period where we were going to go back to real peace. So, as I say, my recollection is that morale was pretty good.

Q: Were there not some postwar investigations, again a congressional one, on Pearl Harbor, and did you get involved in that in any way at all?

Adm. W.: I was not involved in that out there in the CinCPac command. As I recall that one, all of this was done here in Washington.

Q: Yes, it was.

Adm. W.: And they really didn't bother us very much with it.

Q: I imagine that life in the islands was very pleasant at that time, immediately following the war, was it not?

Adm. W.: It was, indeed. During the war, of course, there had been quite a lot of recreational facilities established - both officer and enlisted clubs located on very desirable beaches, and many perquisites of this kind that had remained after the war was over. At this point, there hadn't been any taxpayers' revolt to try to eliminate all the pleasant things that went with the military life and a good many of them remained. So in this atmosphere of hoping for the return of real peace and of a pretty good sufficiency of the things that tended to make life pleasant, it was really quite agreeable in Pearl Harbor during that period right after the war.

Q: You must have been reluctant to leave!

Adm. W.: I was, indeed, although my personal reaction to Hawaii has always been that the longer you stay there the smaller the island gets, so I was about ready to come back to the United States at the end of my tour. That, of course, came -

Q: December 26, 1947.

Adm. W.: Yes. Here, again, it resulted from a change in command. Admiral Denfeld came back to Washington to become chief of naval operations and I came back at more or less the same time to fit into a slot that existed there in the Navy Department. This again was related to aviator and non-aviator possibilities and to various other personnel considerations. But I was due to move anyway. I had to be relieved as a result of the change in command, so it fitted in very nicely all round.

Q: You were deputy chief of naval operations for administration?

Adm. W.: Yes.

Q: What does that entail?

Adm. W.: Well, it is a job that no longer exists. At the end of World War II, as a result of a good deal of planning and some legislation, the office of the chief of naval operations had been organized with a chief, a vice chief, and five deputies. My particular one was that for administration which had originally, I believe, been intended to include intelligence, communications, administration, naval history, Naval Observatory, hydrographic office, and a lot of miscellaneous activities of this kind. There had been a period of more or less continuing change and when I got there I had the office of naval communications, I had naval history, I had the Observatory, I had the hydrographic office, and I had naval missions which, at that time, were mostly in Latin America, and I had the administration of island governments, the trust territories in the Pacific, primarily, and the routine administration of the office of the chief of naval operations there in Washington involving appearance before Congressional committees for our appropriation to support the necessary civilians, who were primarily secretarial in that particular office, but not entirely secretarial. This, in general, is what that job amounted to.

Q: Perhaps you'd talk about some of those categories, one by one? What about the trust territories and the island governments?

Adm. W.: This was a quite interesting phase of the business at that time. The Navy Department was still charged with this administration, although there were plans for turning it over to the Department of the Interior and we were working toward that eventually.

Q: Why would the Interior qualify for this?

Adm. W.: Traditionally, Interior had always administered territories that belonged to the United States but were not states of the United States. They had administered Alaska and Hawaii. Oh, various territories which had not achieved statehood. There had been two exceptions to that general rule in the early days, Guam and American Samoa, and the Navy was administering those along with the trust territories. But all the political side of the federal government seemed to feel quite strongly that this kind of governmental activity belonged in a civilian agency rather than a military one, and although we had been given this trusteeship primarily on the basis of strategic considerations, it still was felt by the high levels of the government that this was a civilian function rather than a military one. There were also some differences in philosophy of how this trust territory should be managed that came to light, and I think that the high levels of civilian government here again were on the side of the Interior Department's philosophy. In the military departments, certainly in the Navy Department at that time, our philosophy was one of letting the natives on those trust territory islands retain their current culture to the greatest extent possible and to limit ourselves as largely as we could to improving their health and to giving them the things that they needed to sustain life, knives, hardware, tools, this kind of thing, providing these things for them, but not trying to do what I think some of the press now calls "bringing them into the twentieth century." We felt that they were probably better off in their particular environment following their current culture. The people in the Interior Department felt that it was an American obligation to make American citizens in every sense of the natives of these islands, to bring them into the twentieth century.

Q: Make them wear clothes and so forth!

Adm. W.: That's right. So we were somewhat at variance in our approach to what the problem was. Eventually the administration of the islands was turned over to Interior, but during my incumbency there the Navy Department did retain it.

Q: The governor was a military governor then?

Adm. W.: The governors in some cases were military and in some cases were civilians. But this was administered through the commander-in-chief of the Pacific. I've forgotten which hat it was. I think commander-in-chief Pacific Fleet, but it was the same individual, anyway, who was the high commissioner of the trust territories at that time. Then, of course, he had commissioners in the various areas and on the various islands who actually did the job.

At that time one of the biggest problems was transportation. There, of course, were no commercial ships operating in the trust territory. There were a few airfields on some islands that were holdovers from military airfields used during the war, but on a good many of the populated islands there were no airfields. We had to use sea planes or amphibians to get in by air, and we had to provide surface shipping through the service force. Eventually, as I recall it, we did acquire some small ships, supply ship types, to operate on a schedule throughout the territory. This transportation was necessary if the natives on the islands were to acquire any income at all. Their income mostly from copra, but we had to get the copra out and the only way to get it out was through the ships that we were providing.

This was the type of problem that had to be dealt with during that period.

Q: What developments were there in the Office of Naval History?

Adm. W.: The Office of Naval History was working at that time most importantly on the 14-volume history of U.S. naval activities in World War II which Professor Sam Morison was writing. We had a contract with him to do that work, and that contract had to be renegotiated a time or two due to inflation and new problems that arose, and the original costs involved simply weren't adequate to support the people that had to work on it. So there was some renegotiation of that contract.

We also had a couple of other contracts for history. One was to be an administrative history of the Navy Department. This one was not progressing well. The Morison contract was making what I thought was plenty of progress and it turned out very well. The administrative history did not make good progress and eventually this contract was canceled, and to my knowledge we never did turn out an administrative history of the Navy Department.

Q: What was the concept there?

Adm. W.: The concept was that this history should cover the activities of the Navy Department during the war - cover its organization, its reorganizations, the people that came and went, the problems that arose. It was essentially a history of the Washington activities of the Navy as opposed to the operating forces of the Navy that Sam Morison was writing about.

Q: I got some of that for you from Henry Williams, who was prominent in running the physical —

Adm. W.: Yes, he was indeed. He was primarily a Bureau of Ships man, as I recall it.

Q: A naval constructor.

Adm. W.: Yes. This history that I am discussing was intended to cover all the activities of the Navy Department and really how the Navy Department's activities were related to the larger picture of the Washington scene. I don't believe this one ever was very successfully completed. There were little parts of it that did get completed. But we had difficulty. This wasn't as glamorous a subject as the operating forces and I think there were a lot of problems in writing this kind of history.

Q: It was bound to be overshadowed by the 14-volume one!

Adm. W.: Yes. At that time, the Navy historical section, too was working on the assembly of documents and things of this kind, the kind of things that historical sections always want. But I think our main projects were these two histories.

Q: Was the foundation in existence then?

Adm. W.: I don't believe it was, no. It came about some years after I left the job of deputy for administration. My memory is a little vague on just when it did start. At any rate, it was not very active if it was in existence. As I recall it, somebody did have Decatur House, so it must have been in existence, but it wasn't exerting a very strong influence at that time.

Q: What about the hydrographic office? Was the Navy beginning to be concerned about coeanography?

Adm. W.: To only a minor degree at that time. The hydrographic office at that time was still mostly involved in the production and distribution of charts and navigational tables and equipment. Ther was some little effort along research lines, largest related to temperature gradients in sea water and things of this sort that affected antisubmarine warfare. But we hadn't got to the point where oceanography was an important aspect of the hydrographic office and what it was doing. They were still principally producers and distributors of charts and navigational equipment. They had moved out of the Main Navy building and had established themselves in new quarters in Suitland, Maryland, but the emphasis had not yet developed on underwater science. You could see the faint beginnings of it but it didn't amount to very much.

The Observatory, similarly, was just sort of beginning to expand and develop as it has now developed, but it was still primarily located at Observatory Circle on Massachusetts Avenue and was involved in the publication of star tables and maintaining the standard time, the kinds of things that it had done traditionally. It at the end of the war was beginning to feel the need for some of the field stations that were established, but it was still basically on Massachusetts Avenue.

Q: What relationship did you have with the Weather Bureau at that time?

Adm. W.: Weather was not in my jurisdiction. Weather in the office of the chief of naval operations was a part of the deputy chief of naval operations for air's jurisdiction, as I think is quite understandable. They were the ones who had the primary interest in weather, so all of our aerological effort and our tie-in with the other branches of government that were interested in weather were through the DCNO, Air. This had a relationship to hydrography and to the Observatory, but it was sort of on a liaison basis that we worked with them.

Q: What about communications?

Adm. W.: Communications were definitely within my jurisdiction at that time and, here again, communications were relatively speaking a lot simpler than they are now. We had managed our worldwide communications during World War II on a basis of, of course, no satellites and getting along pretty much with what we had when the war started. We were thinking in terms of some new high-powered, low-frequency transmitting stations for primarily submarine communications and there was some development of the very high frequencies for relatively secure short-range communications, but at this particular period electronics hadn't quite expanded to the degree it has now. And, of course, money was hard to come by at this particular period for any kind of new installations. We were trying to cut back what we had after World War II rather than to build up very much new.

So, in communications, while we were developing some new ideas, we weren't able to finance very much of this, so communications sort of got along on pretty much the basis that it had existed during World War II. There was a certain amount of security effort attached to communications.

Q: You mean the subject of codes?

Adm. W.: Yes, codes and ciphers, both. What you might call

defensive codes and ciphers and some offensive work against other people's codes and ciphers.

Q: That continued in the postwar era?

Adm. W.: Yes, this continued during the postwar period. Of course, there was no Department of Defense at this time so our work with the Army and with the other branches of government was on a coordination basis. We had pretty friendly relations with them, a certain amount of rivalry, but in this particular field I think they got along pretty well. They had some agreements about which particular governmental branch would handle which particular problem and while, as I say, there was some rivalry there wasn't much bloodletting. I thought it worked reasonably smoothly then. I also thought pretty effectively.

Q: Did you say intelligence was under your jurisdiction?

Adm. W.: No. Intelligence, before I arrived, had been moved. The original concept of intelligence was that it would be a servant not only of plans and operations, but of all the parts of the office of chief of naval operations. And I think this was a pretty sound concept. But it very promptly became apparent that the primary interest in intelligence was in planning and operating parts of the office of the chief of naval operations. So in due course, intelligence was moved to Op-03 which was plans and operations. Subsequently, after a considerable amount of controversy, intelligence became a more or less autonomous part of the office of the chief of naval operation and was set up directly under the vice chief, not going to any of the deputies. Intelligence has always been the subject of a good deal of controversy. Everybody wants to control it. It ended up as an agency that reported directly to the vice chief of naval operations and through him to the chief, at the same time having a chain of command that went directly to the Secretary of the Navy.

Of course, since that time the chain of command has become even more involved because the Defense Intelligence Agency has been established under the Secretary of Defense, and this involves the assistant secretary of defense and the Defense Intelligence Agency which also controls and directs naval intelligence in certain respects. So it's had a history of very involved command.

Q: Tell me about the problem of securing the necessary appropriations from the Congress. This was also in your area.

Adm. W.: Yes, and this had some amusing aspects, too. When you went before Congress to talk about a two-ocean navy and what was needed for it or to talk about very complicated new weapons systems and we were at the time, of course, somewhat involved in the nuclear weapon problem - the average congressman really had not very much understanding of the details of what you were talking about. You could talk in terms of billions and the average member of Congress simply had to accept what you said, because he had no way of contesting it.

My job, however, involved appropriations for the pay of clerks and secretaries and of employees that were understandable to anybody. It involved the purchase of the kind of equipment that went into offices, typewriters and adding machines. This everybody understood. So, whereas the deputy chief of naval operations for air could go up and ask for very large sums of money for a new aircraft that was going to be part of a new air attack system and get away with not-too-detailed a defense of his proposal, when I went up and asked for just a few typewriters or a few clerks, everybody knew what I was talking about and I had to defend them in the greatest detail. So I was subjected to quite a good deal of ribbing in the Department in the face of the detailed defense I had to make - every little item down to dollars and cents!

Q: You were talking the language of the people!

Adm. W.: Yes, I was talking a language that everybody understood, but I found congressmen usually quite sympathetic.

Q: This was before the appropriations committee?

Adm. W.: Yes. This didn't involve an authorization, so I usually had to appear just before three different groups. I always had to appear, of course, before the Bureau of the Budget and once you got by there, then before the House Appropriations Subcommittee, and once the House had passed your bill, then before the Senate Committee. This fell into pretty much of a pattern. The Bureau of the Budget was looking to make sure that whatever proposals you were making were in conformity with what was known as the Program of the President, that is, was this going to fit into his budget which he sent to Congress early in the year. Then when you got to the House, there were a few other considerations, how many employees were going to come from whose district, and so forth, but generally they were pretty reasonable about this. The House nearly always as a matter of principle made a few cuts in what you were asking for. I think probably their basis for doing this was that everybody padded his appropriation requests a little bit and it probably could stand maybe a ten or fifteen percent cut without being hurt. At any rate, there were always some cuts there.

Then, when you went over to the Senate side, the normal drill was to ask the Senate to restore some of what the House had cut, and they quite frequently were sympathetic to this. By this time, the particular order of priorities had been pinpointed and you had an opportunity to put some stress on them, and while you usually didn't come out with the full amount that you had requested originally in the House, some of it normally was restored and you came out with something with which you could live.

Q: Would you say this was an efficient system?

Adm. W.: No, I shouldn't say so. I think that there is involved too much time in going over the same ground. Checks and balances are fine things but to have justified this appropriation in the first instance with your own Navy budget officer, who was always trying to get within a ceiling, then to have done it for the Bureau of the Budget, then to have to go and re-do it to two subcommittees of the Congress seems to me to be more effort, more expensive effort, too, than was necessary.

Q: Redundant, too, wasn't it?

Adm. W.: Extremely redundant, and it's even worse than it was at that time in the present day, because now you have all of the steps that I've outlined and you have an additional one of the Department of Defense analysis of your proposal. So we've progressed I think in the wrong direction in this respect.

Q: That was a very interesting job, I would think.

Adm. W.: It was, quite interesting. Since that time, of course, the job has been revised out of existence. The various elements of it have changed and many of them became independent. Communications acquired a status like that of intelligence and not under any of the deputies. The island governments, of course, went to the Department of the Interior, and the naval missions became part of a larger organization and reorganized out of this office.

Q: So did hydrography?

Adm. W.: The hydrographic office also expanded and acquired a relatively independent status. So a lot of the things that I used to do went elsewhere and subsequently, oh, a number of years after I left, that particular deputy's job was reassigned to I believe it was research at that time, which was expanding, while this administrative office was losing a good many of its functions. So the person who does some of this work now is now called assistant vice chief of naval operations, and he operates directly under the vice chief with somewhat limited functions as compared with what the office had back in my day.

But it was an interesting assignment. There were few dull moments. Of course, there always in any big organization has to be some office that does anything that nobody else wants to do! And this was part of my job. It didn't belong to air or to operations or personnel or to logistics, so it must be administration! So I caught all the dogs and cats. If we had to conduct a drive for the American Red Cross, well, that was mine. It had its amusing moment as well as its important ones.

Q: Well, in January 1952, I see, you went to sea once again.

Adm. W.: Yes. I had been trying for some time to get to sea. During this period, of course, we had what was known as the revolt of the admirals, the great controversy over the B-36, the Air Force airplane, and at this time the Department of Defense came into existence and there was a lot of organizational shuffling back and forth. We had a good many changes in people in the Department. Admiral Denfeld, who had brought me into this job, was summarily dismissed after having been re-appointed, as a result of the so-called revolt of the admirals.

Q: How much before his dismissal had he been re-appointed?

Adm. W.: Just a matter of a month or two. He had originally been appointed for two years, rather than what had been the custom, four. Then he was re-appointed for another two but he –

Q: He fell from grace!

Adm. W.: He fell from grace and was summarily dismissed.

Q: Did you get drawn into that controversy at all?

Adm. W.: Inevitably, to a certain extent, but my particular assignment in administration didn't involve me in the heart of the storm, so I could view this one somewhat more objectively than could, for instance, the deputy for plans and operations or the deputy for air.

Q: But you were close to Admiral Denfeld.

Adm. W.: Yes. I was in that group of a limited number of deputies and things who had to keep pretty close track of what the boss was thinking.

Q: So how did he react to this whole thing?

Adm. W.: Well, he had felt that his advice was not being accepted at face value or at full value, the value due it, in the councils of the Joint Chiefs and his reaction to this whole interservice disagreement was one of "anger" is maybe a little too strong - certainly frustration, and he simply was very unhappy about the situation as it existed. I think he had a very good relationship with Congress and with the civilian elements of the government outside of the military, but I think he felt that this fact tended to produce in some of the people within the military establishment a feeling maybe of both envy and distrust. So he had his problems within the Department.

Q: Had he, up to the point where he was dismissed by the President, had he enjoyed a good rapport with President Truman?

Adm. W.: Yes, although by this time we had a Secretary of Defense, of course, and the relationship with the President was nowhere nearly as close for the chief of naval operations as it had been back in 1939 and 1940.

Q: With Admiral Stark?

Adm. W.: Yes. There were a lot of intervening layers between the chief of naval operations and the president, so I never felt that Admiral Denfeld had the close contact, close relationships, with Mr. Truman. Now, at that time - Mr. Forrestal, of course, was the first Secretary of Defense and his concept of the job was to form a policy and direct it with a very limited staff. His first staff consisted only of half a dozen people. He tried to adhere to this but I think inevitably the people around him and the forces that impinged on him pushed him into assembling more and more people and getting his fingers into more and more details, with the result that by the time he left office the office of the Secretary of Defense was no longer just an office, it had gotten to be a pretty big department and it was directing a good many affairs.

Then, when he was replaced by Louis Johnson, Mr. Johnson's concept of the office never had been one of a small policy organization and he continued the pretty rapid expansion of the office of the Secretary of Defense. I think all of these developments resulted in less and less contact between the chief of naval operations and the president.

Q: It was no longer being at the other end of the telephone.

Adm. W.: That's right. It now became a case of you had to work through the Secretary of Defense.

Q: Would you say that Admiral Denfeld had anticipated what happened when he took this firm stand on the B-36?

Adm. W.: Yes. I think that he had not for any great length of time anticipated that the matter would come to a head as it did, that he would be forced to take a position either on one side or the other. I think he had hoped for quite a long while that the matter could be resolved in an amicable way without an actual confrontation, but shortly before the final explosion I think it had become apparent to him that he could no longer hope for anything except a direct confrontation.

Q: What caused it to get out of control?

Adm. W.: I think this was a combination of personalities and of the objectives of the various services. At this time, the Navy's position was pretty much that it wanted to remain as independent as it could with the Forrestal concept of the office of the Secretary of Defense as a policy agency, with the Joint Chiefs as a coordinating agency for plans and operations. The Army, on the other hand, was holding out very strongly for what then was referred to as "merger" - make everything one big department. The Air Force, while the Army was fighting for merger, was fighting for autonomy from the Army and were busy dividing themselves off from what was originally the War Department and later became the Department of the Army.

So there were three departments that had conflicting objectives and there was Mr. Forrestal who, as the first Secretary of Defense, had one concept of what the office should be, and there was Mr.

Johnson who followed him and had an entirely different concept. Mr. Forrestal had been in the Navy Department before this, during the wartime period, and I think he had really pretty good relationships with military people. Mr. Johnson came in, on the other hand, and his attitude seemed to be that, as you read in the press pretty frequently, "we're going to have to knock some heads together." And he was not a very patient listener to the military points of view. He had his own decisions pretty well organized, and wasn't much interested in hearing other points of view. So there was a change of attitude here.

I think all of this contributed to what happened. You may recall that the Navy secretary at the time was Mr. John L. Sullivan and he was out of Washington - I've forgotten just where now, but on some kind of an inspection or public relations tour - and he first heard of some decisions that affected the Navy Department through the press while he was away from Washington. He was furious about this and submitted his resignation. At this point - a new secretary eventually was appointed, Mr. Matthews from Omaha, Nebraska, I believe, at any rate the middle of the country - and the story that was published was that Mr. Johnson and Mr. Truman had hunted around for somebody that had had no previous contact with anything larger than a rowboat. Mr. Matthews took over the Navy Department with this background and he came in with an attitude of considerable skepticism. He apparently had been briefed that he mustn't believe everything he heard, and this certainly was his attitude during his early days in office. Anything that you told him had to be very thoroughly documented and before it was accepted had to undergo very careful scrutiny. I think this change of command in the Navy Department contributed to the whole thing, too. He was feeling his way, and I think - in fact, I'm sure - when he finally left office he had developed very considerable confidence in the people in uniform and, with the knowledge he had then, would have handled the situation somewhat differently in his early days. But the fact remains that when he first came in he did have a certain degree of lack of confidence in the people with whom he had to deal.

I think Admiral Denfeld taking a strong position in the controversy with a secretary who had just arrived and had a skeptical attitude was part of the picture of his dismissal, too.

Q: There was pretty much unity within the ranks of the Navy, though, on this subject?

Adm. W.: Pretty much, yes. It was not completely unanimous, but, generally speaking, the Navy certainly overwhelmingly felt that its position was right and that it should retain its autonomy to the greatest degree possible. Of course, at this time there were a couple of facets to the whole controversy that were considered of very great importance to the Navy and I think there was almost complete unanimity. The Air Force, of course, was proposing that when it split off from the Army it should take over jurisdiction of anything that flew. Well, I think the Navy pretty unanimously felt that naval aviation was necessarily an integral part of the Navy and that the Navy would be ineffective without it. Similarly, the Army had its eye on the Marine Corps. It was in its plan of reorganization proposing that the Marine Corps cease to exist and simply be absorbed by the Army. We'd have one land force, just as the Air Force was proposing one air force.

I think the Navy was, maybe, not quite as unanimous on this proposition as it was about naval aviation, but it did feel that an effective navy should have a Marine Corps of some sort and that turning over the Marine Corps to the Army would be a naval disaster of considerable proportions.

So, while on all aspects of the controversy there was not complete unanimity, there was a good degree of it all right in the Navy. I think the differences of opinion revolved more on what steps should be taken in trying to save naval aviation and the Marine Corps than to retain as much autonomy as possible. This was the point of disagreement rather than the objective that the Navy was pulling for.

Q: I expect the most prominent spokesman for air was Radford, wasn't he?

Adm. W.: Yes, he was. He at that time was vice chief of naval operations and then became CinCPac during the latter stages. I think he was CinCPac at the time Admiral Denfeld was dismissed. He originally when the controversy developed had been the vice chief of naval operations, but he was pretty much the spirit of the handling of the controversy in the Navy Department. When he left to become CinCPac he was relieved by Admiral John Dale Price and even though he was no longer in the Department he continued to exert a very great influence on the thinking there. He and Admiral Price were very close and consulted on all these things during this period. So I think you're absolutely correct in saying that he was a very important factor in this controversy.

Q: It must have seemed rather good to get away from the vortex!

Adm. W.: Yes! Well, this had subsided somewhat before I got away. You see Admiral Denfeld was relieved by Admiral Forrest Sherman and his approach to the problem was somewhat different from the one that Admiral Denfeld had chosen to take under the - I wouldn't say quite "guidance," but advice of Admiral Radford. Admiral Sherman took one of "conciliation" isn't the right word, but of thoughtful discussion rather than confrontation.

Q: But he didn't relent?

Adm. W.: No. As a matter of fact, I think that he was probably more successful in his efforts than the previous administration had been because the controversy died down and it was possible to discuss these things in a much more reasonable atmosphere. Of course, Forrest Sherman was a master of this kind of negotiation. So I think he was quite successful in handling the problems as they arose. He got the roles and missions pretty well ironed out for each one of the services. We still have a Marine Corps and we still have naval aviation, although at one time, before his arrival, there was a document seen on the desk of the Secretary of Defense which did away with the Marine Corps and re-assigned all the Marine Corps activities to the Department of the ARmy. This document never was put into effect, but it was prepared.

Q: It didn't pertain to naval aviation though?

Adm. W.: No. So far as I know there was never such a document prepared on naval aviation, but it was very clearly proposed and advocated by many in the Department of the Air Force.

Q: Symington was one of the –

Adm. W.: He was Secretary of the Air Force at this time, and he was a very active proponent of the Air Force having jurisdiction over everything that flew.

Under Admiral Sherman, though, the controversy resolved to a much more reasonable negotiating basis, and I think the roles and missions that were determined at that time are pretty much still in existence. There may have been slight variations, but not very much. I think they were pretty well drawn.

I served with Admiral Sherman, then, for some time –

Q: Continuing in the same – ?

Adm. W.: Yes, continuing in the same job, and, in due course, talked him into letting me go back to sea. I was there from 1947 to I think it was 1952.

Q: January 1952.

Adm. W.: Yes. That was longer than a normal tour of duty there.

Q: Not by much. It was only a couple of months.

Adm. W.: Yes, but it was somewhat longer and it was prolonged somewhat by an interesting activity that was going on in the Department of Defense. You will recall that at about this time the Department of Defense had proposed a budget of something like thirteen million dollars and Mr. Johnson, as Secretary of Defense, set up something that he called the Management Committee, which was supposed to pare the appropriation for the Department of Defense to ten million dollars. Those figures seem ridiculous today but this was the fact.

The Management Committee was composed of General Joe McNarney as the chairman and the personal representative of the Secretary of Defense, and either an Under or An Assistant Secretary of each of the three departments, Army, Navy, and Air Force. It was supposed to hunt around through all of the departmental structures to find areas where costs could be cut, unnecessary "fat" could be eliminated, and so forth. At this time the Navy Department felt that to put General McNarney in there as the direct representative of the Secretary of Defense was not giving the Navy enough voice in the operations of the Management Committee, and so in due course the Navy got an agreement that it could send a deputy chairman to General McNarney, and I got tagged as being the deputy chairman of the Management Committee working with General McNarney. This involved some interesting tightrope-walking because I had two hats. One as the deputy chief of naval operations for administration, and I spent my mornings at this usually, and for the operation of this particular job I had to have knowledge of the thinking in the Navy Department, including the controversial thinking. Then mostly I spent my afternoons with General McNarney, where to serve as his deputy on the Management Committee I had to have knowledge of the thinking of the Secretary of Defense on what should be cut, where and why, and in each case the knowledge was supposed to be closely held. The people in the departments were not supposed to be privy to the thinking of the Secretary of Defense, and, of course, the Secretary of Defense was not supposed to know until it was properly disclosed to him what the thinking of the Navy Department was on the controversies.

So, here I sat with a foot on each side, and this called for some very delicate evaluations, but I arrived at an understanding with both Admiral Sherman and with General McNarney that in this particular assignment I did have access to knowledge on each side which was privileged knowledge, but that my proposed way of handling this was going to be that privileged knowledge of this kind I would not disclose to the other side, but that it would be legitimate for me to warn either side that a proposed action would probably result in either favorable or unfavorable reaction on the other side. I think my principal utility in this particular role was in doing this - having knowledge of what was going on in the minds of each side of the controversy, not disclosing the details of it, but simply warning each side "look out, hoist the red flag, you're heading for trouble on this one."

That was an extremely interesting assignment.

Q: How long did this go on?

Adm. W.: This went on for, I guess, the better part of a year. The thrust of it changed somewhat. During the early days the Management Committee decided it needed consultants and it hired Robert Heller and Associates in Cleveland. They appeared with a considerable number of management experts and provided a good deal of advice to the Management Committee. But during the course of the effort to cut the budget from thirteen to ten million, the Korean War started. As a result of this it very promptly became apparent that we couldn't cut that budget, we were going to have to expand that budget, and so the thrust of the Management Committee's effort was redirected from cutting the budget to ten million dollars to more effectively using the dollars that were appropriated.

Q: You were a very flexible committee!

Adm. W.: Well, at this point, I think we could give a good deal of credit to Robert Heller Associates who came up with "a bigger bang for a buck" as the new objective. So the Management Committee did redirect its efforts. We ceased trying to get down to ten million but we continued in our efforts to pare away the fat and prevent "unnecessary duplication and overlap." Those were words that were used ad nauseam in those days.

Q: Didn't you about this time also lose the Secretary of Defense?

Adm. W.: Yes. Mr. Johnson developed some problems and his effectiveness declined for some time. He eventually was hospitalized, as I recall it, and we had quite a series of secretaries of Defense in that period. I've forgotten just who replaced him.

Q: How did you keep abreast of the thinking of the Secretary of Defense? I mean you, as an individual. What were you privy to in order to do this?

Adm. W.: The Secretary of Defense had conferences periodically.

They weren't daily nor were they weekly, but something in between. He would call his group in on call. This comprised his assistant secretaries and his various "family" of whom General McNarney was one, and I very frequently went with General McNarney to these meetings. And this provided you with a pretty good insight into what his thinking was. What his strategy was, first, for getting the budget down, then sometimes even in detail what he thought was a vulnerable area for reduction.

General McNarney was quite close to Mr. Johnson and while I never achieved this kind of closeness I did get by direct contact to a degree and an even greater contact vicariously through General McNarney, a pretty good understanding of what Mr. Johnson was all about.

Q: What was McNarney like?

Adm. W.: An extremely interesting person. A very keen-minded old Scotsman. A very rough exterior. He could be one of the toughest cross examiners of people who were coming up to present cases that I've ever run across. He was very keen at picking the flaws in any kind of a presentation or the holes in an argument. I remember first when I was assigned to this duty -- I didn't know the General and I asked somebody who knew him what he was like. Well, he described him more or less as I have, and I asked, "Has he a sense of humor?" And this person thought a minute, then said, "Yes, if it hurts somebody it's funny." Well, this was his view, and when I first went to work with General McNarney I had tentatively accepted this view. But I found that wasn't correct really. The

General had a delightful sense of humor where it didn't involve hurting anybody, but he gave this impression of "General McNarney, he don't like nobody," and I think he did this quite deliberately.

Q: He wanted to scare people!

Adm. W.: Yes. He actually was a very kind and considerate person and for my money a very able one who had deliberately chosen to project this image of gruffness and disagreeableness. But he was a very keen and a very tough thinking individual, and he was the man for that job on the Management Committee to pare down the appropriation all right.

Q: Well, the service of this management board went somewhat awry, didn't it, with this Korean War?

Adm. W.: Yes. With the advent of the Korean War really it became redundant and unnecessary, and it was abandoned in due course, but more or less as a face-saving proposition after so much publicity had been given to the effort of improving the management and reducing the budget of the Department of Defense, it couldn't be eliminated completely immediately.

Q: And I take it that subsequent secretaries of defense were not so concerned with pinching pennies as was Johnson?

Adm. W.: I think that's correct. When the Korean War started, it was, I think, quite apparent that we were never going to get back to the kind of peace that we had had in the thirties, that we were going to have to maintain a strong military establishment. So the main thrust of the Management Committee at its inception was pretty much outdated, and with the requirement for a military establishment that was able to intervene in conflicts around the world. The idea behind the Management Committee just was inappropriate, so it died pretty much a natural death, but it was an interesting operation while it was going on.

Q: I'm certainly glad you told me about that, I didn't really know. Were there any other facets to this interesting job?

Adm. W.: I think that pretty well covers the activities at the time.

Q: Tell me about your relationship with Admiral Forrest Sherman?

Adm. W.: I had never been really very close to Forrest Sherman. I had known him a great many years. He and I had served at the same time in the old Bureau of Ordnance under Admiral Stark. He had been the head of what was known as the Aviation Ordnance section, the one that bought bomb racks and bomb sights and such things, and I had been, first, a subordinate and later the head of the ammunition section. So we had worked fairly closely together there although we had never become intimate friends. I continued friendship with him, but not a close one over the years and I always had very profound respect for his capabilities.

So when he came in to take over from Admiral Denfeld, we knew one another and I'm sure I had great confidence in him. I don't know whether he had in me or not. I was never that close to him. But at least he kept me there for a reasonable period of time until I finally talked him into letting me go to sea. My relationship with Forrest Sherman, I'd say, was not the kind of a close one that I had with Admiral Stark, for instance, or Admiral Denfeld.

Wellborn #9 - 302

Interview No. 9 with Vice Admiral Charles Wellborn, Jr., U.S. Navy
(Retired)

Place: His residence in the Westchester Apartments, Washington, D.C
Date: Wednesday morning, 26 April 1972
Subject: Biography
By: John T. Mason, Jr.

Q: Well, Admiral, once again as we begin your story back in January 1952 you achieved your burning desire to go to sea. You were put in command of Cruiser Division Four. Will you tell me about its complexion and where you served, and so forth?

Adm. W.: Yes. Of course, going back to sea is always something that any good old sailor enjoys and Cruiser Division Four was one of those very pleasant ones. As I recall it, I relieved Rear Admiral Murray Stokes in Norfolk, Virginia, aboard the cruiser Salem.

Q: She was your flagship?

Adm. W.: She was originally but she very promptly had to go into the shipyard for overhaul and I shifted to the Worcester and stayed in her for the rest of that tour of duty. She turned out to be a very satisfactory flagship. She was one of two ships that differed from almost anything else we'd ever built. They were heavy-cruiser hulls, that is something on the order of maybe 14,000 tons, but their armament, rather than being 8-inch guns which was normal for a heavy cruiser, was a battery of 6-inch double-purpose guns. The

Roanoke and the Worcester, as I recall, were the only two ships of this class that were built.

Q: When were they built?

Adm. W.: They must have been built in the late 1940s. They were conceived during World War II days with the object of producing some heavier caliber projectiles for antiaircraft use than we had available in the various kinds of 5-inch guns. So these two cruisers were turned out and at this point missilery began to come in as a long-range antiaircraft weapon, and no more of thee double-purpose 6-inch batteries were produced. But they were nice ships. They were never tested in battle so we don't know just how successful they would have been.

I stayed in that ship for quite a long while.

Q: Were you attached to the Atlantic Fleet?

Adm. W.: Yes, we were part of the Atlantic Fleet, and it seems to me the first thing we did was to go down to Guantanamo Bay for a refresher training period. The Worcester had just come out of an overhaul as the Salem went in, so we went to Guantanamo Bay and went through the usual gunnery and engineering and damage control exercises of the refresher training of that day. On the completion of that we started off on a Mediterranean tour of duty, which, of course, is always an interesting assignment.

Q: That was with the Sixth Fleet, then?

Adm. W.: Yes.

Q: For a period of what? Three months?

Adm. W.: As I recall, it was about six months. We arrived over there I think in May or thereabouts and got back about November, or something of this sort. So a large part of my duty in Cruiser Division Four was with the Sixth Fleet in the Mediterranean. We sailed from I believe it was Norfolk, at any rate one of our Atlantic coast ports, joined up with the carrier Oriskany and had some destroyers along, did some exercising en route to the Med, and then I think we went in to Gibraltar and relieved the cruiser division commander who had been with the Seventh Fleet, and for the next six months we operated back and forth through the Mediterranean - Greece, Crete at one end, and let's see, we visited Izmir in Turkey also. To the westward we made quite a number of - In those days the Sixth Fleet spent a good deal of time in French ports, which, I believe, is not the case any more. But at that time you would spend roughly a couple of weeks in port, then a couple of weeks at sea exercising, and when you went to sea you usually returned to a different port from that from which you had left, so that over a course of six months, you usually started from the western end of the Mediterranean and ended in the western end of the Mediterranean, and during the six months you worked back and forth from one end to the other visiting these various ports between exercises that were conducted at sea.

Some of these exercises were NATO exercises which involved forces from various other NATO nations, but for the most part they were strictly U.S. exercises. When it was a U.S. exercise, normally they were carrier task force operations with replenishment. Most replenishment was at sea. Supply ships and tankers were available and we did the great majority of our replenishment of all kinds at sea.

Q: Did the same hold true with the NATO forces?

Adm. W.: No. The other NATO navies normally did their replenishment in port. We had some French, we had some Italian, some British, they all had Mediterranean bases, so they normally did their replenishment in port. Most of those navies don't do much replenishment at sea.

Q: Did they seem to have an inclination to learn to do this?

Adm. W.: Not very much, no. I think they preferred their own methods to our replenishment-at-sea method. The British had a little experience with replenishment at sea.

Q: In the Pacific?

Adm. W.: Yes, in the Pacific, but their navy generally had been a shore-based navy. All their Home Fleet was normally operated out of their home bases and this was true in the Mediterranean for them, too. They had Gibraltar and Malta, and they didn't do very much replenishment at sea.

Q: Was Malta a port of call for you?

Adm. W.: I didn't get in to Malta during my period in the Sixth Fleet, but it was one of the ports of call in those days, yes.

Q: Did we resort to any repair facilities in Malta for our ships?

Adm. W.: Occasionally, When there was an emergency repair called for, a ship could go to Malta or to Gibraltar. Normally, our ships did a relatively brief tour in the Mediterranean, six months or so, and no routine overhaul was required. But when there was an emergency, a bent propeller or something, Malta or Gibraltar was made available by the British authorities and our ships would go in there.

In our ports of call, as a security matter, usually the Sixth Fleet would be divided. You'd have a period of exercising at sea, and there were normally two carriers there, and one of the carriers would go to one port and the other carrier would go to a different port, so that should anything unforeseen happen, like a Russian sneak attack, they wouldn't get both carriers with one bomb. At this particular time, for instance if the fleet went to Turkey, usually the Sixth Fleet commander would take one of the carriers and his cruiser flagship in to, say, Istanbul. This was the Number One liberty port in Turkey. That meant that I, as the Number Two senior officer in the fleet, would take my cruiser and the other carrier in to such a port as Izmir. In this way, the fleet was given some security against surprise attack, and of course this resulted, too, in my always getting the Number Two port so far as liberty was concerned! The fleet commander exercised his privileges and took the Number One, so I had a great string of secondary visits to various ports throughout the Mediterranean in the course of that six months.

Q: That was the period when we were active in advising the Turks and helping them to improve their military?

Adm. W.: Yes, we had very good relations with the Turks at this particular time.

Q: We had a whole contingent of American naval officers there.

Adm. W.: Yes, there were lots of American naval officers and lots of American Army and Air Force, as well, in Turkey, and there was a very friendly relationship between the Turkish establishment and our Navy. So visits to Turkey were very pleasant.

I recall an interesting occurrence when we visited Izmir. Of course, you depended very considerably on the local consul general or senior State Department representative wherever you went to advise you on matters of protocol and social activities. And on this particular visit we were entertained appropriately by the Turkish establishment, and, to return the courtesy, we were advised that it would be appropriate to have a dinner aboard the flagship, which we arranged, and the question of whether or not ladies should be included, whether this should be a coeducational dinner, came up. The consul general advised that he thought it was desirable to include the ladies, that the Turks were becoming very rapidly westernized, and that this seemed like the appropriate thing to do at this time.

So, we set up this dinner as a coeducational one and, at first, all the Turkish ladies accepted. Then, as about a week wore on, there usually wasn't very much time between the day you issued the invitation and the day of the party, the Turkish ladies began to fall ill, and one by one, we had to replace the Turkish ladies with ladies of the American community there in Izmir, and by the day of the party we were down to only one wife of a Turkish official, and when she arrived on board, it developed that she was not Turkish at all. She was Russian, but the wife of a Turk. So this effort at furthering the westernization of a Moslem nation didn't work out very successfully.

Q: What prompted the regrets?

Adm. W.: I think simply the old custom in that part of the world that the men and the ladies don't dine together. The men dine and then the ladies dine separately later. I think in the Moslem world and the Near East this custom certainly at that time was nearly universal, and it still remains. But as a gesture toward westernization, they all accept. Then they all fell ill in the meantime and didn't actually come. Whether or not, westernization has progressed beyond this, I don't know! At that time, this was the status of it.

Q: Did you put in at Haifa or places like that?

Adm. W.: I did not. Again now, the Sixth Fleet commander went in to Beirut, as I remember it, in Lebanon. I don't believe he, during my six months of tenancy there in the Mediterranean, visited any Israeli ports. But those ports at that time were being visited. He couldn't make all the ports during the course of six months, so it just happened that during our tour around that end of the Med he didn't make it.

Q: What about the former French bases in North Africa?

Adm. W.: We were not using those bases, we were not visiting them at that time. I had been in those places during World War II, but during the tour in the cruisers we did not visit any of those French North African ports. We did visit European French ports - Marseilles, Villefranche, places along the Côte d'Azur.

Q: There were no upsetting events during that period, were there?

Adm. W.: No. We had, I think, pretty smooth relationships with all the Mediterranean nations at that time. We weren't having much trouble with anybody. We visited Italian ports quite a good deal. I went in to Genoa several times. This was fortunate in that at that particular time there was some kind of a sesquicentennial or something having to do with Christopher Columbus, and one of my cruisers was the USS Columbus, named for Columbus, Ohio, but it served just as well for Christopher Columbus, so this cruiser was a great success in Genoa. There is, of course, a Columbus Museum and a lot of memorial stuff there for him, so the USS Columbus was a great success in Genoa during that visit.

Q: What was the general status of the Italian Navy at that point? What was its condition? Its readiness?

Adm. W.: I would say it was not in a very high state of readiness, but it was improving all the time. They still had ships that were leftovers from World War II almost entirely. There had been a period when the Italian Navy was pretty much in the doldrums right after the war, but they were coming back. We conducted one shore-bombardment exercise during my period in the Mediterranean with some

Italian units. As I recall it was the battleships <u>Andrea Doria</u> and a cruiser, the <u>Garibaldi</u>, and they both did their firing creditably, and they used the NATO communication procedures quite successfully. In fact, they were more accurate in their use of those procedures than we were. They took it more seriously than we did!

But I shouldn't say that at this particular time they had come back to the point of being highly effective units. They were reasonably effective, but I wouldn't have put them in the front rank

Q: How visible was the Royal Navy in the Mediterranean?

Adm. W.: It was really quite visible, but didn't have a great deal of power. We used to quite frequently run into - maybe that's an unfortunate expression - fall in with British units. They had minesweepers, for instance, that visited round the Mediterranean. They didn't have a great deal of military power but they showed the flag all right. In fact, I recall one occasion when a group of my ships was in Taranto and British minesweepers were in I believe it was Bari, one of those little ports on the Adriatic, and we got together for some kind of occasion. At that particular moment Prince Philip, who was at that time not prince consort, he was just a Mountbatten prince, was serving as the commanding officer of one of the minesweepers. This produced a rather amusing situation in which Prince Philip, as a lieutenant commander of the Royal Navy commanding one of these minesweepers, had on board as his personal aide a full eagle colonel who went everywhere with him and took care of his regal and social commitments. He was a good young naval officer, though. He handled his ship well and his crew all thought a great deal of him.

Q: Were there any other, for instance, Russian units?

Adm. W.: At that particular time, no. The Russians had not yet started operating any ships in the Mediterranean. There may have been an occasional Russian merchant ship, but no Russian naval vessels were operating in the Mediterranean. We had it pretty much to ourselves. The only Russian influence that we felt any concern about was air. They, of course, did have planes at bases ashore that could reach us in any part of the Mediterranean.

Q: This was in Arab lands?

Adm. W.: In their own Black Sea area. They had no Arab bases then. You see, at that time, the Arab countries were still sort of loosely connected with Western nations rather than with the Russians or any of the Eastern nations.

Q: That must have been a very pleasant tour of duty. Was Mrs. Wellborn there in the Mediterranean?

Adm. W.: No, she was not there. These tours of six months were such that it wasn't a very attractive proposition to try to bring your family to the Mediterranean. You made one port after another, you never stayed in the same place, and you were in port roughly half the time but when you were in port each of the two senior people, that is the Sixth Fleet commander and the cruiser division commander, devoted a lot of time to official protocol. When you came in to a port, you first exchanged calls with the local governor, and the mayor, and the senior military people in each service that was there. Then there was a certain amount of official entertaining that had to be done. They had to give us a dinner and we had to give them one. So there was really very little time for anything other than official business.

It was pretty busy. It was fun.

Q: Who was then in charge of the Sixth Fleet?

Adm. W.: Admiral Gardner, Vice Admiral Gardner.

There were a lot of amusing things. The Greek royal family, for instance, were all quite nautical and I recall when we visited Piraeus, the port of Athens, we were all together there for a day or two, and King Paul and his wife came out to a dinner I believe - conceivably could have been lunch - aboard Admiral Gardner's flagship. When the king came out, he came out in his own yacht, maybe a 75-footer, power boat, and he put her alongside the flagship himself, handled the wheel and the engine controls. He was a good sailor. That made quite an impression on the crew of Admiral Gardner's flagship, to see the king coxswain his own boat alongside.

There were things of this sort that always kept life entertaining during the course of that cruise, but there wasn't anything of very great consequence that happened, and in due course we came back from the Med to Boston. I left very shortly after the division got back to Boston to go to command the destroyer force with the flagship, the tender Yosemite, based in Newport, Rhode Island.

Q: These were the destroyers of the Atlantic Fleet?

Adm. W.: Destroyer Force, Atlantic Fleet, yes. It was the so-called type command of that day, more or less administrative. The ships of various classes were assigned to the type commanders of those classes, and for operational purposes a good deal of the time your ships, in my case destroyers, were directed to report to the Commander, Sixth Fleet, if they were operating in the Mediterranean, or Commander, Second Fleet, if they were operating as a fleet on the Atlantic coast. And when there were various other kinds of exercises, individual ships were directed to report to other commanders. For instance, when we were having exercises with the submarine force and the destroyers were providing services to them, the destroyers providing these services would report to Commander, Submarines.

So, as the destroyer force commander, you didn't actually control the operations of any of your ships. Those that were undergoing type training were under your type commander's operational control. But except for those and the ones in transit from one place to another, and those undergoing overhaul or maintenance, the ships actually operated under somebody else.

Q: The type commander is a shore-based command?

Adm. W.: It was essentially shore-based. The tender in which you had your flag was alongside a pier in Newport most of the time, although during my period in command we did make a couple of trips. We made one down to Key West for an exercise, and we went to Guantanamo Bay for training. But most of the time the destroyer force flagship stayed in Newport, and this was quite desirable because for a largely administrative command of this kind getting your mail promptly and having good communications with, for instance, shipyards, is pretty essential.

Q: How many destroyers would you have in the fleet?

Adm. W.: At that time, it seems to me, there were something over a hundred destroyers and destroyer escorts in the force. I would guess maybe there were just under a hundred destroyers and maybe twenty-five destroyer escorts. Something of this general sort.

Q: Did you come under CincLant's NATO hat?

Adm. W.: No, this was a strictly U.S. command. We were under CinCLantFlt who was the same individual as CinCLant, the NATO commander, but with a different hat at this particular time.

Q: Were there any interesting assignments for your destroyers?

Adm. W.: At this particular period in history, the Korean War had started and one of the interesting things that these destroyers did was to join the naval force that was operating in Korea. Originall when the fighting started there, of course this was Pacific Ocean and all of the destroyers that operated off Korea were from the Pacific Fleet, and in due course we proposed and action was taken to include some Atlantic destroyers in this, so that the experience of the Korean War would not be limited to the destroyer force in the Pacific but we would get in on some of that experience as well.

So we kept I believe it was a squadron, although it might have been only a division of destroyers operating off Korea. This was always an interesting cruise for the particular batch of destroyers that were doing it, because they would normally start out from either Norfolk or Newport, go through the Panama Canal, and then to Pearl Harbor, then on out to the Western Pacific, and normally return home through Suez or, I think, on one occasion we sent some around Africa. This gave them a good cruise, they saw a lot of the world, in addition to getting some experience in that particular type of operation that they got involved in in the Korean War.

Unfortunately, as the force commander, I couldn't make one of those tours. I had to stay at Newport.

Q: You didn't get to Korea at all, did you?

Adm. W.: No, I didn't get to Korea at all. I was during that whole period in one or another part of the Atlantic. I think that was probably the most active thing that the destroyer force was doing. Otherwise, we were sending units to the Mediterranean's Sixth Fleet and training at Guantanamo Bay.

Q: The routine things!

Adm. W.: Just the routine things, yes. There wasn't very much of particular excitement going on in the destroyer force. Of course, you always have a shortage of destroyers, and there were anti-submarine developments coming along but nothing very spectacular in this. They were getting better sonars and each new group of ships that came along would be a little more effective than the last one. But there weren't any quantum jumps at that time.

Q: Who was CinCLant?

Adm. W.: Lynde McCormick was CinCLant.

Q: He was quite an officer, wasn't he?

Adm. W.: Yes. I had served with him several times before. Out in Pearl Harbor he had been the deputy commander under Admiral Towers. Then he had been the vice chief of naval operations under Admiral Sherman. So I had known him quite well from previous tours of duty and, as you say, he was quite a person. He was a very courtly gentleman and had a very keen mind.

As I recall, it was somewhere round about Christmas time or the first of the year, while I was in the destroyer force, that I was told that I wouldn't stay there very much longer, that I was to be sent to Germany as the senior Navy staff officer in the U.S. European Command with headquarters in Frankfurt, Germany. This was a unified command that had been established shortly before this and Vice Admiral Roscoe Good — he was then Rear Admiral Roscoe Good — had been sent over more or less in a hurry to be the senior Navy representative on this joint command. It was a command that took care of the U.S. part of the command of all of our forces in Europe. The joint commander had as his subordinates the Army commander of all the Army forces in Europe, the Air Force commander similarly of their forces in Europe, and the Navy then known as CinCNelm, our admiral in London, was in command of the Navy component.

The commander of this U.S. joint command was the same person who was SacEur, that is, the NATO Supreme Allied Commander in Europe, and while this commander devoted practically all his time to the NATO command and headquarters, he had as a deputy commander a four-star general who rotated between Army and Air Force who actually exercised the command of the U.S. joint command.

At the outset, the deputy commander of this headquarters who really headed it up was General Tom Handy of the Army, and the chief of staff of the headquarters was an Air Force major general, and later it became a lieutenant general's job to be the chief of staff. At this particular time, it was a major general in the Air Force. The Navy at this time provided the chief of what was called J-3, the operations and plans division of the staff. That was considered to be the Number Three job.

This force in Europe, populationwise, was about seventy percent Army, about twenty percent Air Force, and about ten percent Navy. So I think they had the commanders appropriately designated from the various services. That is, the Army was the boss, the next man was Air Force, and the Number Three man was Navy.

Q: It was a defensive command, wasn't it?

Adm. W.: Very largely, yes. Defensive and logistical. You see, in a combined command such as the European command, the NATO command, each nation is responsible for the logistic support of its own forces. So the U.S. was responsible for providing the beans and the bullets and the people for all of its own forces. Up to the time that this U.S. CinCEur joint command was established, each one of the services was providing its own support without much relationship to the other services, and the ostensible purpose of the establishment of the joint command was to coordinate the logistics of the support of all the American forces in Europe. It actually, too, had some interservice rivalry implications, and these things were being thrashed out during the period that I was in this comma[nd].

Of course, at this time, the Army was still all for merger. The Air Force was getting a little less sure about merger. It wan[ted] independence and to be able to go its own way. And the Navy, as ha[d] been the case right along, wanted just to be left alone. This joi[nt] command, I think, served a useful prupose in getting all the comma[n]ders together every now and then and providing an agency in which representatives from all the services had to talk to one another.

We started off, as I said, in Frankfurt, Germany, and Roscoe Good, who had been sent really only as a temporary naval represent[a]tive came back to another assignment in the United States, and I to[ok] over from him, I think about two months after the command had been set up. So the first formative period was over when I got there. We were still in the stage of feeling our way long pretty much. It wasn't yet quite clear just what the unified command was going [to] do, and just what the component commanders from each of the servic[es] would do.

Q: You were under the over-all command of General Norstad?

Adm. W.: No, not at this particular time. We were under General Ridgway, Norstad was Ridgway's Air Deputy at this time.

Q: This was the beginning of the period when the doctrine of massive retaliation came into effect. Were you able to see any repercussions of this at this early stage?

Adm. W.: Yes. This was always the subject of a good deal of discussion in NATO circles and while in the U.S. European Command as the plans and operations officer I wasn't directly involved in making the NATO plans, we always had our contingency plans which had to be at least compatible with NATO plans. So that we did get involved in this kind of thing. There was always a school of thought that wanted a NATO force that would be a trip wire, simply one that would trigger off a massive retaliation if the Russians attacked and tripped the wire. Then there was another group that felt NATO should assemble enough force to be able to stop any Russian advance with conventional forces in Europe. This was being kicked back and forth and the various sides were being advocated by various people, various nations, all the time, and usually seemed to get resolved on the basis of what was feasible. What would the various NATO nations actually provide in the way of troops? And when you found out what they were going to provide, then your plans had to be based on what was going to be available to you to do your fighting. So it was continually under consideration and under revision, but I don't think anybody was ever completely happy with the plans that evolved and had to be current.

Q: Did you feel the impact of the Russian position in any way when you were at Frankfurt?

Adm. W.: When you say "feel the impact" of it, I think I have to answer this two ways. One, did we actually have any contact with them, did they push? No, they were behaving pretty well except in

Berlin, where, of course, they hadn't built the Wall yet, but there was definite friction in the administration of Berlin as a city. The Russians ran their sector and the Allies, British, French and U.S., ran the rest, and there was always difference of opinion here. But in Frankfurt, of course, there were no Russians in our zone and we didn't actually see Russians frequently. Occasionally they would send a team through and they would be very carefully escorted by our Army forces and we might see them at a lunch or dinner or something, but we had no contact with Russian forces.

Now, when you mention their impact, I think there was an implication that we did feel. We knew, of course, that not very many miles away from Frankfurt there were Russian forces who were in a position to move and had to be watched very carefully all the time for any indication that they were getting ready to move. So they had an impact on our thinking all the time, although we had no actual confrontation with them at that time. Our Berlin commander was continually having verbal confrontations with them.

Q: Harassment?

Adm. W.: Yes, but there was no actual fighting there. Nobody was shooting. We were aware that they were around all right and they made it a point to make us aware of it. Of course, that was a period in Germany when we had become a friendly occupying power. We had pretty good relationships with the Germans, but the United States was still occupying Germany, its sector of Berlin and zone of Germany, and we were in a position to require rather than to request things from the Germans. During the year or so that I wa in Europe this situation changed gradually and the occupation became less of an occupation and more a case of protection. We provided forces which the Germans hadn't yet developed after the war to at least block the Russians off, and during the course of that year the emphasis quite definitely shifted from one of more or less dictatorial powers on the part of the U.S. Army in Germany to a case of providing a force for protecting the country and turning back to the Germans more and more of the decisions regarding administration of the country.

Q: Did they seem anxious to assume these responsibilities?

Adm. W.: Yes, they were always quite happy to take them back as they were ready, and this one worked out really, I think, quite satisfactorily from the point of view both of the U.S. Forces and of the Germans. The Germans were in no position to take over some of the decision-making having to do with administration, but as they got into a position to do it, they wanted to, and pretty generally our people wanted to give it to them. There were exceptions to this where it involved privileges, of course, where the Army, for instance, had some very happy privileges in Garmisch for recreation purposes and Hitler's own retreat at Berchtesgaden and the Army wasn't particularly anxious to give these things back to the Germans, but they did and, of course, the Germans were quite anxious to get them.

But generally I thought this one went along very smoothly. Most of us had very considerable respect for the competence of the Germans. They had demonstrated very little of the old Nazi arrogance.

They were anxious to get their country back on its feet and going again.

Q: You were there during that brief period, that era of good feeling, of the Geneva Conference, weren't you?

Adm. W.: I don't recall that we paid a whole lot of attention to the Geneva Conference.

Q: When President Eisenhower came over.

Adm. W.: Yes. When did he become president? Now I'm trying to recall exactly how this tied in.

Q: 1953. And in December of 1953 he spoke before the United Nations and outlined a program of atomic energy for peaceful means, and then went to Geneva with something of the same concept.

Adm. W.: Yes. Well, this one really didn't seem to have very much impact on us. I don't remember very clearly when he did what in this connection and, insofar as our planning and our operations were concerned, this hadn't really taken hold. We still had our nuclear planning to do. I can't recall that the thrust of this was changed during that particular year. We kept on doing it with much the same ideas that we had had when I arrived. So my recollection would be that it really didn't have much impact.

Q: And I guess it didn't generally speaking after a few months.

Adm. W.: I think that's right.

Adm. W.: Did you have visitations from our State Department, our peripatetic Secretary of State and people like that in Frankfurt?

Adm. W.: Yes. We had a lot of visitations from a great many different people. The president, I don't think, did come during that period. He had been SacEur before he became president, so I think he felt he had a pretty good grasp of the European situation, both from World War II and from his tour as SacEur. We did have, though, the Secretary of State and we had the secretaries of defense, chairman of the Joint Chiefs, and a lot of people of this kind, and visiting ambassadors were pretty frequent. At this time Mrs. Luce was ambassador to Italy and she used to come to Frankfurt every now and then. We had Perle Mesta who was minister in Luxembourg. Perle used to come to Frankfurt every now and then. We had a pretty steady stream of visitations of various kinds, nearly all of them would come to Frankfurt headquarters for a briefing. In Paris at the NATO headquarters they would get, you might say, international briefings which always had to be conducted with the realization that there were a number of powers represented there. Now, when they came to the U.S. headquarters this was strictly U.S. and we could give them strictly the U.S. point of view of what was happening. So they all seemed to like to come to our U.S. headquarters for a briefing and for a chat with the deputy commander.

Q: Did your position entail much entertaining?

Adm. W.: Some, but not a very great deal. Most of this was done by the commanding general, that is, not the commander but the deputy commander. General Handy had been the commander of the Army component before the unified command was established and he was set up in a great big old German house. I remember his dining room could seat forty-two at the dining room table very comfortably. This will give you some idea of the matter of social activities that were conducted. He did most of the entertaining, which is normal, of course. When an ambassador or secretary of state or somebody comes, he doesn't want to be entertained by the second or third boss man, so most of this was done by General Handy and as a normal situation there was Army, Navy, and Air Force representation at whatever entertainment was given. So I did get involved as the senior naval officer in most of this, although very little of it was done in my own name.

Q: And you had your family there?

Adm. W.: Yes. Families were encouraged and Mrs. Wellborn did come. She joined me I think a month or so after I'd arrived in Germany. At this time we were all provided with German houses and they were really very pleasant places to live in. At that particular time there was a good deal of unemployment in Germany and servants could be employed quite reasonably, so between having a German house assigned as military quarters and having the capability of employing at a reasonable rate enough people to take care of the house, I thought it was quite pleasant there.

Q: You must have been loth to leave it, then?

Adm. W.: Well, yes, although I don't believe I'd want to live in Germany permanently.

Q: You came back to your old bailiwick, only temporarily though.

Adm. W.: Before we returned to the United States, headquarters was moved out of Germany. The U.S. European Command headquarters about the middle of my tour of duty moved from Germany, Frankfurt, down to France and was set up at a former French Army establishment, Camp des Loges, just maybe ten miles from SHAPE, the NATO headquarters.

Q: And that was the reason for it.

Adm. W.: Yes, the reason for this was to get the two commands located close together so that there could be an easier interchange between the NATO headquarters and the U.S. Command headquarters. This involved, of course, not only shifting the headquarters itself with all its paraphernalia but all of us finding new places to live in the Paris vicinity.

Q: You weren't allowed to take over French houses!

Adm. W.: No, here we couldn't just have French houses taken over. We had to get out in the French market and find places to live, and that was an interesting experience, too. French tax collection being what it is, or as it was at that time any way, we had a rather peculiar arrangement. We rented a house from a Frenchwoman who was a widow and French law said that she had to maintain ownership of this house until her only son was twenty-one years old and could participate in the disposing of it. So she had the house in which she didn't want to live and which she could not dispose of, so she rented it to us. It was a pleasant house, but we had no lease, no written arrangement, because this would have subjected her to some taxes that she had no intention of paying. So, she wrote us a letter which said that she would be very much pleased to have us occupy her house from a certain day to a certain other day. There was no mention of any kind of compensation. This apparently was just an invitation. She took it on faith that I was going to pay her what we had agreed on, which I did, but I was not permitted to pay her by check. At the end of each month her daughter rode up on a bicycle and I handed her daughter the right number of francs, as paper money, not checks, and her daughter took it in this way. I did insist on getting a receipt. The daughter signed a little slip of paper saying that she had on this date received from me a certain number of francs. This was the accepted way of renting a house in Paris at that time.

Q: Did this fool the tax collector?

Adm. W.: I don't think really, but the tax collector at least didn't have any papers on which he could base a law suit or some effort to collect due taxes. French taxes are assessed a little differently from the way ours are. I don't recall exactly how it worked, but the tax collector would try to determine how many radio sets a particular individual owned, if he owned a car and, if so, how many, whether or not he had an electric refrigerator. These things apparently were used to determine the scale of living and then his tax was assessed in some way based on his scale of living. Owning a house that was being rented at a profit would have apparently materially increased the scale of living of my hostess, I guess, so she was not anxious to have this established. This was accepted by the U.S. authorities as being a reasonable way to rent a house and certainly whether the French government accepted it, the French people did! So this is the way it went.

We lived very pleasantly in Paris and I think both Mrs. Wellborn and I thoroughly enjoyed that tour of duty.

Q: Was there any noticeable improvement in the liaison between the two outfits?

Adm. W.: Yes, I think there was. As long as we were in Germany it was quite a chore to get down to Paris and to talk with your counterparts in the NATO headquarters. Of course, telephones are completely insecure and when you're talking plans and various other things that had to be classified, you needed security. Well, this meant one day to fly down and another day to fly back, and weather in that part of the world isn't too good. At that time we didn't have the reliability of air transportation that we have now. So it did give us lots better contact with the NATO headquarters.

During the couple of years that I was in the European command, of course, up at NATO headquarters Field Marshal Montgomery was staging his annual CPX, command post exercise, as it was called. Actually it was no such thing as a command post exercise. It was a meeting at which a lot of the NATO senior commanders were able to express their views. It was a very interesting performance, but not really an exercise at all. The military chiefs of most of the NATO nations would come to this thing and Field Marshal Montgomery, of course, was the star of the show and did most of the talking, but he would give most of these national chiefs a chance and most of the NATO commanders at the high level, that is the NATO areas and striking fleets and things a chance to talk. So, while it really wasn't a command post exercise, it was I think a worthwhile interchange of ideas. It was completely dominated by the Field Marshal, but he let the other people speak enough so that their ideas did come through.

Q: So they were willing to come again the next year?

Adm. W.: Yes, and of course I think most of them always relished three or four days in Paris, which is very pleasant. The old Field Marshal was really quite a character. He was acutely aware of the fact that he was always the deputy in the headquarters. He considered himself to be the world's leading general at that time, and he held in somewhat less than very high esteem any other general who would contest this with him, and he was always acutely aware of the fact that he was not the supreme allied commander, he was only the deputy. This showed through in all of his presentations. He always looked a little disdainfully at his boss and sometimes he was even outright insubordinate, but his bosses during my period there chose to ignore this. First Ridgway and then later Gruenther, took the tack of getting along with the Field Marshal inspite of his eccentricities, so there was never any open hostility, although every now and then when the Field Marshal got a little out of line and made public statements that were at variance with the commander's policy, the supreme commander would have to straighten that out. But always very politely.

Those were interesting get-togethers in that there were people from all parts of NATO who came together. Of course, some of them spoke English and some didn't, and even though this was conducted in France, English was the language of the meeting and it was translated by use of earphones, as is done at the United Nations, so that regardless of what language people spoke you could participate. Of course, all French commanders, even though they understood English would speak in French!

Well, in due course, I finished off that tour of duty and came back, reporting initially to the Bureau of Personnel.

Q: That was just a waiting —

Adm. W.: That was just a holding assignment until I went down to Norfolk and relieved Vice Admiral Woolridge as commander of the Second Fleet.

Q: Did you have any interesting assignments while you were in BuPers? What did you do?

Adm. W.: I really wasn't there long enough to do anything worthwhile. I arrived and I had some accrued leave, which I took, and then there was a period when I had a chance to go over papers and documents and sort of get myself acclimated to the Second Fleet. So it was really just preparatory to taking over the new job. I didn't do anything in the way of duty independently of the Second Fleet assignment while I was assigned to BuPers.

Q: The Second Fleet assignment was a considerable command you were taking over?

Adm. W.: It was odd procedurally, but at this period in time the Atlantic Fleet didn't have very many ships and for the most part the Commander, Second Fleet, operated from shore-based headquarters in Norfolk in the same complex as CinCLantFlt. The Second Fleet commander was a two-hatted gentleman. His U.S. title was Commander, Second Fleet. His NATO title was Commander, Striking Fleet, Atlantic. And in these two hats he was subordinate to, respectively, CinCLantFlt as the SEcond Fleet commander, and SacLant, the NATO commander, when he had on his Strike FleetLant hat. So this was one of those jobs where I did have a NATO connection again, a direct one, and again our planning had to be both U.S. and NATO.

Q: You had two staffs?

Adm. W.: No, it was all one staff, but we had to have two sets of plans, one a NATO plan and the other one a contingent U.S. plan. You see, in nuclear planning you couldn't have all the details spelled out in a NATO operations order. All this had to be U.S. So we had to have two sets of plans to take care of one set of operations.

Q: As Commander of the Second Fleet, did you have amphibious forces under you?

Adm. W.: The Second Fleet was what was called a task fleet. It had no permanently assigned forces. When the Second Fleet was to conduct an operation, for this particular operation forces were assigned and very rarely were the same forces assigned for two consecutive operations. The Commander, Second Fleet, was responsible for fleet training, fleet operational training, of the forces on the Atlantic coast and, in order to accomplish this, periodically forces would be assigned. The type commanders were responsible for training their ships as individual ships. Then the various types of ships would be assigned to the Commander, Second Fleet, for training as a fleet. These ships would go through their training in the Second Fleet, then normally these ships that had completed their fleet type training would be sent to the Sixth Fleet where they would operate for their tour of duty in the Sixth Fleet. Then the ships would return to the Atlantic coast, usually to go into overhaul or maintenance for a period, and there'd be a lot of personnel turnover. After this maintenance period they would come back for an assignment with the Second Fleet for training. So there was a rotation usually involving three parts -- an assignment to the Second Fleet for training, an assignment with the Sixth Fleet for Mediterranean operation, and an overhaul and maintenance period.

So the Second Fleet commander was involved very largely in training ships for assignment to the Sixth Fleet, although, of course, he had a wartime operational job for which he had to plan. So most of your actual peacetime operating was training ships for Sixth Fleet operations, but in wartime you'd have to have forces that would have had their own jobs to do. The ships you were assigned were given to you on more or less the same kind of a basis that in World War II Admiral Halsey and Admiral Spruance's Third and Fifth Fleets got ships. The operation that was being conducted and the availability of ships determined what ships were assigned as parts of the Third and Fifth fleets, and that was true in the

Second Fleet at this time, too. What you had under your command varied from zero during period of no activity to a full-sized operating fleet for certain exercises.

Q: Did this put you in contact with Latin American navies also?

Adm. W.: A little bit but not a great deal. During the period that I was Commander, Second Fleet, we had a fleet review in Norfolk as a part of a centennial celebration. This was in 1957, I think, and it was a sesquicentennial, rather than a centennial, and at this time we re-staged a fleet review similar to the one that had been staged in 1907 when Theodore Roosevelt was president and they had a great exposition in Norfolk and had navies from a great many nations represented for this fleet review. There was another one staged in 1957 and most of the foreign navies represented in this instance were Latin American navies. I had a good deal to do with them at that time, but for our normal operations we had not very much Latin American naval contact.

Our contact was rather NATO than Latin American in our foreign business.

Q: Tell me about some of the NATO exercises.

Adm. W.: There was an annual NATO exercise in the Atlantic and in alternate years there were some pretty sizeable forces assigned. The other year, the off year, it was largely a command-post-type exercise. The commanders went through the motions but there were no actual ships operating.

During my more or less two years in the Second Fleet, we ran off one of each kind. On the actual exercise I took some ships from our Atlantic coast to various ports. The operation was in the Norwegian Sea largely and we visited a number of Norwegian ports and some British ports. The exercise involved Norwegian and British forces. In the other parts of the exercise there were Dutch, Belgian, and French forces, but in the striking fleet we had only U.S. and British forces, and our contact with the Norwegians was largely the result of our visits to Norwegian ports.

Q: At that time, were any of the Scandinavian nations a little squeamish about participating in NATO exercises?

Adm. W.: Yes. Norway was fairly hearty in its cooperation. Denmark was a member of NATO, but they were not very enthusiastic about it. Of course, Sweden had never been in NATO, so we didn't see anything of them, although at this time the Swedes were much more friendly than they are now. We had a certain degree of understanding on a personal basis with various Swedish commanders, but there was no official relationship with the Swedes.

I would say Norway was fully cooperative. Denmark something less than enthusiastically cooperative, and Sweden on the outside. Of course, there was a NATO headquarters at Oslo, just outside of Oslo, and Norwegian ships were active in participating in NATO exercises. During this period I had the present King of Norway, who was then the Crown Prince, off for lunch in the flagship. He was an old sailor man and very much interested in NATO exercises.

Q: Olaf?

Adm. W.: Olaf, yes.

Q: Were there any problems language-wise in these joint exercises?

Adm. W.: Not in these particular exercises because our striking fleet was composed, as I say, of British and U.S. forces and we all spoke English, although it might have been a different version of the English language but we could understand one another and the Norwegians all speak - at least their military people, all speak English as a second language. So we had no trouble at all with understanding.

Q: At that point there was no attempt to experiment with a joint crew, however, was there?

Adm. W.: No. We had liaison officers aboard one another's ships, but there was no effort made to man ships with crews that came from the various nations. Each ship had its own national identity. We had operated enough with the British Navy so that this was very smooth and easy.

Q: There was sometimes a bit of difficulty, I believe, in terms of who was in command of the NATO forces and who was deputy?

Adm. W.: Yes. This always was a subject of a certain amount of maneuvering between British and U.S. forces. There were the old Churchillians who felt that the British Empire would never go down, that they knew more about the management of world affairs than anybody else, and that it was perfectly normal for any kind of important international command to be in British hands. Then there was always the American point of view of yes, we agree you know quite a lot about military affairs and the management of world affair but after all you don't provide much in the way of forces. Most of these are American and, since we're providing most of the forces and know the idiosyncrasies of most of the forces, we think we'd better command. This was always a matter of some pushing and pulling. In these particular instances, for the same reason that the little boy that owns the baseball usually gets to pitch, the U.S. usually won these arguments because we had the forces and without the forces there wasn't anything to command. But the British always were quite anxious to take command, regardless of whether or not they provided anything in the way of forces. And my own personal view was that they were pretty good commanders. There were certain American officers who took this one as deadly serious and other who felt it didn't make too much difference. But when the chips were down, usually the command went to the nation that was providing most of the forces and that usually was the United States.

Q: Tell me, since you were based in Norfolk, you must have been the recipient of many visits by congressmen and others. What was your program for them?

Adm. W.: There were a good many visits of this kind. However, I didn't get particularly involved in this. At the time I was down there, SacLant, CinCLant, and CinCLantFlt was Admiral Gerauld Wright and he was the Number One man, just as General Handy was in Germany, and most of this handling of VIPs fell to him. Only when there was an overflow did I get involved in it. This happened occasionally. There'd be a big NATO convocation or something of this sort and there would be too many visitors for him to handle it all and in this case some of the overflow might have to be put up in my quarters or something of this kind. But, for the most part, this was something that he handled himself.

Q: Did you have an established public relations policy?

Adm. W.: Well, now, here again, public relations was very largely in his hands. He had a public relations staff. My staff normally did not include a public relations officer. When we went on a NATO exercise, a big one, we sometimes would get assigned a temporary duty public relations officer, but normally the Second Fleet commander didn't handle very much in the way of public relations. This was always handled by the commander-in-chief.

Wellborn #10 - 337

Interview No. 10 with Vice Admiral Charles Wellborn, Jr., U.S. Navy
(Retired)

Place: His residence in the Westchester Apartments, Washington, D.C.

Date: Wednesday morning, 10 May 1972

Subject: Biography

By: John T. Mason, Jr.

Q: It certainly is good to see you this morning, Admiral. Last time, you completed your remarks, I believe, about command of the Second Fleet and on July 31, 1957 you went down to Norfolk to take the assignment as commandant of the Armed Forces Staff College there.

Adm. W.: Yes. That really didn't involve moving out of Norfolk. Second Fleet headquarters was in Norfolk, so I simply turned my hat around and went over to the Staff College to relieve Air Force Lieutenant General Schlatter. The commandant of the Staff College rotates between Army, Navy, and Air Force and it's a three-year assignment. And there is a deputy from the services who is not providing the commandant at any particular moment, and the tour of duty of the deputy is two years and through the combination of numbers it comes out just right that with the three-year rotation for commandants and two-year rotation for deputies, they all have to be relieved at the right time so that you keep a commandant from one service and the two deputies from the two others.

Q: That's a clever arrangement, certainly.

Adm. W.: It's one of those mathematical peculiarities that works out to everybody's advantage.

Q: It certainly gives full coverage to the services, too, doesn't it?

Adm. W.: It does, indeed. Of course, the Marines are considered as part of the Navy. This is departmental, rather than service, so while I don't believe there's ever been a Marine commandant at the Staff College this could happen. He would then take the place of the Navy rotation. But there are, of course, Marine officers on the staff and faculty. The Marines are well represented at the College.

Q: Perhaps it would be well before you tell me about your career there to give me a picture of the Armed Forces Staff College. What purpose does it serve and what is the intention of it?

Adm. W.: The Staff College was established during World War II. Its original name was, I believe, The Army and Navy Amphibious College or something like that. It was not originally called the Armed Forces Staff College. It was set up by the Army and the Navy to give officers training in joint operations.

Q: And that was amphibious operations?

Adm. W.: Yes, that was primarily amphibious. Subsequently it was broadened a little bit because it developed very promptly that we had not only joint operations and joint operations are defined as ones in which more than one U.S. services participate, but we also had combined operations, and they're defined as ones in which forces of more than one nation participate.

So, the College was broadened a little bit and then when the Department of Defense was set up the Staff College came under the aegis of the Department of Defense and specifically the Joint Chiefs of Staff, and it was renamed the Armed Forces Staff College and given the mission of training officers in the planning and conduct of joint and combined operations. That, I think, is quite an accurate description of what it does.

Q: How large a student body does it have and how are they selected, and how long do they stay?

Adm. W.: At that time - and I think still - it had a student body of something on the order of two hundred and fifteen. They stay there for about five months. There are two courses a year with a brief interval between each of the two courses. The student body comes from the three services equally plus a small contingent from a few allied countries - Britain, Canada, Australia, New Zealand, France, and, I think, West Germany has been added to it since my day.

Q: No Latin Americans?

Adm. W.: No Latin Americans. The nations I have named were the ones that were there during my period, and there's a limited number of those. Of the two hundred and ten or fifteen that we had in each class, I would guess there may be about a dozen foreign students and the rest of them were equally divided between the Army, Navy, and

Air Force with Marines forming part of the Navy contingent.

Q: And there are no other representatives from government departments, other than the military?

Adm. W.: Oh, yes, there were and I'm glad you brought that up. We had one State Department student in each class and we had a USIA student, and I believe the CIA was represented on occasions. But the State Department and USIA were regularly represented. On the faculty, when I arrived there, we didn't have a State Department representative but during the course of my tour of duty we did manage to get the State Department to send us a faculty member.

Q: How is the faculty selected and what percentage is military figures?

Adm. W.: The faculty was really entirely military. The staff was not entirely military. We had a number of professional people, librarians and the people who prepared the art work for visual aids and training, a lot of this kind of people. But primarily since the object was to train in planning and execution of military operations, the faculty was a military faculty. The services each provided approaimxately equal contingents for the staff and the faculty, and each one of the services assigned officers to fill these particular billets and their assignment was more or less negotiable, as all assignments are. Normally the service would propose to assign somebody who was quite suitable for the job, but in the rare instances where they proposed somebody that didn't seem to be quite suitable for the job, the commandant could always negotiate with the service for somebody else. Or, if they needed somebody with a particular qualification they could generally negotiate that with the service, too, to get the kind of an officer that was needed.

The Army and, to a somewhat lesser extent, the Air Force took the assignment of officers to this faculty quite seriously and assigned quite good officers. The Navy, as I think is frequently the case, didn't consider this kind of faculty assignment at a school as a very desirable one, and you had some difficulty getting from the Navy officers who were on the way up the promotion ladder.

Q: That doesn't pertain, however, to the Navy's attitude toward the Naval War College?

Adm. W.: To a very much lesser extent. But I think even there the Navy tends to assign its really top-notch officers either to Pentagon duty, where they are in the midst of both interservice rivalries and appropriation efforts, operational planning that's for real rather than for instruction, and this kind of assignment I think still gets higher priority in the Navy than assignment to faculties and jobs of this kind.

Q: The point you make about the Navy's attitude toward faculty assignments at the Armed Forces Staff College, would you say that this underscores the statement made to me by a man who is a Rhodes scholar and a naval officer, "You know there's really not much place for that type of training in the Navy"?

Adm. W.: I think there is a degree of truth in what he says. On the other hand, my own feeling after being commandant of the Armed Forces Staff College for three years is that the Navy doesn't give due weight to some aspects of education. I think the Army does a better job, maybe, in this respect. I believe the Navy overstresses what you might call training and actual experience and understresses education in the sense of mental development - developing orderly thought processes. The Army does a great deal of this and their whole educational philosophy seems to be more of starting off with a young man, giving him education as opposed to training, then after he has completed what you might call a basic education, the Army starts to train him, that is, they send him to an infantry school or an artillery school, whereas the Navy attempts to put its education and training all into one pot and the Naval Academy is supposed to turn out a young man who is not only educated but also trained to be a junior officer.

It's not for me to say who's right on this one, but my own view is that the Navy could do well to move a little in the direction that the Army has moved and give somewhat more attention to developing orderly thought processes in its naval officers and in giving them a somewhat broader background of education, somewhat less ordnance and gunnery, let's say, or steam engineering, and a little more liberal arts simply to provide a little more background of knowledge of the rest of the world.

Q: It's curious that within the same country two separate services should develop such a different philosophy and approach to the education of their young officers.

Adm. W.: Yes, there are a number of differences in the approach of these two services to their problems. I've tried to figure this one out and the only explanation I could give you which may or may not be correct is that in its early day the Navy was essentially an operating force that was on its own the minute it left port. Now, the Navy went to sea in the days before radio communications or even cable communications, and you had to be trained, you had to know how to do things, whereas during the arly days Army officers, generally, were on posts, with more senior officers and could pick up this kind of training much more easily. They were always within some kind of a community even though it might be mostly Indians! And I think it was more readily apparent to Army people that there was a need for shall we say general culture than it was to the Navy, which was off on its own at sea where it was quite apparent that you needed knowledge of sails and ropes, but some of these other things seemed a little extraneous.

This may or may not be an explanation for the way the services have developed, but this was my rationalization of it at any rate, and I think with the unification that we've developed between the services - they're all getting closer together now - their educational philosophy is much more nearly alike today than twenty years ago.

Q: And, of course, now the superintendents of the service academies meet on a regular basis.

Adm. W.: Yes.

Q: To compare their curricula.

Adm. W.: Of course, the Staff College, to get back to that, was not under the Navy Department directly, it was for command purposes under the Joint Chiefs of Staff directly. As commandant, I reported to the Joint Chiefs, not to the chief of naval operations or the Chief of Naval Personnel.

Q: How vital and how active was that connection with the Joint Chiefs?

Adm. W.: Not very active! The Joint Chiefs gave you your mission, then they were involved with other things and you proceeded pretty much on your own.

Q: Did they serve on your board in any way?

Adm. W.: No. There was a Joint Educational Committee that was composed of the commandants of the Armed Forces Staff College, the National War College, and the Industrial College, who were supposed to meet regularly and to supervise the curricula of the three colleges. And we did meet reasonably frequently, but again each one of the commandants pretty much went his own way and the other two commandants agreed with him that that was the way to run his college. So they operated more or less freely, but we did have close contact with the Joint Chiefs through our speakers who came to talk to us and I think that this helped us to stay in the lines that they wanted. Also our faculties were always very alert to keep abreast of the thinking of their own particular planners. The way our curriculum was set up, we had an Army week, a Navy week, and an Air Force week very early in the curriculum during which we had either the chief of staff of the respective services or what they called the "little chief," the operations and planning deputy speak to the student body. Then we had various others during the course of this week, probably six or eight speakers from each of the services who would explain their views on a great many things, research and development, for instance, new weapons that were coming along and what their personnel problems and policies were.

So I don't think we had too much trouble with being unsupervised and getting off the track, thinking in directions that were not the same as the Department of Defense and the military departments were thinking. There was plenty of liaison.

Q: Since you've introduced the subject of your outside speakers, do you want to say something more about that?

Adm. W.: Yes. Here we did have a great deal of civilian representation. The regular schedule of events was normally on each day to have two speakers in the morning. EAch speaker would speak forty-five minutes, then have a short break, and then a question period of forty-five minutes. There would be two of these sessions, two speakers, in the forenoon, then the afternoon would be devoted to seminar sessions.

Q: Based on the same subjects introduced in the morning, or what?

Adm. W.: Generally, yes. Speakers would speak on something that was relevant to what was going on in the way of problems and seminar work. Of course, it was a little difficult to make each one directly pertinent to the afternoon's work, but that developed then into quite a goodly number of speakers. Of course, we didn't have two speakers five days a week every week. There were periods when you were working with a good deal of intensity on problems where you wouldn't have speakers, and there were periods of visits to typical installations of each one of the services. Things of this sort would interrupt your speaker program.

But it all added up to a very considerable number of speakers who talked to the student body and they covered a pretty wide field. We always started off to set more or less of an intellectual tone for each class with a law professor, Hardy Dillard from the University of Virginia. He was an interesting person. He graduated from West Point and had served in the Army for a little while, then resigned from the Army, I guess, shifted to the Army Reserve, rather than resigned, and studied law. He practiced law for a time and then became a professor of law at the University of Virginia, and he had something in common with Hubert Humphrey in that he was a congenital talker! He loved to speak and was one of the best speakers I've ever listened to. He always opened up each class on an intellectual plane that stimulated them. He was interesting and he made them think and he, I think, is representative of the kind of civilian speaker we tried to get.

Q: How did you go about getting these speakers? Was this within your purview as commandant?

Adm. W.: As the commandant, I had some say in it, advised and signed all the letters, but for each of our lectures some faculty member was given the responsibility for locating someone who was both a competent speaker and a knowledgeable person in this particular subject, and then making the initial approach usually, as to whether or not he might be amenable to come down. to Norfolk

For non-Defense speakers, we were allowed to pay an honorarium. I think it was three hundred dollars. So those speakers who were accustomed to accepting fees of that kind could get them from us. And it was, at that time, considered quite a desirable thing for a good many of the people whom we wanted to have speak to us to be able to add to his credentials that he was a lecturer at the Armed Forces Staff College. As a general rule, those whom we wanted to come were quite willing to do so.

Q: Were they largely from academic communities or were they government people?

Adm. W.: Well, we had quite a variety. Of course, we had a good many military speakers on military subjects, but we also had, for instance, the civil servant who is the historian of the Department of Defense and his name gets away from me at the moment — a German name and he speaks with a little bit of a German accent. He spoke to us on the history of the Department of Defense and how it got the way it is. He was a very interesting speaker and one who stirred up thought. We tried to get this. Someone not who would simply tell you facts but would engender a lot of thinking and maybe even controversy in the student body and would produce a good lively question-and-answer period.

The type people we had, for instance - I mentioned Hardy Dillard and I mentioned Rudy Winnacker - that's the name of the man. We had the ambassador from France to tell us about how it was that France acted as it did in Algeria and in Vietnam, Indochina.

Q: Who was he?

Adm. W.: That was - oh, I'll think of his name in a minute. We had Admiral Sir Michael Denny who was at that time the chairman of the NATO Military Committee, who spoke to us on the NATO problems. We had the secretary general at that time of the Organization of American States [Dr. Mora,] to explain the thinking of that organization to us. We had to tell us about highly classified intelligence matters always one of the civilian intelligence experts either from the Central Intelligence Agency or from one of the military departments.

So we had quite a diverse group in addition to some pure academicians. For instance when we wanted information about situations in, let's say, the Soviet Union we found the most knowledgeable people on this and they were nearly always civilian professors at, say, Princeton or Columbia, or something of this kind.

Q: Or else diplomats like Kennan and Thompson?

Adm. W.: Yes. Occasionally, a diplomat would turn up. We had a man named Wright, who was one of the best. He was both an academician and an ex-diplomat, but he could explain the petroleum situation worldwide probably better than anybody else I've ever listened to. We didn't try to get our speakers from any one particular source. What we tried to get was good and challenging speakers who had the best knowledge of the particular field on which we wanted a discussion.

Q: The name of the French ambassador you finally decided was Hervé Alphand?

Adm. W.: Yes, and there was an amusing situation that arose once when we asked him to come and speak to us. We almost invariably originally extended the invitation to our speaker and his wife to come to Norfolk, have dinner in the quarters with us, and to spend the night there, then the speaker would talk to the College in the morning and we'd have a luncheon the next day, that is, after his lecture. Then he would depart after lunch.

Well, when we asked the ambassador we asked Madame Alphand also and he replied that Madame Alphand was now in France and would be unable to accompany him. Under these circumstances, we then offered our speaker the use of our airplane that was assigned to the College for this purpose to fly him into Norfolk because Norfolk's a very difficult place to get to commercially. The ambassador accepted this with some gratitude, and we had it all set up. Then the ambassador went home to France for a visit, and he returned in several weeks and communicated with the Staff College that now Madame Alphand would be very happy to attend. Well, it developed that the original Madame Alphand had been in France busily engaged in acquiring a divorce from the ambassador, and after his return to France for a few weeks he acquired a new bride and when she returned to this country with him, she would be very happy to attend our lecture and dinner and so forth.

This created a complication because Navy rules wouldn't permit the wife of the ambassador to fly in our Navy airplane, and we had an international crisis over this. The Navy Department was adamant. They wouldn't waive the rule, which didn't seem to me to make very much sense, but that was the way it was and so we had to disinvite Madame Alphand or we had to tell the ambassador that he'd have to make his own way down to Norfolk.

Q: Or provide a plane on your own!

Adm. W.: Yes. The upshot of the whole business was that the ambassador was furious and he never would come down again to speak to us after that. But with the advent of the new ambassador when Mr. Alphand went home I think the breach was healed and everything turned out all right in the end.

But this is illustrative of the kind of problems that did arise when we were trying to get speakers who were all somewhat conscious of their prerogatives and somewhat sensitive to any apparent slight.

Q: Admiral, you mentioned earlier the fact that you always had a lecture dealing with sensitive and security matters. This must have created a problem for you having in the student body representatives from allied countries. How did you deal with this?

Adm. W.: This was a problem, but it was solved without very much difficulty because during the course of the class the foreign students were all sent on a tour that was not made by the American students. They visited several installations that were of interest to foreign students and while they were all off on their tour we had our highly classified lectures which were for U.S. eyes and ears only.

Q: Were they cognizant of the fact that you - ?

Adm. W.: Yes, they knew what it was and they all understood it. They all had their secrets, too, that they wouldn't tell us. This was no problem, it worked out very nicely. We were doing something that was worthwhile for them, while the American students were getting their "U.S. only" part of the course. In fact, the foreign students, I thought, made quite a contribution to the effort there. They each had some points of view to introduce and they each had a little humor to introduce every now and then which kept things going pretty well.

The Australians I recall as being particularly ones who livened things up.

Q: They would!

Adm. W.: We had really something of a difficult problem from an educational point of view because it was a short course - five months - and we had a very specific mission which, on the face of it, was more training than it was education, that is, to train officers in the planning and execution of joint and combined operations. We did try, though, to keep this on an intellectual level that would prevent it from becoming pure training. Whether or not we succeeded, I don't know. Maybe the students would be able to give a better answer than I could, but I think that most of them seemed to feel that we weren't dealing strictly in reading regulations and policies and learning how to comply with them.

For instance, in our problem work we had established a policy that the solutions to problems didn't necessarily have to follow service doctrines. If the students thought they could develop a better doctrine than the service doctrine, go ahead and try. They had to be aware of what the service doctrine was and then had to justify their using one of their own. In ways of this kind we did manage to introduce some thought process rather than simply memorizing service doctrines and learning how to apply the service doctrine

Q: Well, now, when a solution other than the application of the service doctrine was applied to a problem, it was an original solution and, in your eyes, highly successful as a solution, was this then made available to the services?

Adm. W.: Oh, yes. You could count on this without any specific action on the part of the commandant. As soon as something of this kind developed the service members of the faculty would all get the word right back to their own services that here was a thought that was developing. We had no trouble at all with this kind of knowledge being passed.

This, though, brings up an interesting point. At the time I was there, there still was pretty strong service rivalry and I think there still is a good deal of it, but back in 1957 it was quite strong and the student officers would arrive with generally little knowledge of the other services and with some pretty strong biases. I watched six classes there arrive with this kind of a feeling generally. After about a month you could begin to see that these officers were suddenly realizing, well, those people from the other services aren't too different from me. They think pretty much the way I do and live pretty much the way I do. Their families all lived in little apartments there at the College so that they got to know one another pretty intimately very quickly. And about the end of the month you'd begin to see these people were thinking "these people aren't such ignorant and stupid individuals as I had thought they were." Then you'd begin to see very strong friendships develop across service lines, and along towards the end of the course you would begin to get some thinking that was pretty objective as regards the interservice rivalry.

I think that this was one of the purposes that the Armed Forces Staff College served, maybe even to a greater extent than it did its primary mission of training officers in joint and combined operations.

Q: It's an interesting point to make and I've heard the same story in connection with the National War College. This cross fertilization is a valuable part of the whole course.

Adm. W.: Yes, and I watched this develop in every class that came and went while I was there. It was invariable. The officers would arrive - they were all generally lieutenant colonel and commander rank - and the students from all the services were very carefully selected, much more so than the faculty.

Q: Would you say a word about the selection? How was this done?

Adm. W.: Each service did it in its own way.

Q: How did the Navy do it?

Adm. W.: The Navy did it through a selection board process that was set up in the Bureau of Personnel. They established this informal board - this was not a statutory board but it was one that was ordered by the Chief of Naval Personnel and usually included the director of officer personnel and several other individuals who varied, but flag rank people.

Q: What were their specific criteria for selection?

Adm. W.: I think, generally, it involved a record that indicated promotion potential. This I'd say was probably the primary consideration. Then, previous educational background was considered, too, I think. In the Navy they tried to spread the higher education around among as many people as they could, and as a rule if somebody had been to one college he wouldn't be sent to another college. This was not true of the Army. The Army tried to pick their best people and they'd start them off at one of the lower-level colleges and then put them in the next echelon, and so on up.

Q: Again underscoring that philosophy you mentioned earlier.

Adm. W.: Yes. But the Navy generally found that if an officer had gone to the Armed Forces Staff College he might not be eligible for the War College and so forth. But they all did seem to me to try to send only top-notch people who had potential for going on to higher rank, and I was really very happy with the quality of the student body. Assignment to the College was in demand among the officers of the proper rank, and I think that's always a pretty good indication of whether or not good people are being selected.

Q: And it also, I would think, would be gratifying to a man

selected. He knew he had the stamp of approval!

Adm. W.: Yes.

Q: And the opportunity to go on.

Adm. W.: Very much so.

Q: Tell me about some of your moments of triumph as commandant.

Adm. W.: Well, now, I'm not sure I had very many moments of triumph down there! You always had a lot of amusing incidents happening. I recall each class, for instance, used to give some sort of a pretty good-sized social affair during the latter part of their stay at the Staff College, and one class decided that they were going to have a costume party and the theme should be the "Roaring Twenties." I was supposed to attend this thing and supposed to attend in a costume appropriate to the Roaring Twenties and I neglected it till the last monute and realized that I had neither a costume nor a very good idea, and then all at once somebody suggested, well, how about an old frock coat, the kind that the Navy used to wear in the Roaring Twenties? So I dug out my old frock coat with epaulettes and full-dress belt and things, found I could still get into it -

Q: Were you garbed in a boat coat also?

Adm. W.: Yes, the whole outfit. When I arrived and met the very pretty young wife of one of these young lieutenant colonels, she looked at this outfit, she'd never seen anything like that before in the flesh, and she asked me where in the world I acquired that old Admiral Farragut uniform! That really put me in my place and made me realize that I belonged to a different generation from that little girl.

For the most part I thought that was a very stimulating and very interesting assignment. There weren't many crises. As I say, we were permitted to run our own show pretty freely. I guess maybe my best feeling of triumph came when we finally got an appropriation from Congress to build a new academic building on the Staff College grounds down in Norfolk. The idea was not an original one of mine by any means. The plan had been made for a good many years when I arrived, but it had always died from lack of funds. I was fortunate enough to be able to talk the Department of Defense controller and the Congress into appropriating enough money to build the new building.

Q: Did this mean an appearance before a congressional committee?

Adm. W.: Yes, quite a lot of appearances. As I guess you know, the process for something of this sort calls for, first, a justification of the authorization for the spending of the money with the department that's going to do the work - in this case it was the Navy Department because they owned the land. Then you go over to the Department of Defense to justify the authorization before the Department of Defense controller. Then you go to the House Armed Services Committee and justify the building. Then you go over to the Senate and appear to justify the authorization before the Military Affairs Committee. Oh, I left out one step. You go to the Bureau of the Budget after the Department of Defense.

Once you've got all this accomplished and you've got your

authorizing legislation for the building, then you have to start the process all over and go through each one of these steps again for the appropriation before you actually get the money. So you have to have two pieces of legislation, and to get these through you have to appear before the departmental - Defense, the Bureau of the Budget, the House and the Senate - authorities, all of whom have to act on your request. So this is a very involved process.

Q: Takes infinite patience, I assume!

Adm. W.: It does indeed.

Q: I would think in your own particular case you knew your way around Washington, you had contacts, you had done these things before.

Adm. W.: Yes, I had been involved in this kind of thing in some of my previous assignments, so I knew the process and knew some of the people. They changed from time to time. I think probably the key man in my getting this appropriation through was Wilfred McNeil who was the controller in the Department of Defense at the time. I had known him well in the past and was able to talk on a friendly personal basis with him, and when he agreed that we should have first the authorization and then the appropriation, the rest of it fell into place pretty easily.

Q: What did it mean, the new quarters, in terms of the effectiveness of the school?

Adm. W.: On this one I like to quote Father Hesburgh, then

the president of Notre Dame. You may recall at one stage of the game he fired his football coach, Terry Brennan, who was coaching a losing football team. Somebody asked him why and he said, "Well, Coach Brennan wasn't maintaining an atmosphere of excellence and this we must have at Notre Dame."

My feeling was that it was difficult to maintain an atmosphere of excellence at the Staff College in a bunch of ramshackle old buildings that made it physically uncomfortable for the students to do their work. I think that second-class environment tended to produce second-class work.

Q: Is this something that you were aware of before you went to the College, or did the situation there bring this upon you?

Adm. W.: I was, I think, aware of this fact of life before I went there, but certainly the experience there at the Staff College strengthened my belief in this theory.

Q: That was very interesting. Was it actually completed and available in your regime?

Adm. W.: No. This process took quite a long while. The process of getting the authorization and appropriation took about two years. Then, once the money became available, the construction took another couple of years, so the new building was actually put into use a year or so after I left. I have been to see it and I think that it turned out quite well. That started also a program of replacing all the old buildings. Once we got the ice broken with the first appropriation, the rest of it came easy. All the old buildings that were converted temporary barracks buildings that had been used for apartments have now been replaced by housing that was built as housing and, while it's not plush by any means, it's very much more satisfactory than what we had.

Q: Since you've talked about your moment of triumph, were there any difficult time and frustrating times that you couldn't unravel?

Adm. W.: As I recall, the frustrating items were all rather minor ones. There were such things as the Alphand incident where for various reasons people would get temperamental and not do just what you wanted. Occasionally you'd have one of your students, or even one of your faculty, get a little bit too ardent in support of his own service views. But my recollection of that tour of duty is distinctly one of being very pleasant, working with people who were highly cooperative, and one in which there weren't very many frustrations.

Q: I imagine the president would have been very much interested in the Armed Forces Staff College - that is, President Eisenhower - did he pay a visit there at any time during your regime?

Adm. W.: We did not have the president there. We had several - and I can't remember just which ones now - secretaries of defense speak to the student body. You recall at that time the President who had been one of those instrumental in setting up the original college, of course -

Q: And the National War College as well.

Adm. W.: Yes. He was in rather bad health a good deal of this time and he was making a minimum of appearances at this time, through most of the period that I was there. You remember, he had an attack of ileitis, he had a stroke, and there were various other things that happened physically to him at that time. So we never did get the President down there, although we always felt that he had an interest in us.

Q: Your three-year term came to an end in 1960 and your next assignment began on the 31st of March when you went as commander of the Eastern Sea Frontier and had other duties as well.

Adm. W.: The duty in New York was one that involved originally five different hats. The primary one when I first took over was Commander, Eastern Sea Frontier, with additional duty as Commandant of the Third Naval District, the CNO's representative on the Military Staff Committee of the United Nations, the Commander of the Atlantic Reserve Fleet, and Commander of the New York Naval Base.

Q: And how many staffs did you have to maintain in order to do this?

Adm. W.: There actually were three separate staffs. The Eastern Sea Frontier staff was one separate staff, but it also included a few members who worked primarily on the Atlantic Reserve Fleet matters, and a Third Naval District staff was separate from the Eastern Sea Frontier and Reserve Fleet staff and it also included some members who worked on the Naval Base. So these were two strictly naval staffs, with a chief of staff in each one of these headquarters. Then there was a third staff, a very limited number, one Army, one Navy, and one Air Force officer plus a few civilians, primarily secretarial, who formed the staff of the Military Staff Committee of the United Nations. So there were three separate staffs, one of them was very small and tri-service, and the others were a pretty good size naval staffs.

After I had been there for maybe a year, it developed that the Military Staff Committee assignment had become somewhat more important in the eyes of the Joint Chiefs of Staff, and they discussed with me making that my primary duty and having me devote most of my time to that rather than to the strictly naval jobs. When I arrived the Military Staff Committee was moribund. It hadn't done anything for a good many years. When the United Nations first set up the Military Staff Committee was envisaged as being a military staff for the secretary general and for the Security Council. It very promptly developed, however, that the members of the Military Staff Committee couldn't agree on anything because their nations weren't politically in agreement on anything. So what they invariably did was to send a split version of the solution to the problem up to the Security Council who couldn't agree on it either because still they got instructions from their own nations and they weren't in agreement.

Q: In other words, the Russians stood out against all the rest?

Adm. W.: Yes. There were on the one hand the U.S., the British, the French, and the Nationalist Chinese, and the fifth member was the Russian and they vetoed everything in the Military Staff Committee just as they did in the Security Council.

So it had become moribund. It met every two weeks. We had an agenda with no active items on it. It was something of a contest among the various chairmen - the chair rotated between the five nations each month - and each chairman tried to get the meeting over more quickly than the previous chairman had done. I think when I arrived the French held the record by conducting a meeting in four and a half minutes on one occasion.

But, as a sideline of the Military Staff Committee work, it developed that keeping the ambassador and the rest of the State Department delegation to the United Nations aware of military problems was becoming more important. When I arrived, the head of the delegation was Henry Cabot Lodge, who had a good deal of military experience and a good understanding of military problems. He was succeeded by ~~Henry Wadsworth~~ - Jerry Wadsworth who had neither interest nor understanding of military problems, and very shortly after he took over from Mr. Lodge he made some statements in speeches before the Security Council that were quite at variance with Department of Defense thinking. So at this point the Joint Chiefs called me in and said that they wanted me to spend most of my time in the delegation trying to make sure that the things that our delegation said in various kinds of meetings were in keeping with Pentagon thinking.

Q: Well, you were, in effect, the military adviser to Wadsworth, then?

Adm. W.: This is what I became, although by the time all the arrangements had been completed Mr. Wadsworth had gone. He didn't stay there very long. He left, of course, with the Eisenhower administration, and when the Kennedy administration came in Adlai Stevenson took over. Of course, he was an entirely different character too.

Q: Was Wadsworth very amenable to advice of that sort?

Adm. W.: Not very, but fortunately it developed that there wasn't much in the way of controversy during the period that he stayed there. After the first few incidents nothing much came up where he had to express views along the military line. So after my orders were changed to make the United Nations the primary one I had no real problems with him, but he was succeeded by Adlai Stevenson who said in his speeches frequently that he felt the primary mission of the United States should be to share its very great wealth with the less fortunate nations of the world. Now, I'm quoting this quite accurately from his speeches. He made this statement repeatedly and I had difficulty believing that he really meant it, but I did become convinced that he really did mean it, that this was his thinking, and you can imagine with somebody whose thoughts were these that I had some difficulty presenting effectively a military point of view!

Q: The Joint Chiefs understood this, of course?

Adm. W.: More or less, yes. He was a delightful individual. While he and I disagreed completely on certain facts, certain philosophies maybe, rather than facts, nevertheless we had a very pleasant relationship and I was devoted to him as an individual.

He was a bright, witty, pleasant person, but his philosophies were very different from mine.

But to go on with my story about the way the assignments in New York worked out: I felt that I couldn't adequately handle the job at the U.S. delegation to the United Nations, keeping track of what was going on and what the thinking on the part of all the diplomats was, and still devote the right amount of time to the Naval Reserve, for instance, and the Third Naval District, which involved inspecting some forty Naval Reserve units scattered around New York and Connecticut.

Q: The job had grown too big for one man?

Adm. W.: Yes, it was just too time-consuming. There weren't enough days in the year to do both jobs. So we arrived at an agreement that I would turn over the Third Naval District and the Naval Base, New York, to another flag officer, and it turned out to be Admiral George Wales, and I continued as Eastern Sea Frontier, Atlantic Reserve Fleet, and the United Nations. This was an entirely feasibl combination job. The Reserve Fleet was pretty much a routine maintenance job and didn't involve very much that consumed a lot of time. The Eastern Sea Frontier, in wartime, was a very active assignment but in peacetime it didn't amount to very much. So it was possible to devote most of my time to the United Nations assignment without really doing any violence to the other jobs.

Q: Where did you live?

Adm. W.: This was an interesting proposition, too. The quarters for the officer in this particular assignment were over in the Brooklyn Navy Yard.

Q: In that old house!

Adm. W.: In the old house that was up in the corner of the yard.

Q: An historic mansion!

Adm. W.: Yes, it was said to be a Bulfinch house, but I don't think it really was. It had some Bulfinch characteristics. It wasn't a thing of beauty outside, but it was a beautiful old house inside. It had been originally built in 1806, I think it was, then added to and modernized at various times, but it was one of the show places of the New York area. Living in that house was really quite a pleasure once you got into it. The neighborhood through which you had to drive to get through the gate into the shipyard and the house was just about the worst there was in New York City.

Q: Yet, you had to do a lot of entertaining there?

Adm. W.: Yes, we had to do a great deal of official entertaining. United Nations entertaining particularly was pretty extensive and this involved people from all sorts of places. I recall, for instance, the grandson of the Emperor of Ethiopia appeared in New York. He had come to this country as the chief of Ethiopian Navy to accept a lend-lease ship, and he had to be entertained appropriately. He turned out to be a very pleasant young fellow.

Q: (Just for the record, the young Ethiopian was Prince Desta.)

Adm. W.: I think he was one who was very highly regarded by his grandfather, the Emperor. He's just an example. We had all sorts of people. As I remember, we entertained people from some forty nations during my tour of duty up there, and they ranked from princes and ambassadors on down.

Q: Did you have anything to do with my friend Mary Lord?

Adm. W.: I did not in connection with the UN, but I have in connection with USO lately. I have known her. I think probably the one time that having a military adviser up there on the staff of the U. S. delegation paid off to the greatest extent was during the Cuban missile crisis. This, of course, involved quite a lot of military activity, principally naval, and at this time I think it was really quite helpful to Mr. Stevenson as well as a lot of the others who were dealing in this particular matter to have somebody who understood what was going on and could make it all clear to them, and who also had access to some of the strictly military intelligence that made the situation much more understandable.

During the rest of the time it was interesting and we made mi× contributions at various times. "We" being our military staff there in the U. S. delegation. But I think on that missile crisis we really provided an essential service.

Q: How early in the game were you in cognizance of what was going on in terms of the missile crisis?

Adm. W.: We were, I think, fairly well current. We were a little behind. You may recall that Mr. Stevenson made a speech first that indicated we didn't think there were any missiles out there. Pretty soon we reversed our field, and I think he wasn't alone in being not quite current on things.

There was an interesting international situation that you historians, I'm sure, know a lot better than I do. The Russian foreign minister, Gromyko, had come to this country. He had talked personally to the President. He had told the President that there are no offensive Russian weapons being sent to Cuba, and the President had agreed with him. About the same time that this was going on, Senator Kenneth Keating from New York had been insisting on the floor of the Senate that the Russians were sending missiles to Cuba, and this had developed into quite a partisan controversy in Washington, each one getting his own version of the intelligence available, and it turned out that Keating was right. Shortly after Mr. Gromyko had assured the President that there were no offensive weapons in Cuba, reconnaissance by air produced some pictures that showed them very clearly.

Well, the President had what I think is a typical Irish tempermament. When somebody double-crossed him this way, he got angry, very angry, and when he was angry he took very positive steps. The steel companies learned about this, you remember. He got very angry with the Russians at this point, and he took very positive steps.

While all this was going on, I would say up at the mission we were not completely up to date with what was happening in Washington because it was happening pretty fast. But we learned about it pretty quickly. There was a secure telephone in the embassy building there in New York and there was quite a good deal of conversation back and forth between State and various levels of the mission, and although I didn't have a secure telephone in the Third Naval District headquarters, I did have an airplane and got down to Washington pretty regularly to discuss with the Joint Chiefs and the Joint Staff what the situation was. So we all, I think, were fairly up to date.

The initial position that the President took on this was a very firm one and as long as he continued to take this firm position the Russians just backed off every time they were told to back off. And several days after the crisis started, it seemed to me from where I sat that the President was no longer angry and he got a little apprehensive. "Maybe the Russians won't continue to back off," and he eased pressure on them somewhat. After that I think each nation stood its ground pretty firmly.

Q: How did Stevenson react to the whole thing? I mean other than his official reaction?

Adm. W.: My feeling on it was that he was pretty frightened, that he thought that this inevitably means World War III with nuclear weapons, that there isn't any way out of it. And I think a good many of the diplomatic representatives in the delegation felt this same way. They were counseling more or less continuing caution on the part of the U.S. government. We mustn't do anything to arouse the Soviets because, if we do, it might result in World War III. This may have had something to do with the fact that after several days the U.S. position did become much more conciliatory than it had been originally.

Q: Were there other crises in your period of duty there?

Adm. W.: Crises used to arise but most of them didn't have very much in the way of military connotation. There were many times, for instance, when the Congo situation arose while I was up there. This had some military connotation all right, but in this kind of a crisis the major powers were never permitted to provide any of the military forces. They always came from places like Sweden and India, the minor and, hopefully, neutral nations.

Q: Did the military advisers have any say, however, in the situation?

Adm. W.: We were never consulted as a military staff committee because, as usual, we couldn't agree any more than the Security Council could agree, and you remember the Russians continually fought the Congo operation. In fact, they refused to pay their share of the money to support it.

By this time the secretary general had acquired something of a military staff of his own. He had an Indian, Rikye, first he was a colonel and he got promoted up to lieutenant general during the time he was there, and he had several military assistants usually whose rank was about a major or so - one from Ethiopia and I think there was either a Norwegian or a Swede -

Q: This was Dag Hammersjold?

Adm. W.: No, this was U Thant, at this time. Hammersjold was killed, you remember, at the start of the Congo episode. U Thant used this Indian general. We had very close relations with the general and the U.S. provided most of the logistics for the Congo operation, although none of the military forces. We had a transport that was just continually assigned to transporting various forces from wherever their home country was to the Congo and returning them after they'd done their tour there.

This introduced some amusing problems, incidentally. On some occasions you'd turn up with some Pakistani forces who were Moslems and had certain dietary rules. You'd have Indian forces and they got along pretty well in those days. They were Hindu and had some other dietary restrictions. We had a few Israelis participating and they had their own dietary restrictions. And putting all of these people in the same transport and having to feed them all in accordance with their own dietary laws required a little doing. Fortunately, those people in the transport rose to the occasion very well and were always highly commended for adhering to everybody's rules.

Q: The Navy had a little experience with that in terms of the success in the Claude V. Ricketts.

Adm. W.: Yes. They had a mixed crew there. Of course, our crew was all American but the passengers, the people who were being transported in the transport, were from various nationalities and this caused quite a lot of effort. But it was this kind of thing that we were involved in a good deal of the time in the other crises. The United States as a possible belligerent nation was not involved in any of the Congo-type operations.

During this period there was a lot of military staff activity, not in the special meetings of the Military Staff Committee, but on the side, trying to plan just what kind of a military staff the secretary general should have and whether or not it wouldn't be advisable for various member nations to provide either on a permanent basis or on a standby basis forces that could be used for such operations as the one in the Congo.

Q: Was Alan Kirk brought into this discussion?

Adm. W.: No. As I recall, Alan Kirk was not alive at this time.

Q: Yes.

Adm. W.: He was?

Q: He was brought into the discussion at the White House.

Adm. W.: Oh, wait a minute, yes. I'm completely wrong. He was alive, of course and Alan Kirk was involved, not in the military side of the Congo controversy - my memory is coming back on it - he was involved in liaison between the Belgian interests -

Q: With the corporation there?

Adm. W.: Yes, that were suffering some pretty heavy losses as a result of the action taken by the newly independent government of the Congo. I can't remember the name of the corporation now, but maybe I'll think of that later.

Admiral Kirk - you're right - was very much alive. He died

shortly after this. I remember this particularly because in the particular assignment that I had up there I was called upon for all sorts of unusual services and one of the things that I had to do when Admiral Kirk died was to help Mrs. Kirk ensure that his old naval uniforms were properly preserved in a naval museum. There didn't seem to be any great demand for these particular uniforms but we finally did get proper disposition of them. I think this is what had confused me about Admiral Kirk not being alive at the time.

Q: This must have been a really pleasant assignment.

Adm. W.: It was, indeed. There were occasions when you felt you were doing something very much worthwhile -

Q: It took you out of the Navy orbit, didn't it?

Adm. W.: Yes. And as a final assignment, just before reaching the statutory age for retirement, I think it was quite an appropriate assignment. It gave you an opportunity to do something useful and at the same time you weren't involved in too much routine and weren't too carefully supervised by a lot of people that otherwise might have been looking over your shoulder all the time, but you did have a spot in which you were both kept advised by the Joint Chiefs of Staff as to what they wanted and you kept them advised of the things that were going on in the United Nations that might be of interest to them.

Q: Your liaison was directly with them. The U.S. representatives at the United Nations directly with the White House and the State Department? There were parallel lines.

Adm. W.: Yes. Actually, the Military Staff Committee, as established by the charter of the United Nations, was composed of the chiefs of the military services of the five permanent member nations of the Security Council.

Q: You were Admiral Anderson's representative, then?

Adm. W.: Well, whoever happened to be CNO, and at that time I guess it was Admiral Burke.

Q: Burke and then Anderson, and probably on to MacDonald.

Adm. W.: Yes, but the individual chiefs very seldom acted as individuals. They acted as the Joint Chiefs. Instructions that you'd get would be from the Joint Chiefs through the Joint Staff, rather than from the individual chiefs.

Q: Did you get called to the White House ever?

Adm. W.: During the Cuban crisis, yes, I was down at the White House, but normally Governor Stevenson was the one that went to the White House regularly. Yost used to go to the State Department, Patterson went to the State Department relatively frequently, but normally Mr. Stevenson would be the only one that made the White House.

Q: What was the occasion of your visit there? What sort of information were you called upon to give, or advice?

Adm. W.: The occasion involved trying to decide just what to do in the way of, first, blockade to prevent any more weapons getting into Cuba. Then there was also, in the background, just what was going to be done in the way of preparing for an assault on Cuba. You may remember that a great deal of force was sent down to Florida and to our southern East Coast in case we did have to invade Cuba, and the planning involved getting these forces into position and how they might be used and how this tied in with the intelligence effort and the blockading effort that was under discussion at the time. A group that was called, I think, the Executive Committee or some such expression. It was the Secretary of State, the Secretary of Defense, the Chairman of the Joint Chiefs, Ambassador Stevenson, and the National Security Council and a few people of that kind.

Q: Was Robert Kennedy on that also?

Adm. W.: He used to attend, yes. In just what capacity he was there - I think just brother of the President. But there was this relatively small number of people who were actually making the decisions at the time. I used to attend just as kind of a back-up for the Governor because the state he was in, while he could still speak clearly his memory wasn't very clear, and things would happen in the meeting and when he got back to New York he wouldn't have them quite clearly in mind. We all used to be sure that there was somebody there with him who was taking notes and being sure that when he got back to New York he would have the correct picture of what had transpired.

Q: Was he in failing health at that point? Or was it just his emotional state?

Adm. W.: No. The emotional state and the nervous tension that was involved in it had this effect.

Q: Did you in the committee discuss the fine point of distinction between the blockade and the quarantine?

Adm. W.: There was some discussion of this but by the time I got into it that point had been resolved, call it what you will and we'll avoid use of the word "blockade," but this is what it's going to be!

One of the points, for instance, that seemed necessary for discussion was just how were we going to tell whether or not these weapons are actually in those ships. There was some discussion, first, of actually sending boarding parties on board and inspecting the weapons. Well, the Russians would not agree to this. Castro was acting up quite a good deal. He wouldn't permit any inspection on Cuban territory, of course. Finally, by the time this thing got resolved, the U.S. position had gotten somewhat less intransigent and we agreed simply to inspect the ships from another ship close aboard.

Q: By helicopter?

Adm. W.: Yes, there were helicopters used, but it was a visual inspection from some distance and no actual contact with the weapons, but there was a good deal of discussion as to how closer inspection could be made without producing World War III and with the agreement of both the Cubans or the Russians or both.

Q: Who conceived the inspired idea of having a Russian-language officer on each of our naval warships involved?

Adm. W.: I don't know just where that one originated, but I would expect a lot of people thought of that one about the same time, because this is more or less normal when you're working with any kind of a foreign nation. One of the first things you do is to get someone who can speak the language available to you in case you have to communicate with the forces of the other nation. So I would not guess that that was something that anyone could claim as an original idea.

Q: I wonder if you'd be willing to give some sort of a judgment on the effectiveness of the United Nations as a world organization?

Adm. W.: Yes. This is a personal view.

Q: Exactly.

Adm. W.: People may or may not agree with it. The United Nations, I think, is highly effective in an area that doesn't get any publicity. It's the clearing house for a lot of different kinds of things, such as the exchange of hydrographic information, the UNESCO-type operation, the health standards throughout the world, when various kinds of immunization should be required or should not be. There are just any number of this kind of activity that requires international coordination. It doesn't involve, as a rule, cold war problems.

Q: These are peripheral to the political?

Adm. W.: Yes, they're practical matters that have to be solved. Well, the assignment of radio frequencies is another good example. Radio doesn't know international boundaries and some agency has to be set up to coordinate this. The United Nations does a superb job in this kind of thing.

When it comes to political friction between nations, I think the United Nations can do a creditable job, providing mediation and even in some cases force, as it did in the Congo, where there is no clear conflict of interest among the big powers. Where there is a conflict of interest among the big powers, the United Nations is powerless, and I think that this is understandable, because the United Nations would fall apart if it were not supported by the powerful nations of the world. So it avoids getting into the controversy that involves the major powers. Where they are not involved it can be quite effective in settling things where minor powers are involved.

I think lots of people don't understand the United Nations either. The charter set up the Security Council as the decisive body, and the General Assembly, which is the one where nations vote, has no power, no authority at all. It's simply an advisory body.

Q: And it's a forum!

Adm. W.: Yes, so when it passes a lot of harsh resolutions about taking measures against South Africa, it has no real meaning except as an expression of the views of a lot of little nations. But if the Security Council acts, then, presumably, all member nations have to abide by this decision. So the Security Council is where the real action is and here is where all of the five permanent members have veto power.

Q: Admiral you haven't said very much about the Reserve Fleet and your responsibilities with them. You did tell me off tape that there was some activity in that area at the time of the Cuban crisis.

Adm. W.: Yes. We recommissioned some ships from the Reserve Fleet about that time. Tankers, I think, were the principal ships that we got out of mothballs, but there were also some cargo ships. This proved to be more expensive and more time-consuming than we had thought it would be, I think. Ships didn't come back into commission as readily as we had hoped they would, but they did manage to get back into service all right. There was a continual goage and comage into and out of the Reserve Fleet. Ships were being decommissioned and put in reserve, and occasionally one would come back out. So the art of doing this was being kept alive but it wasn't a very active business. There was a certain amount of activity all the time, but the Reserve Fleet was declining. As the ships got older and older some of them would be disposed of.

Q: How was this determined? What was the line of demarkation?

Adm. W.: The Navy Department determined this through the action of the Board of Inspection and Survey and, of course, appropriations. The budget was set up and you had the money to take care of a certain amount, and when the available money wouldn't permit you to take care of all the ships in your Reserve Fleet, some of them had to be disposed of. This determination was made in the logistics side of the Office of the Chief of Naval Operations. Then we were told which ships would be disposed of. This involved a certain amount of shifting ships around. If you acquired some new additions in one of your Reserve Fleet groups, you might overload it and have to shift some of those ships to another group, and this involved towing at sea. So there were problems of this kind that arose.

Q: How many areas were designated as places for the Reserve Fleet?

Adm. W.: It varied from time to time. The whole Reserve Fleet operation was declining and occasionally you'd close down one of your Reserve Fleet activities. As I remember at the start we had one in Boston, we had one in New York Harbor -

Q: On the Hudson?

Adm. W.: That was the merchant marine, ours was over at Bayonne, New Jersey. We had one in Philadelphia, one in Norfolk, and we had one in Green Cove Springs, on the river that goes by Jacksonville, the St. John's River, in Florida, and we had one in Orange, Texas. It seems to me we had one in Key West. There were quite a number of them scattered around, as this list will indicate, and as the Reserve Fleet grew smaller during the time I was there we closed out the operation at Green Cove Springs, we shut down on the scope of the activities of the one in Orange, Texas, we closed the Bayonne one, and the Boston one had been cut way down. Philadelphia and Norfolk continued to be the primary active Reserve Fleet areas.

But this was an effort that changed from time to time for various reasons, the number of ships you had, the amount of money you had, the age of the ships and their potential usefulness.

Q: I would think that it could be accomplished with less expense if it were attached to a naval base and personnel could serve in several capacities?

Adm. W.: Well, really, I think it was being done with about as small a number of people as was possible. Most of the Reserve Fleet groups were at places where there was a naval shipyard. Philadelphia and Norfolk, for instance, New York, Boston, all had naval shipyards that were available to them if the ships needed work to be accomplished by a shipyard it could be done. But most of the maintenance didn't involve shipyard-type work. It involved inspections, pumping out bilges, maintaining dehumidifying machinery, keeping it operating, and whether the people who were doing this work were nominally attached to a shipyard or Reserve Fleet group didn't make much difference. It was the same number of people either way.

I personally thought, along towards the end of my tour of duty there, that most of the ships had got to the point where their usefulness had declined and we were overdoing it.

Q: Did you make a recommendation in this area?

Adm. W.: Yes, and in some cases the recommendations were accepted. In other cases the Navy Department didn't agree with me that we should let these ships go. But that's perfectly legitimate. It was their decision. I think the Reserve Fleet concept initially was a very good one, but after a ship's been out of commission for a certain length of time, it becomes so expensive and so time-consuming to put it back into commission and have it able to operate effectively with other units of the fleet, that there comes a time when it's cheaper to let 'em go and start all over again. All of your electronic equipment, for instance, after two years or so is so out of date and not compatible with what's being used by operating ships. And it's these things that usually are the controlling items timewise.

Q: We learned that, did we not, in terms of the reconditioning of the destroyers - I've forgotten the term for that operation?

Adm. W.: Modernization, they called it, but they had another expression too that I can't recall at the moment. The updating of the World War II destroyers was quite a project and a very expensive one.

Q: Well, Sir, your retirement came?

Adm. W.: Yes, I reached sixty-two. I was sixty-two on the 30th of January and retired on the 31st, 1963. That was the end of my active career, although I did come back to active duty for one assignment after I had retired.

Q: What kind of assignment was that?

Adm. W.: That was to make an inspection of the Defense Intelligence Agency for the Joint Chiefs of Staff. This was something that was triggered off by the Secretary of Defense. There were several agencies that the Joint Chiefs supervised: the Defense Intelligence Agency, the Defense Communication Agency, and an agency that provides logistics in relation to atomic weapons. None of these had been subject to any kind of inspection because they didn't belong to any one of the services and at that time there wasn't an inspector general of the Department of Defense. There is now. To give some kind of surveillance to these joint agencies, the Joint Chiefs called back from retirement an officer from each of the services and each one of the services drew one of the agencies. The Navy drew the intelligence agency.

Q: Is this a periodic thing?

Adm. W.: Not any more. This was the first time it was done, and after this was done an inspector general of the Department of Defense was established and he does this kind of thing now.

Q: On a permanent basis?

Adm. W.: Yes, he does it regularly.

Q: The merits of the act were justified by the special assignment?

Adm. W.: Well, I'm not sure where the chicken and the egg come in this cycle, but at any rate some of the Secretary of Defense's staff felt that it was mandatory to have an inspection of these agencies, and so, in the first instance, it was done by calling back retired officers.

Q: I would think it would be salutary to the agency itself.

Adm. W.: Oh, it, I think, was. I think we did a few things for the Defense Intelligence Agency that were helpful, and as far as our inspection was concerned, I think we found that they were doing a pretty good job. They had some deficiencies that seemed to us to need correcting but none of them were the kind that were either venal or terrifically important from the point of view of accomplishing the mission.

Q: How long did this tour of duty last?

Adm. W.: This went on for three or four months, I think.

Q: In retirement have you been involved with any boards or anything of that sort?

Adm. W.: Not any official Navy or Defense boards.

Q: Any industry?

Adm. W.: Since retirement I have got interested in armed services

YMCA work which led me into USO work, but this was strictly unofficial, volunteer type of work. There's some contact with the military in doing it but it has no direct connection to the Navy or Defense.

Q: Well, I thank you very much for this very interesting series.

Adm. W.: It's been fun for me. I think we've now just about cooked it dry.

Index

for Series of Interviews with

Vice Admiral Charles Wellborn, Jr.

U. S. Navy (Retired)

ABC Conference in Singapore: 114-115, discussion of U. S. attitude towards a two-ocean war (and Admiral Stark's plan), 115-117

Administration: Wellborn becomes Deputy CNO for, 273, description of duties by title, 273-286

Administrative Aide: Wellborn serves Admiral Stark, 79, duties as Aide, 79-80, relations CNO has with army and with President, 80-81

Algiers: British Naval Base for N. African-Sicily operations, 175

Alphand, The Hon. Herve: incident involving Alphand, the French Ambassador to U. S., 349-350

Amphibious Operations: contrast between amphibious operations in Mediterranean and in the Pacific, 199-200, contrast between the concept of the Marines and that of the army in the Pacific, 200-202

USS ANCON: 261

Anderson, VADM Walter Stratton: 83-84

USS APPALACHIAN: Command ship for Admiral Conolly, 197, off the beach at Kwajelein, 209, 211, discussion of command ships, 211-213, becomes command ship for Adm. Harry Hill, 218

Armed Forces Staff College: Adm. Wellborn takes command, 337, rotation of command system, 337-338, history of school, 338, what it does, 338-339, complexion of student body, 339, complexion of faculty, 340, discussion of educational philosophy as it pertains to army and navy, 342-343, influence of Joint Educational Committee, 344, discussion of curriculum, 344, program of speakers, 345-346, discussion of security problems, 350, problems in teaching, 351-352, inter-service friendships develop in student body, 352-353, Navy's selection of students, 353-354, social activities, 355-356, funds for new academic building, 356-358

Athletics, for fleet morale: 42-46

Azores: 170

Bdger, Admiral Oscar Charles: 235, 240, 248, 255-256

Battle Force: manner of operating, 47-48

Bermuda: 158

USS BISCAYNE: converted A/C tender, flagship of Adm. Conolly for Sicilian operation, 182-183, Capt. Dyer hit by projectile on her deck at Salerno, 196

Bizerte: one of U. S. naval bases, N. Africa, 175

Blisters: underwater protection on naval ships, 37-38

Block, Adm. Claude C.: 69, telephone call from Adm. Block to Adm. Stark after attack on Pearl Harbor, 128, 134

British Island bases: exchange for 50 U.S. DDs, 97-98

Browning Shots: name given the random firing of six torpedoes, 161, 163

Buckner Bay, Okinawa, 251-253

HMS BULOLO: Royal Navy Command ship at Casablanca, 211, prototype for some U. S. models, 211, discussion of command ships, 211-21

Camp des Loges, France: U. S. European Command headquarters relocated there, 325-326

Carney, Admiral Robert B.: 257

Casablanca: 161-162, air raid on, 172

USS COLUMBUS: 309

Command Ships: special requirements and limitations, 210-213, as targets for the kamikaze, 213

USS CONCORD: 62-63, 65

Congo: The Congo Crisis in the U.N., 369-371

Conolly, Adm. Richard: in command of Sicily landings, 182, new Chief of Staff at Salerno, 196, ordered to command amphibious group 3 in Pacific, 196, 202, 212, outstanding impressions of Kwajelein operation as personified in Conolly himself, 214-215, relations with Adm. R. Kelly Turner, 215, further efforts in Pacific war, 216, 218

Convoy Escort Duty: 165-168, techniques and problems, 168-175

Cooke, Adm. Charles Maynard, (Saavy): 130

Cruiser Division Four: Wellborn in command, 302

Cuban Missile Crisis: 366-368, White House activity, 374-376

Davidson, VAdm. L. A.: engaged in operation for Sicily, 187

Denfeld, Adm. Louis: 61, becomes #2 in BuPers, 218, 228, 232, named CinCPac, 259, Wellborn Chief of Staff, 259, problem of training new personnel to man ships after Magic Carpet, 271, becomes CNO, 273, "revolt of the Admirals" and his dismissal from office, 286-288, 292-293

Defense Intelligence Agency: inspection of, 382-383

USS DELAWARE, BB: 13

Denmark: attitude towards NATO command, 333

Denny, Adm. Sir Michael: Chairman of the NATO Military Committee, 348

Destroyer Division 8: Wellborn takes command, 165, escorting slow convoys, 165-167, at Oran becomes part of Naval Forces, North Africa, 175

DD Division 19: Wellborn takes command in USS HAMBLETON, 151, becomes unit of Home Fleet, 153-154, 155-156, rejoins the U.S. Atlantic Fleet, 158, trains for TORCH operation, 159, participation in TORCH, 161-165

Destroyer Force, Atlantic Fleet: 313, duties of Command, 313-316

Dyer, VAdm. George C.: injured in Salerno operation, 195-196, Wellborn replaces, 196

Eastern Sea Frontier: Wellborn becomes commander, 360

Eberle, RAdm. Edward Walter: Superintendent of U. S. Naval Academy, 14

Eisenhower, President Dwight D.: his interest in Armed Forces Staff College, 359-360

Fechteler, Adm. William: 61

Fedala: fueling station for DDs in operation TORCH, 161

Fire Control Equipment: Wellborn has temporary duty at General Electric as Inspector, 34, new equipment contrasted with that used previously, 34-35

Flag Rank: method of promotion, 256-257

Forrestal, The Hon. James: his concept of office of Secretary of Defense, 288

Frankfurt, Germany: headquarters of U. S. European Command, 316, 318-319, 323

Gardner, Adm. M. B.: CinC 6th Fleet, 312

General Board: comments on effectiveness and purpose, 142-144

Genoa, Italy: 309

German raiders: 67-69

Ghormley, VAdm. Robert Lee: 83, 87-88

USS GILMER, DD: 29-30

Good, VAdm. Roscoe: senior navy representative on U. S. European Command in Frankfurt, 316

Grew, The Hon. Joseph C.: U. S. Ambassador to Japan, 123-124

Gromyko, Andre, Soviet Foreign Minister: 367

Gruenther, General Alfred M.: 328

Guam: Amphibious Group #3 designated for landing on, 218, 274

Guantanamo Bay: base of cruiser under Adm. Stark, 71-72

Hall, Adm. John Leslie, Jr.: 203

Halsey, Ft. Adm. William F., Jr.: message to fleet after notice of Japanese surrender, 239

USS HAMBLETON, DD: flagship for Commander, Destroyer Division 19, 151, German SS torpedoes her off Fedala, 161-162, repair job in Casablanca and New York, 162

Handy, General Tom: 317, 323-324

Hart, Adm. Thomas C.: role in RAINBOW planning, 92-94, state of Asiatic fleet, 121-122, Hart's interpretation of "the war is imminent" messages, 126

Hesburgh, Fr. Theodore Martin: 357-358

Hewitt, Adm. H. Kent: 158, training for TORCH, 159, 180-181

Hill, Adm. Harry W.: takes over USS APPALACHIAN as his Command Ship after Kwajalein, 218

Hitler, Adolph: U. S. Navy reaction to him, 70-71

Holloway, Adm. James L., Jr.: 234-235

USS HONOLULU: 66

Hornbeck, The Hon. Stanley: 101, differences of opinion between Secretary Hull and Hornbeck, 103

Horne, Adm. Frederick Joseph: named as Deputy CNO, takes over duties performed by Adm. Stark after King's appointment as COMINCH, 148

Hull, The Hon. Cordell: Secretary of State, 100, relations with Adm. Stark, 101-103, 119

Hydrographic Office: 278-279, new location in Suitland, Maryland, 279

Ingersoll, Adm. Royal E.: 96, mission to London prior to our entry into World War II, 96-97, 137, 153

USS IOWA, BB: Wellborn named skipper of, 233, 237, in Tokyo Bay at time of surrender, 238-240, serves as transmitting station for press messages to United States, 241-243, state of readiness in case of perfidy, 244-245, second in line into Tokyo Bay, 245, display of air power, 246-249, a unit in Magic Carpet, 251-252, problem of maintaining discipline of SeaBees enroute home, 252, skipper speaks on Navy Day in Davenport, Iowa, and accepts silver service from original BB IOWA, 255-256, turns over command to Capt. Entwistle, 257

Istanbul: liberty port in Turkey for 6th fleet, 306-307

Italian morale: state of, at the invasion of Sicily, 183-184, incident of two Italian cruisers, 190-191, state of, at Salerno, 193

Italian Navy: status of, 309-310

Izmir: visit of 6th fleet units, 307-308

Jacobs, VAdm. Randall: 231-232

Japanese Surrender: state of wariness and lack of trust on part of U. S. forces taking over, 245-246, 248-250

Johnson, The Hon. Louis: 288-290, sets up Management Committee, 295-296, out as Secretary of Defense, 297, 299

Joint Educational Committee: of three inter-service schools, 344

Keating, Senator Kenneth: 367

Kennedy, President John F.: The Cuban Missile Crisis, 367-368

Keyport Torpedo School: 17, requirement to qualify as divers, 18-19, discussion of torpedoes, 19-20, 21

Kimmel, RAdm. Husband E.: 126-127, discourse on nature of Washington dispatches prior to Pearl Harbor attack and their interpretation, 126-128, 134, Kimmel's removal from command, 137-139

King, Fleet Adm. E. J.: circumstances surrounding his appointment as COMINCH, 141 ff, Stark had him named as CinC Atlantic Fleet, 142, called to take command as COMINCH, title he selected, 146, various duties remain with Adm. Stark, 147, remarks about King the man, 149-150, King's attitude towards Pacific War, 203, meetings with Nimitz on Flag Officer assignments, 227-228

HM King Paul of Greece: 312

Kirk, Adm. Alan: 203, 371

Knox, The Hon. Frank: Secretary of the Navy, role in navy affairs, 102, Pearl Harbor day, 132-133, 137, removal of Adm. Kimmel, 137-139, recognizes Adm. King's ability as CinCAtlantic, 144-145, sees King as type to replace Adm. Stark, 145

Korean War: changes direction and purpose of Management Committee, 297, 299, DDs from Atlantic Command participate, 314-315

Kurusu, The Hon. Saburo: special Japanese emissary to Washington, 105

Kwajalein: destination of Amphibious Group #3 from Oceanside, 198, Marine vs Army, 200-201, armada sails from Pearl Harbor, 207, lessons from Tarawa experience, 208, clean up from main operation, 216, failure of Japanese to respond to propaganda leaflets, 216

Leahy, Fleet Adm. William Daniel: 69-70, retirement assignments, 77-78

Leapfrog Operations: General Patton's plan for quick capture of Sicily, 186-189

Lee, VAdm. Fitzhugh: 243

Lee, Adm. Willis A.: skipper of USS CONCORD, 63, ability with mathematics, 63-66, 234-235, 259

Limitation of Armaments Treaty: discussion of varients achieved on men of war, 39-41

Lodge, The Hon. Henry Cabot: 362

USS LONG ISLAND, CVE: first of small carriers, 169

MacArthur, Gen. Douglas: role in RAINBOW planning, 92, flies up from Philippines for Japanese surrender ceremony, 245-247, 260

MACOMB, DD: replaces HAMBLETON as flagship of DD Division 19, 164

Magic Carpet, Operation: Battleship IOWA becomes unit in this operation, 251-252, planning demobilization on CinCPac Staff, 266-26?

Majuro, regrouping after Kwajalein: 205

Malta: 305-306

Management Committee, Department of Defense: 294-297, Wellborn serves on Committee as Deputy Chairman, 295, purpose of Committee, 295, with Korean War came reversal of purpose, 297, manner of keeping informed on thinking of SecDef, 297-298, dissolution of committee, 300

Marine Corps: status becomes a part of 'revolt of the admirals' controversy, 291-292, document prepared for dissolution of

Marine Corps, 293

Marshall, Gen. George C.: 109, army's attitude towards preparation for war, 109

USS MARYLAND, BB: returned to P.H. from Kwajalein, 217

Massive Retaliation, doctrine: 319, problems for NATO and U. S. European Command, 319

Matthews, The Hon. F. P.: appointed by President Truman, entertained attitude of skepticism when taking office, 290

McAfee, Captain Mildred, 224-225

McCormick, Adm. Lynde D.: 316

McNamee, Adm. Luke: Commander of Battle Force, 41, 44, 46

McNarney, Gen. Joe: Chairman, Management Committee and personal representative of SecDef, 295-296, characterization of, 298-299

McNeil, RAdm. Wilfred James: Comptroller in Department of Defense, 357

Mediterranean: problems encountered by U. S. fleet in connection with operation for Sicily - weather, temperature gradients, air attacks, etc., 178-179

Messina: rivalry of Patton and Montgomery to see who got there first, 186, Patton's leapfrog landings, 186, 189

Military Staff Committee of United Nations: Wellborn serves on as representative of CNO, 360-361, assignment grows in importance, 361-362, residence, 365, entertaining as requirement, 365-366, Cuban missile crisis, 366-368, Congo crisis, 369-71, liaison with Joint Chiefs of Staff, 372-373

USS MISSOURI, BB: (old battleship) used as Naval Academy cruise ship, 10-11, (new BB) transfer of marine guard from IOWA in preparation for Japanese surrender, 240, remarks on maneuverability of this class BB, 240-241, leads way into Tokyo Bay, 245-246

Mitscher, Adm. Marc: 259-260

Mohammed V, Sultan of Morocco: visits DD WAINWRIGHT in Casablanca harbor, 172-173

Monroe Doctrine: 69, 72

Montgomery, Field Marshall Sir Bernard: during landing on Sicily engaged in race to reach Messina, 186, 327-328

Moore, Capt. Samuel Nobre: head of foreign intelligence, ONI, 130-13[?]

Moreell, Adm. Ben: Chief, Bureau of Yards and Docks, 107, efforts before Pearl Harbor to prepare for war, 107-108

Morison, RAdm. Samuel E.: cites Adm. Stark's opposition to any interruption of fleet training agenda, 117-119, 122, writing history of naval events in WW II, 276-277

Munitions Board: 110

Munn, Gen. J. C.: 262-264

Murmansk Convoy run: 156-157

Murray, Adm. S. S.: 248

NATO Command: 316 ff. (as it has bearing on U. S. European Command)

NATO Exercises, Atlantic Fleet: 332-333, question of Command, 334

NATO Forces: with Sixth Fleet, 305, refueling at sea, 305

Naval Academy: appointment, 1-3, difficulty with physical exam, 4-5, orientation, 5-6, scholastic requirements, 6-7, rules, 8, athletics, 9-10, cruises, 10-14

Naval appropriations: 282, procedure for obtaining yearly appropriations for navy department, 282-283

Naval Communications: 280, efforts in post-war period, 281

Naval History, Division of: 276-278

Naval Intelligence: discussion of interpretation, ONI vs War Plans, 84-86, 281-282

Naval Observatory: 279

Naval Officers, Careers: comments on Atlantic theatre and Pacific, WW II, 202-204

USS NEVADA, BB: Wellborn has duty in, 38, blisters added, they create problems, 38, 41

USS NEW MEXICO, BB: 15, new type of electric propulsion, 15-16, torpedo tubes, 21, other fittings, 22, unit of Pacific Fleet, 23, 25, Wellborn has five years duty in N. M., 27-29, 31, second tour of duty, 36

Nimitz, Fleet Adm. Chester: discussion of his appointment as CinCPac, 136-137, 140, meetings with Adm. King on Flag Officer assignments, 227-228, present for surrender ceremony in Tokyo Bay, 246-247, 258

Nomura, Adm. Kichisaburo (Japanese): Ambassador to U. S., Adm. Stark's relationship with, 103-15, Nomura's knowledge of developments in Japan, 105-106

Norway: attitude towards NATO organization, 333

Noyes, VAdm. Leigh: head of Naval Communications, 83-84

Oceanside, California: training center for Amphibious group #3, 196, vicissitudes in getting there from North Africa, 197, Camp Pendleton, 197, nature of training period, 204-206

Officer Personnel Branch: Wellborn comes in under Roper and Wooldridge, 219, duties and objectives, 219-220, type billets, 220, priority of MANHATTAN project, 221-222, line officers vs aviators in top billets, 222-224, Nimitz-King meetings on placement and replacement of high ranking officers, 227-228, difficulties with assignments for contemporaries, 228-229, requirements for officer advancement, 230, wartime speed-up in advancement, 230-231

Okinawa: BB IOWA embarks contingent of SeaBees from, for demobilization, 251

Oran: destination of troop convoy, 175, DD Squadron 8 becomes part of Naval Forces, N. Africa, 175, troop transport out of, for Sicily campaign, 177

Ordnance Bureau: duty in, 48, discussion of ammunition production, 49-52, use of live ammunition, 53-55, move towards automation in production of ammunition, 55, comparisons with Royal Navy and Japanese Navy, 55-56, night fighting, 57, maximum effectiveness of various guns, 57-58, problems of ordnance in pre-Pearl Harbor days, 111

Osborne, The Hon. Henry Z., 4

U.S. Pacific Fleet: routine of 1920s, 23-24, personnel limitations, 24-25

Palermo: an objective during invasion of Sicily, 182-184

Panama Canal: 26, problems of defense, 26

Patton, Gen. George: escorts Sultan of Morocco, 172-173, Sicily operation, 182, rivalry with Gen. Montgomery to reach Messina, 186-187, Messina gained, 189

Pantelleria: Island in Mediterranean, 179

Pearl Harbor: 25, question of basing fleet at P.H. in light of what happened to Italians at Taranto, 94-96, telephone communication with P.H., 128, basic responsibility for defense lodged in army, 129-130

Pearl Harbor Day, December 7, 1941: 131-132, confusion in Navy Department, 133-135

USS PERRY, DD: Wellborn has command of, 60-62

PG (Postgraduate) School: 33-36

Pichilinque Bay: 27

Polish Destroyers, with Home Fleet, R.N.: 157

Price, Adm. John Dale: 292

HRH Prince Phillip: 310-311

Pye, VAdm. William S.: 138-139

The QUEENS _ HMS QUEEN MARY and HMS QUEEN ELIZABETH: used as troopships by British, 172

Radford, Adm. Arthur: Tactical Commander of Task Group, illustration of his manner of acting, 235-237, involvement in "revolt of the Admirals," 292

RAINBOW Plans: 88-91, FDR's role, 89-90, role of field commanders in planning, 91-92

Ramsey, VAdm. Paul H.: 257-258

Reserve Fleet: 360, recommissioned ships at time of Cuban Missile Crisis, 378, disposal of old ships, 379, designated places for reserve fleet units, 379-380

Revolt of the Admirals: controversy over the B-36, 286-287, development of this controversy and reasons thereto, 289-290, attitudes within naval cricles, 291-292, attitudes on naval aviation, 294

Richardson, Adm. James Otto: Wellborn discusses question of basing fleet at Pearl Harbor, 95-96

Ridgeway, Gen. Matthew: NATO Commander, 318, 328

Rikye, Lt. Gen.: head of Secretary-General's Military Staff, U.N.: 3(

Robert Heller Associates: 296-297

Roberts Commission: special commission headed by Justice Owen
    Roberts investigates Pearl Harbor situation, 124-126, 138

Rodman, Adm. Hugh: 16

Roi and Namur: in Kwajalein operation landings assigned to Adm.
    Conolly, 198, SeaBees accompany Marines on landing, 210

Roll-Up: name applied to closing of bases and slavage operation in
    Pacific, post WW II, 269

Roosevelt, The Hon. Franklin Delano, President of the United States:
    convictions about U. S. Navy, 73-74, 75, 82, FDR and prepara-
    tions for war, 89-90, 93, attitude towards British needs,
    110, 115-116, agreement with Adm. Stark's estimate of grand
    strategy for a two-ocean war, 116, proposals originating in
    fertile imagination of FDR and Churchill, 119-120, Adm. Stark
    keeps him informed about P.H. attack, 132-133, recognizes
    ability of Adm. King as CinCAtlantic, 144-145, at Casablanca
    Conference, 173

Roper, Vice Adm. John Wesley: Chief of Officer Personnel Branch, 219

USS ROWAN, DD: sunk by torpedo, 195

Royal Navy: in Mediterranean, 310-311

Russian Influence in Northern Europe: 319-321

Sagami Wan: little bay south of Tokyo, 244

USS ST. PAUL, Cruiser: 234-235

USS SALEN: cruiser flagship, CruDiv 4, 302

Salerno Landing: 192, effects of Mediterranean storm, 193, Germans use guided missiles, 194, use of torpedo boats, 194

Salvage, materials: post WW II roll up, 268-269

Samoa, American Samoa: 274

San Pedro: 23-24, 256-257

Scales, RAdm. Archibald H.: Superintendent of U. S. Naval Academy, 14

Scapa Flow: 153, U.S. DD Division 19 becomes unit of Royal Navy's Home Fleet, based on, 154

Schenectady: 34

Schlatter, Gen. David Myron: commandant of Armed Forces Staff College, 337

Second Fleet: description of command duties, 330-331

Shapiro, Isaac: 263-264

Sherman, Adm. Forrest: 293, his role in settling controversy surrounding "revolt of the admirals," 293-294, Wellborn serves under him when Sherman becomes CNO, 294, 300-301

Sherman, VAdm. Frederick: becomes Commander of 5th Fleet, 259, VAdm. A. M. (Mac) Bledsoe becomes Chief of Staff, 259

Sicily: invasion of, 175 ff, training in preparation, 176, landing ships of various kinds added to fleet, 176-177, 179-184

Sinews of War: attitude in U. S. towards curtailment of Japanese supplies prior to Pearl Harbor, 112-114, Adm. Stark's attitude, 114

Singapore: British request for U. S. naval units to help defend, 116-117

Standley, Adm. William H.: 125-126

Stark, Adm. Harold R.: 59, Wellborn's association with in BuOrd, 66, commander, cruisers, 66-67, concern with German Raiders in Atlantic, 67, his handling of Cruiser Command, 72, friend of Secretary Claude Swanson, 73, 76, takes up duties as CNO, 78, RAINBOW planning, 91-94, impact of Taranto attack on Italian fleet, 94, attitude towards DD-British Base exchange, 99, Congressional Committee dealings, 99-100, relationship with Dept. of State in pre-war period, 100-103, with Japanese Ambassador Nomura, 103-105, Stark's effort before Pearl Harbor to get the navy ready for war, 106-109, attitude towards British needs, 110-111, attitude towards ordnance matters in pre-P.H. days, 111-112, attitude towards sinews of war, 114, his general plans for strategy to fight two-ocean war, 115-116, attitude towards British request for naval units at Singapore, 116-117, does not want any interruption in training agendas for fleet, 117-118, way of handling 'left field' proposals of FDR on war matters, 119-120, Adm. Wilkinson asks Stark to telephone Adm. Kimmel, 128-129, accessibility to DNI and others in pre-P.H. period, 130-131, Pearl Harbor day, 132-133, Stark's reactions, 134-135, Stark previously had Adm. King recalled from duty with General Board to command Atlantic Fleet, 142, King called to take operational command of Navy after Pearl Harbor, 146, Stark remains for some months as CNO but it becomes a logistical job, 147, named to London to coordinate U. S. and British activities, 147, Stark had not anticipated his replacement, 149-150

State Department: relations with Chief of Naval Operations, Joint Liaison Committee, 100-101, attitude towards Fleet at Pearl

Harbor, 103, suggestion of fleet units in Pacific, 118

Stevenson, The Hon. Adlai: U. S. Ambassador to United Nations, 363-364, 366, his attitude during Cuban crisis, 373-374

Strategic Bombing Survey, Japan: 261-262

Submarines: enemy activitires in U. S. coastal waters early in 1942, 151-153

Sullivan, The Hon. John L.: resigns as Secretary of the Navy, 290

Sullivan, RAdm. William A.: salvage operations at Palermo, 184-185, at Bizerte, 185, at Naples, 186

Swanson, The Hon. Claude: Secretary of the Navy, 73

Sweden: 333

Symington, Senator Stuart: attitude towards naval aviation while serving as Secretary of the Air Force, 294

Taranto: air attack on Italian Fleet, 94-95

Tarawa: lessons learned there are applied at Kwajalein, 208-209

Terranova: a minor landing on Sicily coast in General Patton's drive to capture Messina, 187-188

Third Naval District: Wellborn named Commandant, 36 $ U.N. duties become so heavy he is directed to turn over District Command, 364

TIRPITZ, German BB: 156

Tokyo Bay: 238, 244-245, 248, 251, 258

TORCH: code name for N. African landing, 159, movement of ships across Atlantic to North African coast, 160, high degree of security maintained in Washington for operation, 160, Wellborn participation in operation, 161-165

Towers, Adm. John: becomes Commander of Fifth Fleet, 257-258,

Wellborn Chief of Staff, 257, Towers named CinCPac, 259, Wellborn his deputy for plans, 259, 264, post war planning on CinCPac Staff, 265-268, problem of salvage of materials, 268-269

Truman, President Harry: 287-288

Trust Territories, Island governments: 274-276

Turner, Adm. Richmond Kelly: 83, War Plans and ONI, 84-85, impact of Taranto event, 95, 130

United Nations: opinion about its effectiveness, 376-378

U. S. European Command: Wellborn replaced VAdm. Good, 316, nature of the command, 317-319, making of contingency plans to be compatible with those of NATO, 319, Russian influence on Command actions and plans, 320, VIPs to Command Headquarters, 324, problem of quarters when Command moved to Camp des Loges, France, 325-326, improved liaison with NATO, 327

Ustica: island off Sicily, necessity for supplying water to populace there, 189-190, incident involving water barge and Italian cruisers, 190

U Thant: Secretary-General of the United Nations, 369

Vinson, The Hon. Carl: 99, cooperation with Adm. Stark on legislation, 99-100

Wadsworth, The Hon. James J. (Jerry): U. S. Ambassador to the United Nations, 362-363

USS WAINWRIGHT, DD: with DD Division 8, 172

Wales, RAdm. George: becomes Commander of 3rd Naval District, 364

Walsh, The Hon. David I., U. S. Senator: 100

WAVES: 224-227, Wellborn feels they did not serve any great purpose

225, they impeded BuPers policies of rotating men at sea to shore billets for a rest, 225

Wellborn, VAdm. Charles, Jr.: early history, 1-2

Welles, The Hon. Sumner: Undersecretary of State, 100-101

Wellings, RAdm. Augustus J.: in charge of salvage of materials in Pacific, 268

Welsh, Robert Henry Winbourne: 12

Wilkinson, VAdm. Theodore Stark: requests Adm. Stark to telephone Adm. Kimmel on morning of December 7 (e.s.t.), 128-129

Willard, RAdm. Arthur Lee: as Captain was skipper of BB NEW MEXICO, 16-17

Williams, RAdm. Henry: 277-279

Winnacker, Rudy: historian, Department of Defense, 347

Wohlstetter, Barbara: her book titled Pearl Harbor cited by Wellborn, 123-125, 127

Wooldridge, Adm. Edmund Tyler: Chief of Officer Personnel Branch, 219, relieved as Commander of 2nd Fleet by Adm. Wellborn, 329

USS WORCESTER: becomes flagship of CruDiv 4, 302, description of armament, 302-303, to Mediterranean as part of 6th fleet, 304-312

Wright, Adm. Jerauld, 335, 336

Yokosuka, Japan: U. S. Navy takes over Japanese Naval Base, 239-240, 248-249, Japanese turn over navigational charts, etc., 249, 262

USS YOSEMITE: DD tender based on Newport, flagship for Commander, DD Force, Atlantic, 312

Yuan Debt: 269

www.ingramcontent.com/pod-product-compliance
Lightning Source LLC
Chambersburg PA
CBHW080622170426
43209CB00007B/1496